REVOLUTION OR
RENAISSANCE

LIBRARY AND ARCHIVES CANADA CATALOGUING IN PUBLICATION

Schafer, D. Paul (David Paul), 1937-
    Revolution or renaissance : making the transition from an
economic age to a cultural age / D. Paul Schafer.

(Governance series ; 16)
Includes bibliographical references and index.
ISBN 978-0-7766-0672-9

    1. Economics--History. 2. Culture--Forecasting. 3. Human
ecology--Forecasting. 4. Sustainable development--Forecasting.
5. Environmental protection--Forecasting. 6. Culture. 7. Internationalism.
I. Title. II. Series: Governance series (Ottawa, Ont.) ; 16

HM636.S42 2008   306   C2008-901444-8

Published by the University of Ottawa Press, 2008
542 King Edward Avenue
Ottawa, Ontario K1N 6N5
www.uopress.uottawa.ca

The University of Ottawa Press acknowledges with gratitude the support extended to its publishing list by Heritage Canada through its Book Publishing Industry Development Program, by the Canada Council for the Arts, by the Canadian Federation for the Humanities and Social Sciences through its Aid to Scholarly Publications Program, by the Social Sciences and Humanities Research Council, and by the University of Ottawa. We also gratefully acknowledge the Faculty of Arts at the University of Ottawa whose financial support has contributed to the publication of this book.

REVOLUTION OR RENAISSANCE

MAKING THE TRANSITION FROM AN ECONOMIC AGE TO A CULTURAL AGE

D. Paul Schafer

Governance Series

Governance is the process of effective coordination whereby an organization or a system guides itself when resources, power, and information are widely distributed. Studying governance means probing the pattern of rights and obligations that underpins organizations and social systems; understanding how they coordinate their parallel activities and maintain their coherence; exploring the sources of dysfunction; and suggesting ways to redesign organizations whose governance is in need of repair.

The Series welcomes a range of contributions – from conceptual and theoretical reflections, ethnographic and case studies, and proceedings of conferences and symposia, to works of a very practical nature – that deal with problems or issues on the governance front. The Series publishes works both in French and in English.

The Governance Series is part of the publications division of the Centre on Governance and of the Graduate School of Public and International Affairs at the University of Ottawa. This volume is the 16th volume published within this Series. The Centre on Governance and the Graduate School of Public and International Affairs also publish a quarterly electronic journal www.optimumonline.ca

Editorial Committee

Caroline Andrew
Linda Cardinal
Monica Gattinger
Luc Juillet
Daniel Lane
Gilles Paquet (Director)

The published titles in the Series are listed at the end of this book.

Preface

This is a book about economics and culture: two of the most powerful forces at work shaping our world.

The first of these forces - economics - gave rise to the economic age we are living in at present. It is an age that has made economics, economies, and economic growth in general, and the production and consumption of material and monetary wealth, consumerism, materialism, and the marketplace in particular, the centrepiece of society and the world system. It has done so because this is deemed to be the most effective way of dealing with people's needs and wants in all areas of life.

While the economic age has produced many benefits, particularly for people and countries in the West, it is not capable of coming to grips with the fundamental problems confronting humanity. This is because it is based on theoretical, practical, and historical foundations that are incompatible with solving these problems. This is especially true with respect to the environmental crisis, climate change, the gap between rich and poor nations and rich and poor people, and, most notably, the escalating pressure of human numbers on the finite carrying capacity of the planet.

Hence the need to create an age that is capable of confronting these problems, and others that have loomed up on the global horizon in recent years. Of all the possible forces upon which such an age could be founded, culture provides the most promising possibilities. This is largely because culture possesses a number of properties that are of crucial importance to the world of the future. Most prominent among these properties is the capacity for holism, sharing, cooperation, conservation, creativity, and the ability to provide a bridge between human beings and the natural environment. Clearly we have only begun to realize the rich potential culture possesses to create the conditions for a better world.

It is to a cultural age, then, that attention is directed in the second part of the book. How would a cultural age function? What foundations would underlie it? What priorities would drive it? How would it flourish most effectively? These are the tough and demanding questions that must be asked - and answered – in order to make the cultural age a reality.

In order to answer these questions, it is necessary to delve deeply into the domain of culture, both as a concept and as a reality. What emerges is a portrait of the world system of the future where culture and cultures are developed in breath and depth, situated effectively in the natural, historical, and global environment, and the necessary safeguards are established to ensure that culture and cultures are used for constructive rather than destructive purposes. This is imperative if global harmony, environmental sustainability, economic viability, and human well-being are to be achieved in the future.

While this is not specifically a book about governance or public policy, it is very much concerned with these matters in the final analysis. For it is concerned with the need to reduce the demands human beings are making on the natural environment, as well as to make it possible for people in all countries of the world to enjoy reasonable standards of material living and opportunities for a great deal of creative and spiritual fulfilment. And it is concerned with doing this without straining the globe's finite resources and fragile ecosystem to the breaking point.

I would like to thank Gao Xian and the Social Sciences Academic Press for translating this book into Chinese and publishing it in China in 2006. I would also like to thank a number of people whose contributions to my work over the years have meant so much to me, especially Walter Pitman, Biserka Cvjeticanin, Jack Fobes, Guy Métraux, Eleonora Barbieri Masini, Ervin Laszlo, Erika Erdmann, John Gordon, Bill McWhinney, Prem Kirpal, André Fortier, Sheila Jans, Joy MacFadyen, Arthur Witkin, Attila and Elfriede Bimbó, Tony Saadat, and Réal Bédard. A special note of thanks is due to the team at the University of Ottawa Press - Dr. Gilles Paquet, Eric Nelson, Marie Clausén, Jessica Clark, Patrick Heenan, and especially Alex Anderson - for the key role they played in editing, publishing, and promoting this book. Finally, I would like to thank my family - Nancy, Charlene, Susan, and Cinnamon - for their support and understanding during the writing of the book. While recognizing these contributions, I nevertheless assume full responsibility for everything contained in the text.

D. Paul Schafer
Markham, Canada
2008

Table of Contents

Part II – THE AGE OF CULTURE

Prologue

Ours is possibly one of the most critical periods in human experience. Poised in the transition between one kind of world and another, we are literally on the hinge of a great transformation in the whole human condition.—John McHale (1969), p. 15

There is mounting evidence to confirm that humanity has arrived at a crucial turning point in history. One piece of evidence is the environmental crisis and, with it, climate change and growing shortages of strategic resources such as wood, water, coal, electricity, oil, fish, rice, corn, and, especially, arable land. Another piece of evidence is the persistent gap between rich and poor countries, and between rich and poor people. Still other pieces of evidence are alarming levels of pollution, poverty, famine, and unemployment; the spread of infectious diseases; increased violence and terrorism; the threat of biological, chemical, and nuclear warfare; and the failure to achieve "development with a human face." It does not take a great leap of the imagination to visualize the kind of world that could result if solutions to these problems are not found.

Standing behind these problems is an even more dangerous and potentially life-threatening problem. With the world's population at six billion and growing rapidly, and with the carrying capacity of the Earth severely limited, the entire global ecosystem could collapse if ways are not discovered to prevent it.

It is for reasons such as these that more and more people throughout the world are coming to the conclusion that a major transformation is needed in the human condition to set things right. Can this transformation be achieved in peaceful ways? Or will it be necessary to resort to a great deal of violence?

In the past, transformations in the human condition have come about in both peaceful and violent ways (see, for example, the works by Boulding, de Waal, Eibl-Eibesfelt, Keeley, Margalis and Sagan, Sahtouris, and Watson cited in the Bibliography). There have been times when transformations in the human condition have been achieved by peaceful means, largely through general evolution or a renaissance. In the twentieth century, for example, substantial improvements were made in living standards and people's lives, primarily in the western world, through evolution. This occurred as a result of phenomenal advances in commerce, business, industry, science, technology, communications, and agriculture. Moreover, a renaissance occurred in Italy in the fourteenth and fifteenth centuries, and fanned out to encompass the whole of Europe and other parts of the world in the sixteenth, seventeenth and eighteenth centuries, sweeping away one established order and introducing another through peaceful means. It was predicated on major advances in the arts and sciences, incredible bursts of creativity and imagination, and new ways of looking at the world, acting in the world, and valuing things in the world.

In contrast, the revolutions that occurred in France in the eighteenth century, and in Russia and China in the twentieth century, were not achieved without a great deal of violence. They were also predicated on sweeping away one established order and introducing another. They stand as vivid testimony to what can happen when political and military leaders, governments, and countries conclude that transformations in the human condition can be achieved only through bloodshed, brutality, and oppression.

What makes the encounter with developments such as these so pertinent to the present situation is the fact that once again we have arrived at a crucial turning point in history. Can the changes that are needed in the human condition be achieved through a renaissance or general evolution? Or will it be necessary to resort to a great deal of violence and revolution?

What is bringing this situation to a head is the conflict that is raging throughout the world at present over glaring inequalities in income and wealth, globalization, free trade, capitalism, the profit motive, the division of the world into two unequal parts, and fundamental differences between religions, cultures, and civilizations. As the terrorist attacks in the United States, Britain, Egypt, and Spain, hostilities in Iraq, elsewhere in the Middle East, and Afghanistan, and the reactions to globalization and free trade in Seattle, Quebec City, Gothenberg, Genoa, Cancun, and elsewhere in the world have demonstrated, and demonstrated convincingly, the world is divided into opposing camps. On the one hand, there are those who believe that the transformation that is needed in the human condition can come about through peaceful means, largely through acquiescing to the present world system, and allowing the forces of globalization, free trade, capitalism, democracy, corporatism, and technological development to run their course. On the other hand, there are those who believe that the transformation that is needed in the human condition can be achieved only through conflict, confrontation, and revolution. The evidence seems to be mounting on the side of the latter group. The protests are getting more frequent, the barricades are getting higher, the security measures are getting tighter, violence and terrorism are more commonplace, and the rhetoric is more high-pitched.

It is impossible to understand the reasons for the present situation without examining the economic age that underlies the current world system and has given rise to it. Violence, terrorism, globalization, free trade, capitalism, corporatism, profit maximization, inequalities in income and wealth, and the division of the world into two unequal parts are deeply embedded in the economic age in which we live. It is an age that has made economics and economies in general, and products, profits, technology, specialization, consumption, competition, economic growth, the marketplace, capitalism, and materialism in particular, the centrepiece of society, and the principal preoccupation of municipal, regional, national and international development.

Many may question the contention that the present age is an economic age, preferring to call it an information age, a technological age, a scientific age, a communications age, a capitalistic age, or a materialistic age. However, while information, technology, science, communications, capitalism and materialism have played powerful roles in shaping the age we are living in, it is economics, more than any other factor or set of factors, that plays the dominant role in the world, as it has for more than two hundred years. It is the magnetic force around which all other forces have galvanized and coalesced, thereby shaping the entire way the world is visualized, understood, and dealt with today. There is a logical reason for this. Economics and economies in general, and economic growth and development in particular, are seen as the principal means for increasing material and monetary wealth, and making improvements in society. This has produced an economic age that draws heavily on information, science, technology, communications, capitalism, and materialism, but incorporates these and other factors within its gargantuan grasp.

How did the economic age originate? How has it evolved over the past two hundred years and more? What worldview underlies it? What model of development drives it? What forces dominate it? How does it function throughout the world? These are the tough questions that must be asked, and answered, if justice is to be done to the economic age. In order to answer these questions it is necessary to delve deeply into the domain of economics. This makes it possible to examine the theories, ideas, policies and practices that have been and are most instrumental in shaping the economic age, and giving it its form, content, and character. These theories, ideas, practices, and policies have been developed by countless individuals, institutions, countries, and governments throughout the world, especially the western world, as well as by such well-known economists as Adam Smith, David Ricardo, Thomas Robert Malthus, John Stuart Mill, Karl Marx, Alfred Marshall, John Maynard Keynes, John Kenneth Galbraith, Milton Friedman, and others. However, while the origins, evolution, and functioning of the economic age make for fascinating reading in their own right, that is not the real reason for delving deeply into the domain of economics. The real reason has to do with determining whether the economic age is capable of producing the changes that are needed in the human condition and world system to address the difficult, demanding and debilitating problems that have loomed up on the global horizon in recent years.

In order to ascertain this, it is necessary to subject the economic age to vigorous evaluation. On the one hand, this means examining the numerous strengths of the economic age, strengths that many people and countries in the world enjoy today. On the other hand, it means analyzing the many shortcomings of the economic age, shortcomings that many people and countries are compelled to endure every day. If, as John McHale contended (1969, p. 3), people survive, uniquely, by their capacity to "act in the present on the basis of past experience considered in terms of future consequences," then it makes sense to assess the economic age in order to determine whether it is capable of delivering the changes that are needed in the human condition and the world system to set things right.

When this process is completed and the balance sheet is composed on the economic age, the overriding conclusion that emerges is that the economic age is not capable of delivering the changes that are needed. In fact, the longer the economic age is perpetuated, the more dangerous the consequences will be, particularly in terms of further degeneration of the natural environment, consumption of the world's scarce renewable and non-renewable resources at an alarming rate, multiplication of consumer demands and expectations that are impossible to fulfil, substantial inequalities in income and wealth between rich and poor countries, and between rich and poor people, failure to achieve "development with a human face," and the potential collapse of the entire global ecosystem. This makes it imperative to ask what type of age would be capable of addressing these problems and producing the changes that are needed to deal with them.

Needless to say, there are many different views and opinions on what type of age this should be. For some, it should be a totally different kind of economic age, based on knowledge, information, ideas, services, and "the global economy" rather than machines, industry, products, and municipal, regional and national economies. For others, it should be an environmental age, capable of conserving resources, controlling pollution, reducing global warming, protecting the biosphere, and radically changing people's attitudes towards nature, the natural environment, and other species. For still others, it should be a technological or communications age, capable of capitalizing on the computer revolution, the shift from verbal to visual literacy, global networking, the internet, electronic highways, cyberspace, and mind-boggling changes in communications. For still others again, it should be a political, social, scientific, artistic or spiritual age, based on preventing terrorism, providing safety and security, promoting democracy, reducing the production of nuclear, biological and chemical weapons, conquering outer space, capitalizing on major advances in science, biotechnology and genetics, creating new social and legal structures, fashioning new moral and ethical codes, and evolving new aesthetic and religious values.

While all these views and opinions have a legitimate claim to the type of age that is most needed in the future, many signs point in the direction of a "cultural age." Most prominent among these signs are the holistic transformation that is taking place in the world today, the environmental movement, the encounter with human needs, the struggle for equality, the necessity of identity, the quest for quality of life, the focus on creativity, and the rise of culture as a crucial force in the world.

What makes a cultural age so compelling is the fact that it possesses the potential to bring about a transformation in the human condition and the world system in peaceful rather than violent ways, through a renaissance rather than a revolution. Its potential to achieve this is based on taking a comprehensive and egalitarian approach to the world system, rather than a partial and partisan approach, instituting the safeguards and precautions that are essential to ensure that culture, cultures, and civilizations are dealt with in positive rather than negative ways, and focusing on "ends" as well as "means." This makes it possible to place the priority on the whole (rather than a part of the whole, as is the case with the economic age), as well as to achieve balanced, harmonious and equitable relationships between the parts and the whole, economics and all other activities in society. Not only would this help to reduce the demands human beings are making in the natural environment, but also it would place humanity in a stronger position to make sensible and sustainable decisions about future directions in planetary civilization.

Whereas Part I of the book is largely descriptive, factual and explanatory in nature, primarily because we are living in an economic age at present, Part II is much more exploratory, analytical, and prospective. Its purpose is to sketch out a general portrait of a cultural age and put enough flesh on it so that it can stand alongside other portraits of the future age, and act as a guide to human development and decision-making in the years and decades ahead.

In order to sketch out this portrait, it is necessary to delve deeply into the realm of culture. On the one hand, this means examining the theories, ideas, insights, and works of many cultural scholars and practitioners, since it is on these that the foundations for a cultural age would be established. On the other hand, it means building up an understanding of the way a cultural age would function in fact, especially as it relates to the mechanics, priorities, and flourishing of such an age.

What stands out most clearly when this portrait is completed is how different a cultural age might be from an economic age. Not only would it be based on different theoretical, practical, historical and philosophical foundations, but also it would flow from different principles, priorities, policies, and practices. This is essential if humanity is to come to grips with the life-threatening problems of the present and cross over the threshold to a more exhilarating future.

Part I

THE AGE OF ECONOMICS

1

Origins of the Economic Age

The task is far from simple, yet understanding ourselves and the world we have created—and which in turn creates us—is perhaps the single most important task facing mankind today.
—Edward Hall (1976), p. 195

If the origins of the economic age can be traced back to a single year, surely that year would be 1776. In that year, three events occurred that were destined to have a profound effect on the human condition for centuries to come.

The first event was the signing of the American Declaration of Independence. It transformed the way people, countries and the world viewed government, governments, freedom, democracy, politics, and the political process. It also set the stage for the development of the United States as the most powerful nation on Earth, a nation that many would say is the epitome of the economic age. The second event was the first use of James Watt's steam engine in the blast furnaces and manufacturing ventures of John Wilkinson and Matthew Boulton in Britain. This opened the doors to a profusion of technological inventions and innovations in science, industry, agriculture, and transportation that had a profound effect on the world situation, largely by making it possible to shift from dependence on animal power to dependence on machine power. The third event was the publication of Adam Smith's *An Inquiry into the Nature and Causes of the Wealth of Nations*. It opened the doors to new ways of thinking about and looking at wealth. With this came new attitudes to the nature, creation, and significance of wealth, as well as the way wealth could be used to increase people's standards of living, make improvements in society, and increase the power and prestige of countries in the world.

As important as the signing of the American Declaration of Independence and the introduction of Watt's steam engine were in contributing to the origins of the economic age—and there is no intention of downplaying or diminishing their importance here—it is the publication of *The Wealth of Nations* that was by far the most powerful of these three events. Anyone who doubts this need only reflect on the impact that books such as Darwin's *On the Origins of Species* or Marx and Engels's *The Communist Manifesto* have had on the human condition to realize what a powerful effect a book can have on the world. Those who doubt the ability of a scholar such as Adam Smith to have a profound effect on the world situation need only reflect on the following statement by John Maynard Keynes, one of the twentieth century's most respected economists (1936, p. 383):

> the ideas of economists and political philosophers, both when they are right and when they are wrong, are more powerful than is commonly understood. Indeed, the world is ruled by little else. Practical men, who believe themselves to be quite exempt from any intellectual influences, are usually the slaves of some defunct economist. Madmen in authority, who hear voices in the air, are distilling their frenzy from some academic scribbler of a few years back. I am sure that the power of vested interests is vastly exaggerated compared with the gradual encroachment of ideas.

What makes *The Wealth of Nations* and Adam Smith's theories so powerful is the fact that they paved the way for the economic age we are living in today. It is an age predicated on such fundamental forces as economics, economies, economic growth, production, consumption, specialization, competition, profit maximization, capitalism, trade, materialism, and the marketplace. If we are to understand the impact that Smith and his book have had on people and countries in every part of the world, and on the world as a whole, since 1776, we must examine the subject matter of this seminal publication and the thoughts of this remarkable individual in depth. Contained here are the keys that are necessary to understand the origins of the economic age and the nature of the present world system.

The Wealth of Nations

Of course people had been concerned with wealth for hundreds of years before Adam Smith's arrival on the scene. Military campaigns were organized to acquire it, geographical expeditions were mounted to discover it, political leaders were obsessed with it, and countries were invaded, conquered and colonized to procure it. Think, for example, of all the geographical explorations mounted in the fifteenth, sixteenth and seventeenth centuries to enhance the flow of gold, silver, and other precious metals into Europe, as Spain, Portugal, Britain, France, the Netherlands and other countries endeavoured to find trade routes to East Asia to capture the wealth of the Orient and the spice and silk trades. The whole world was being turned topsy-turvy in an effort to discover and acquire wealth.

Even immediately before Smith's time, politicians, practitioners, planners, and countries were preoccupied with wealth, especially national wealth. In Europe an elaborate system called mercantilism was created to show how wealth in general, and national wealth in particular, could be increased most effectively (see, for example, the studies of mercantilism by Heckscher and by Wilson). Mercantilism, created at a time when there was a great deal of rivalry and warfare between nation states, was developed most fully and successfully in Britain. It was based on the conviction that wealth and power could be enhanced most effectively through an elaborate system of domestic development, international relations, colonialism, and the maintenance of a favourable balance of trade. The object was always to ensure that more gold, silver, and other precious metals flowed into a nation state than out of it, since this would tip the balance of trade, and hence the balance of power and wealth, in that state's favour.

This was particularly important when rivalry and warfare between nations were viewed as a "zero sum game," with one nation's loss being another nation's gain. Thomas Mun, who, along with Edward Misselden, Sir William Petty, Sir Josiah Child, Sir Francis Bacon and others, laid the theoretical and practical foundations for the mercantilist system, wrote (as cited by Spiegel, p. 108): "The ordinary means to increase our wealth and treasure is by foreign trade, wherein we must ever observe this rule: to sell more to strangers yearly than we consume of theirs in value." According to mercantilist theory, this was best achieved by such measures as increasing exports and decreasing imports; imposing rigid state control of industry, commerce, and manufacturing; granting monopolistic privileges to manufacturers under royal charters; and, especially, having the government intervene in the economy through regulation of production, promotion of international trade, the levying of duties on imports, the signing of treaties with well-defined objectives with other countries, providing exclusive trading privileges to specific companies, and exploiting the resources of other nations.

In France, a different system, physiocracy, was devised to show how France could increase its wealth, power, and prestige in the world (see works by Meek and Turgot). It was called physiocracy because it was based on the idea that there is a natural order in the world, an order best realized through domestic rather than international development. This was largely because the French believed in the supremacy of the natural world, which accounts for the prominent role that agriculture has always played in the economic and cultural life of France. Victor Mirabeau, François Quesnay, Anne-Robert-Jacques Turgot and other physiocrats were appalled by the idea that one nation's wealth, power, and prestige in the world might be achieved at the expense of other nations. According to the physiocrats, wealth was created in agriculture rather than in manufacturing or commerce. This was because seeds and livestock could be multiplied many times over when cultivated and mated. Moreover, the physiocrats believed that a *produit net*, a surplus of production over consumption, could be realized in agriculture but not in manufacturing or commerce. This led the physiocratic thinkers to devise an elaborate *tableau économique* to show how wealth was created in agriculture and then circulated throughout the entire economy, much as blood flows through the human body.

Adam Smith admired many aspects of physiocracy. What particularly attracted him were the quest to find scientific and empirical laws capable of explaining economic behaviour; the *tableau économique*, which shed light on the circulatory nature of the economy; the idea of the *produit net*, which showed how a surplus of production over consumption could be created, resulting in capital accumulation; and, especially, the idea that minimal government involvement in the economic and the social affairs of nations, expressed in such physiocratic slogans as *laissez faire, laissez passer* (roughly, "leave things alone and let everything happen of its own accord"), was the best way to create and increase wealth.

Unlike the physiocrats, Smith believed that the origins of wealth lay largely in manufacturing and commerce, not in agriculture. This was due to the fact that productivity in manufacturing and commerce could be increased many times more than in agriculture. It should be remembered that Smith was writing at a time when Britain and France were still largely agricultural and agrarian in nature, although Britain was standing on the cusp of an industrial revolution about to assume gigantic proportions. In fact, a number of writers have contended that Britain had already achieved one industrial revolution when Smith arrived on the scene, and was about to realize another (see Nef). The major reason given for this was that Britain placed a much higher priority on commerce and manufacturing, whereas France placed a much higher priority on agriculture.

While Smith was attracted to many aspects of physiocracy, he was strongly opposed to mercantilism, for two reasons. First, he objected to the idea that wealth is synonymous with gold, silver, and other precious metals. Smith defined wealth in terms of "the necessaries and conveniences of life": if they were decreasing, or if they were increasing at a slower rate than the population was declining, then wealth was declining and people were becoming worse off, regardless of the flow of precious metals into or out of the country. Second, Smith was convinced that the key to the creation and augmentation of wealth lay in minimum rather than maximum state intervention in the economy. This led Smith to conclude that economic and political liberalism was a prerequisite for creating and increasing the wealth of nations, and therefore also their power and prestige in the world.

The combined effect of these two objections led Smith to create an elaborate economic system to show how wealth could be created and enhanced most effectively. The key elements in this system were as follows: making the economy the centrepiece of society, and the principal preoccupation of public and private policy- and decision-making; the recognition of labour as the principal source of all value and wealth; the promotion of "the division of labour," or labour specialization, as the key to the creation and augmentation of wealth; the expansion of the size of the market to facilitate the division of labour; the assertion of the importance of "productive" as opposed to "unproductive" labour; the use of the market as the main vehicle for discharging economic functions; facilitating as much capital accumulation, international trade, and colonial development as possible; relying on "enlightened self-interest' on the part of individuals and institutions; and depending on an "invisible hand" to guide the economy and society more generally. If nations wanted to increase wealth, enhance the standard of living of their citizens, make improvements in society, and play powerful roles in the world, they should commit themselves to these essentials and build an economic system equal to the task.

In order for Smith's system to function effectively the economy had to be made the principal preoccupation of policy-making. This, in his view, was the key to increasing the "necessaries and conveniences of life," and making improvements in society. If the economy was expanding, particularly at a faster rate than the population, then people would become better off because the "necessaries and conveniences of life" would be increasing *per capita*. However, if the economy was contracting, people would become worse off, again *per capita*. (The only exception to this general rule was when a population was decreasing at a faster rate than the "necessaries and conveniences of life" were. In this case, people would be better off, but only slightly.)

Given the importance of expanding the "necessaries and conveniences of life," it was natural for Smith to ask who was primarily responsible for this expansion. Smith's unqualified answer was *labour*. In his view it is labour, more than any other factor or factors in society, that is responsible for creating wealth. This is how *The Wealth of Nations* begins (p. 104):

> The annual labour of every nation is the fund which originally supplies it with all the necessaries and conveniences of life which it annually consumes, and which consists always either in the immediate produce of that labour, or in what is purchased with that produce from other nations. According, therefore, as this produce, or what is purchased with it, bears a greater or smaller proportion to the number of those who are to consume it, the nation will be better or worse supplied with all the necessaries and conveniences for which it has occasion.
>
> But this proportion must in every nation be regulated by two different circumstances; first, by the skill, dexterity and judgement with which its labour is generally applied; and, secondly, by the proportion between the number of those who are employed in useful labour, and that of those who are not so employed. Whatever be the soil, climate, or extent of territory of any particular nation, the abundance or scantiness of its annual supply must, in that particular situation, depend upon those two circumstances.

Given the importance of labour to the functioning of Smith's entire economic system, it was necessary for Smith to deal with labour in abstract, theoretical terms as well as in specific, practical terms. In order to do this Smith evolved a version of the labour theory of value that was to dominate economic thinking for more than one hundred years following the publication of *The Wealth of Nations*. It is a theory based on the conviction that there are really two types of value. First, there is "value in use" (or use value). This type of value results when people use the things that they produce or that are provided for them by nature. Second, there is "value in exchange" (or exchange value). This type of value results when people exchange things with other people in a marketplace. There is a significant difference between the two, according to Smith (pp. 131–32):

> The things which have the greatest value in use have frequently little or no value in exchange; and, on the contrary, those which have the greatest value in exchange have frequently little or no value in use. Nothing is more useful than water: but it will purchase scarce anything; scarce anything can be had in exchange for it. A diamond, on the contrary, has scarce any value in use; but a very great quantity of other goods may frequently be had in exchange for it.

Smith's distinction between the two kinds of value may be further illustrated in our own time with his example of water: as water becomes scarce and there is more demand for it, its exchange value increases correspondingly, and there is considerable evidence to suggest that the exchange value of water will be very high in the future.

While use value is important, it is exchange value that is by far the more important of the two as far as the economic system is concerned. This is because the large majority of people are unable to make the things they need and must therefore engage in exchange in a marketplace. According to Smith, enlightened self-interest, not benevolence or compassion, lies at the heart of this process. In one of the most telling passages in *The Wealth of Nations* Smith states (p. 119): "It is not from the benevolence of the butcher, the brewer, or the baker that we expect our dinner, but from their regard to their own interest."

If enlightened self-interest, exchange value, and labour are the key ingredients in Smith's economic system, it is essential to understand how they function within it. In order to do this it is necessary to deal with Smith's convictions concerning labour in general and the division of labour in particular, since the creation and augmentation of wealth are largely a function of labour, and especially of labour specialization, or the division of labour.

The division of labour occurs when labourers specialize in one or two production functions, rather than generalizing across many production functions. Smith uses the example of the pin factory to drive this point home with startling clarity and conviction (p. 110):

> I have seen a small manufactory of this kind where ten men only were employed, and where some of them consequently performed two or three distinct operations … they could, when they exerted themselves, make among them about twelve pounds of pins in a day. There are in a pound upwards of four thousand pins of a middling size. Those ten persons, therefore, could make among them upwards of forty-eight thousand pins in a day. Each person, therefore, making a tenth part of forty-eight thousand pins, might be considered as making four thousand, eight hundred pins in a day. But if they had all wrought separately and independently, and without any of them having been educated to this peculiar business, they could certainly not each of them have made twenty, perhaps not one pin in a day; that is, certainly, not the two hundred and fortieth, perhaps not the four thousand, eight hundredth part of what they are at present capable of performing, in consequence of a proper division and combination of their different operations.

If the division of labour is of vital importance in the creation and augmentation of wealth, because people can increase their output substantially when they specialize, what is it that limits specialization? According to Smith, it is "the size of the market." The larger the market, the more specialization is possible; the smaller the market, the less specialization is possible. The solution, therefore, is to expand the size of the market as fully and rapidly as possible, in order to realize as much specialization or division of labour as possible.

This cannot be accomplished, in Smith's view, when there is a great deal of state intervention in the economy. It can only be accomplished when there is as little state intervention as possible, since this allows the economy to be as free as possible from restrictions and constraints. It is clear from this why Smith was so opposed to mercantilism. Whereas the mercantilists advocated state control of the economy and a great deal of intervention in the marketplace, Smith advocated freedom from the state. This was best accomplished, according to Smith, by pursuing a policy of economic and political liberalism, allowing "an invisible hand" to govern the actions of individuals, institutions, the economy, and society generally. It is this "invisible hand" that causes individual and societal interests to converge rather than conflict. This is because, according to Smith, there is a "natural order in the world" that brings this about, even if individuals, institutions, and society as a whole are totally unaware of it. As Smith contends (quoted by Wesley Mitchell, Vol. 1, p. 52):

> As every individual, therefore, endeavours as much as he can both to employ his capital in the support of domestic industry, and so to direct that industry that its produce may be of the greatest value, every individual necessarily labours to render the annual revenue of the society as great as he can. He generally, indeed, neither intends to promote the public interest, nor knows how much he is promoting it. By preferring the support of domestic to that of foreign industry, he intends only his own security, and by directing that industry in such a manner as its produce may be of the greatest value, he intends only his own gain; and he is in this, as in many other cases, led by an invisible hand to promote an end which was no part of his intention. Nor is it always the worse for the society that it was no part of it. By pursuing his own interest he frequently promotes that of the society more effectually than when he really intends to promote it. I have never known much good done by those who affected to trade for the public good. It is an affectation, indeed, not very common among merchants, and very few words need be employed in dissuading them from it.

Smith's notion of the harmonious convergence of individual, institutional and societal interests caused him to believe fervently in political and economic liberalism (quoted by Wesley Mitchell, Vol. 1, p. 53):

> the individual would get on best if he was left alone by the government. But the income of the nation as a whole is nothing but the sum of the incomes of the individuals who comprise the nation; therefore, the policy which is most

advantageous to individuals must be one which is best for nations. This is the fundamental argument for *laissez faire*.

This belief in *laissez faire* caused Smith to conclude that there is a self-regulating mechanism at work in the economy that causes everything to work out for the best in the end. When labour and capital are free to move wherever and whenever their interests are best served, and when the economy is left free to make the adjustments that must be made as the supply and demand for products and factors of production change, an equilibrium is achieved that is in the best interests of individuals, institutions, and society as a whole. It was this belief that came to dominate economic thinking until well into the twentieth century, when John Maynard Keynes arrived on the scene to challenge it, although many would contend that it has returned today.

If *laissez faire*, labour specialization, market expansion, enlightened self-interest, an invisible hand, and the self-regulation mechanism play crucial roles in Smith's view of the creation and augmentation of wealth, so too does capital accumulation. This results when wealth produced in a given period is not entirely consumed. This yields a surplus of production over consumption in one period that can be ploughed back into further expansion, and the production of more "necessaries and conveniences of life," in the following period. Naturally, the larger the surplus, the greater the potential for capital accumulation, and therefore the greater the possibility of economic growth. The accumulation of capital therefore plays a crucial role in Smith's system because it provides the wherewithal that is needed to increase wealth.

This, in the main, is Smith's theory of production. However, Smith also had a theory of distribution. It is necessary to examine this theory, since, as Karl Marx pointed out in the nineteenth century, the creation and augmentation of wealth are affected not only by the production of wealth, but also by the distribution and use of wealth by the various classes and interest groups in society. If wealth is squandered rather than used productively, production can be affected adversely rather than favourably.

In order to show how wealth is distributed Smith divided society into three classes. First, there were the labourers. These were the people who worked on the farms and in the factories that were beginning to evolve in Smith's day. They received wages for their work. Second, there were the capitalists. They owned the machinery, equipment, and capital used in production, and received profits. Third, there were the landlords. They owned the land used in production, and received rents for its use. In most societies, and particularly in economically advanced societies, these three classes contribute their factors of production in varying proportions to create wealth. According to Smith, the wages, profits, and rents that they receive in return vary depending on many factors, including the productivity of labour, the suitability of land, the size and character of the stock of capital, the growth of the population, the extent of the market, the division of labour, the dexterity and skill of workers, and so forth.

Generally speaking, Smith believed that wages, profits, and rents would all rise as wealth increased and economic growth took place. This would mean that all classes would be better off. Labourers in particular would be better off because their wages would increase as wealth increased, thereby giving them more purchasing power. The one exception to this rule for Smith was when labourers increased the size of their families more quickly than their wages increased. In this case wages might remain constant or even fall somewhat, despite the fact that wealth was increasing for society as a whole. Rents would also increase as wealth increased, according to Smith, since more land would be brought into cultivation as population increased and landlords would be able to charge higher rents, both for the use of their existing land and for the use of the new land they brought into cultivation. Profits would also increase as wealth increased, although not as fast as wages and certainly not as fast as rents. This was because competition among producers would tend to drive profits and profit margins down rather than up.

It is this optimistic view of distribution, particularly when it is combined with the optimistic view of production, which explains the enormous popularity of *The Wealth of Nations* and Adam Smith's theories, which has lasted ever since they were first propounded. Everybody gains, in Smith's system, as wealth increases. Standards of living improve for labourers, capitalists, and landlords alike as the size of markets expands, the productivity of labour increases, more specialization and division of labour takes place, and capital accumulates.

Nevertheless, according to Smith there are a number of exceptions to this general rule. One, as we have seen, is when a population is growing at a faster rate than wealth is being created. Another is when more wealth is withdrawn from the income stream through squandering and frivolous expenditure than is returned to the income stream through capital accumulation and reinvestment in production. Smith thought that landlords might be particularly guilty of this, since most of their land was inherited and they were able to "reap where they had not sowed." Yet another exception, as we have also seen, is when the state interferes with the free functioning of the economy.

A final exception, and an exception that worried Smith a great deal, is when there is too much "unproductive labour" in society. Before we can determine what "unproductive labour" means, it is necessary to examine what Smith meant by "productive labour." According to Smith, labour is productive when one or both of two conditions prevail: either a tangible product or material commodity of lasting value is produced, or a surplus of production over consumption exists and can be reinvested in production and capital accumulation. Labour is "unproductive" when either or both of these conditions do not prevail. Smith illustrates what he means by "unproductive labour" with the example of the menial servant. Whereas a labourer in manufacturing adds to the value of the materials on which he or she works, because a tangible product is produced or a surplus of production over consumption is created, the menial servant adds to the value of nothing, since he or she produces neither a product nor a surplus. This led Smith to conclude (p. 430) that "A man grows rich by employing a multitude of manufacturers: he grows poor by maintaining a multitude of menial servants." The reason for this is clear. The menial labourer must be paid for his or her labour and receive wages, despite the fact that there is no real contribution to production and nothing of lasting value is created. (Note that it was not until systems of national accounts came into existence that services and service providers were recognized as making important contributions to the economy.)

This distinction between "productive" and "unproductive" labour led Smith to differentiate between labourers who are productive and labourers who are not. Included in the latter category, in Smith's view, were the sovereign and all the officers of justice and war who serve the sovereign, and thus the whole of the army and the navy, as well as (p. 431) "some of the gravest and most important, and some of the most frivolous professions: churchmen, lawyers, physicians, men of letters of all kinds; players, buffoons, musicians, opera-singers, opera-dancers, etc." Their services, however honourable or useful they might be, produce nothing for which an equal quantity of service can be purchased or commanded in a market, yet they are (p. 430) "the servants of the public, and are maintained by a part of the annual produce of the industry of other people."

Given his views on "unproductive labour," it is easy to see why Smith was so concerned about increases in the number of people he deemed "unproductive," as opposed to "productive," as well as the ratio between them: by acting as a drain on the economy, unproductive labourers take wealth out of the system without providing anything of equal or lasting value in return. While these views are discounted today by economists, they were exceedingly popular in Smith's lifetime, had a profound effect on economic theory and practice during the hundred years or so following his death, and linger on in the minds of many people throughout the world.

There is one final aspect of Smith's system that must be examined if justice is to be done to it. This is the problem of determining when increases in wealth are "real" and when they are "illusionary." It is impossible to determine this without examining Smith's theory of prices, since prices in general, and changes in prices in particular, have to be taken into account in determining actual increases and decreases in wealth. Smith tried to get at the problem of prices by making a fundamental distinction between the "natural prices" of commodities and the "market prices" of commodities.

For Smith, the natural price of a commodity is determined by the amounts of labour, capital, and land embodied in it. When the price is neither more nor less than what is sufficient to pay "the rent of the land, the wages of the labour, and the profits of the stock employed in raising, preparing, and bringing it to market according to their "natural" rates, the commodity is sold for what may be called its "natural" price." (Barber, p. 33).

The commodity is then sold for what it is worth, or for what it really costs the person who brings it to market. Smith's preoccupation with the "natural" prices of commodities can be traced back to the medieval Scholastics, and their concern with "the just price," the price that reflects the actual amounts of land, labour, and capital that go into production and therefore determine the "real value" of commodities. This was also a fundamental concern for Smith, given his preoccupation with exchange value, the role that labour and labourers play in wealth creation, and, especially, the need to ascertain the "real" value or worth of everything. This is not surprising in view of the fact that Smith was primarily a philosopher (as well as what we now call an economist), and his other major book was *The Theory of Moral Sentiments*, which reveals a strong background and interest in ethics, morality, and determining the intrinsic worth of everything that is produced and consumed in society.

In contrast to the "natural" prices of commodities, the market prices of commodities are those that people actually pay for them in the market. According to Smith, these can vary from the "natural" prices according to a variety of institutional and non-institutional factors, including charging what the market will bear, and deliberately withholding a product from the market in order to drive its price up and receive a profit that is higher than the cost of producing it.

In retrospect, it is easy to see why Smith was so concerned with differentiating between market prices and "natural" prices. On the one hand, he was anxious to get at the "real" value or worth of everything, as opposed to its monetary value or worth. This necessitated lifting the veil of superficial changes in prices in order to get at real changes in prices. On the other hand, he was interested in determining whether wealth was increasing or decreasing from one year to the next, in real terms as opposed to monetary terms. This could only be ascertained when adjustments were made for changes in the price level and the purchasing power of money, since this was the only way to determine whether people were better off or worse off in real terms as opposed to monetary terms.

With this examination of real and monetary changes in prices and wealth, our examination of Smith's economic system is complete. The two main features of the system that account for its lasting power and popularity are its comprehensive character and its optimistic nature. It stands as a vivid exemplar of Victor Hugo's statement that "greater than the tread of mighty armies is an idea whose time has come." The world was ready for Adam Smith and *The Wealth of Nations*, which is why Max Lerner concluded, in his introduction to a modern edition of the book (p. v), that:

> Like all great books, *The Wealth of Nations* is the outpouring not only of a great mind, but of a whole epoch. The man who wrote it had learning, wisdom, a talent for words; but equally important was the fact that he stood with these gifts at the dawn of a new science and the opening of a new era in Europe.

While Smith made many original contributions to the origins of the economic age, these contributions should be seen in their context rather than in isolation from it. Many of the ideas and theories contained in *The Wealth of Nations* were already popular in Smith's day, or even earlier, including the circulatory and interdependent nature of the economy, the perceived need for minimal rather than maximal involvement of the state in the economy, the desire to find laws capable of explaining economic behaviour, and the importance of "enlightened self-interest" in driving people, institutions, economies, and societies. One only has to read the works of other economic, political and philosophical scholars— such as Mun, Bacon, Petty, Child, Locke, Cantillon, Quesnay or Turgot, or Smith's fellow Scots David Hume and James Steuart, or Smith's own teacher, Francis Hutcheson—to realize that many of the ideas contained in *The Wealth of Nations* were of concern to many others besides Smith.

Moreover, many of the issues that have preoccupied economists, governments, and countries since Smith's day—such as short-term and long-term fluctuations in economic activity, gluts in markets, the possibilities of overproduction and underconsumption, business cycles, the role of entrepreneurs and technology in economic development, and particularly the demand side of the economy, the marketplace and price determination—were left largely unexamined or unattended by Smith. Indeed, if *The Wealth of Nations* is deficient in one very important respect, it is in Smith's failure to give the demand side of the economy, including the determination of prices, the same attention as the supply side.

Despite this, *The Wealth of Nations* had an extremely powerful impact on the origins and evolution of the economic age. Five factors account for this impact. First, Smith was concerned with a very practical problem, namely, how to create and increase wealth, enhance people's standards of living, and make improvements in society. It was this concern that prompted Smith to write the book in the first place, as well as to develop an elaborate theoretical and practical system to show how these aims could be realized in fact.

Second, Smith was concerned with the wealth and well-being of all people and classes in society, and not just the rich and privileged. A great deal of attention is directed in *The Wealth of Nations* to determining how the labouring class can profit from the creation and augmentation of wealth through higher standards of living and increases in the purchasing power of money, thereby putting Smith in the vanguard of all those who have been concerned about the development of an economic system that is egalitarian and inclusive, rather than elitist and exclusive. This fact is often ignored or downplayed by people who view Smith as the main architect of the current world system, contemporary capitalism, and the main forms of conservatism.

Third, Smith was able to pull together all the diverse threads and arguments that were needed to make a coherent, comprehensive and compelling case, primarily because he had a very eclectic mind. There is something for everyone in *The Wealth of Nations* and Smith's economic system. What counts is the design, development, scope, subject matter, and spirit of the system as a whole, rather than its individual parts. This is why Smith has done more than any other economist or social thinker to shape the way of life of the economic age we live in today.

Fourth, Smith was an optimist rather than a pessimist. He was excited about the possibility of increasing wealth for all people and classes, as well as making improvements in society. While this could not be achieved without losses and gains, Smith believed that the long-term prospects for social improvements and higher living standards for everyone were very favourable. This helps to account for the popularity of *The Wealth of Nations* in Smith's own day, as well as its ability to withstand the test of time.

Finally, Smith's thoughts and writings on the subject that we now call economics, and on the functioning of economies, societies, and countries, make a great deal of sense. His thoughts are logical, straightforward, practical, well-ordered, and very relevant to people and countries in every part of the world. This helps to explain why Lerner calls Smith "a gentle sage with dynamite flowing from his pen." It certainly explains why Smith and *The Wealth of Nations* deserve a prominent place at the forefront of the economic age.

The Industrial Revolution

While the publication of *The Wealth of Nations* was by far the most important event in laying the theoretical and practical foundations for the economic age, other developments were taking place in Britain and elsewhere in Europe that were also destined to play seminal roles. One of the most powerful of these developments was the industrial revolution.

While there is a great deal of controversy over when the industrial revolution actually began, there is no controversy over the fact that Britain and other parts of western Europe experienced an industrial revolution in the eighteenth and nineteenth centuries. Most authors place the dates for this revolution between 1750 and 1850, although, as indicated earlier, the prominent economic historian John Nef argued that Britain experienced two industrial revolutions rather than one, the first occurring between 1540 and 1640.

Despite this, in 1776, when *The Wealth of Nations* was published, Britain was still a largely agricultural country, more than fifty percent of the working population being engaged in farming, fishing, and forestry . Nevertheless, there were signs that an industrial revolution was rapidly evolving and was about to assume gigantic proportions. As evidence of this, by 1850 Britain was primarily industrial rather than agricultural in character, with more than half the labour force working in manufacturing and less than a quarter working in agriculture.

The story of how this industrial revolution occurred is a fascinating one that has filled numerous books (see, for example, those by Mantoux, the older Arnold Toynbee, Hartwell, E. R. Chamberlin, and, most recently, Ashton and Hudson). In the first place, there were phenomenal changes taking place in farming, such as the enclosure movement, the introduction of new methods and techniques, and, strange as it may sound, the introduction of the turnip. These changes, and particularly the introduction of the turnip, made it possible to increase the fertility of the soil, rotate crops more effectively, increase yields and productivity substantially, bring much additional land into cultivation, release people to work in manufacturing, and make the transition from an agrarian society to an industrial society. These changes were matched by corresponding advances in manufacturing, finance, commercial development, and international trade. By the time Adam Smith arrived on the scene capital goods and raw materials were circulating throughout Britain and the rest of western Europe, and, indeed, throughout the world, in volumes and at speeds hitherto unknown in history.

An extensive battery of colonies existed by this time in North and South America, the Caribbean, Asia, Africa, and the Middle East. These colonies provided resources, raw materials, and markets for Britain and most other

European countries. New ways of financing, marketing, and commercial development were also evolving rapidly, as were new modes of transportation. The movement of goods by horse and cart along mostly unpaved roads was giving way to the movement of goods by ship, canal boat, and, eventually, the train. In addition, there was a dramatic increase in population. After several hundred years of more or less constant or nominal population growth, the population of Britain, as of most other European countries, swelled considerably between 1750 and 1850. For example, the population of England and Wales was roughly seven million in 1770, but by 1850 it had increased to roughly eighteen million.

These changes were so phenomenal in size, scope, significance and influence that such terms as "the agricultural revolution," "the commercial revolution," "the transportation revolution" and "the population revolution" have been used to describe them. Despite this, it is the broader and older term, "the industrial revolution," that is usually used to convey the fact that something far more fundamental was occurring in Britain and elsewhere in Europe at this time, subsuming all the other changes, and a great deal else, in its gargantuan grip. What was at the root of these changes was the colossal transformation of industrial production.

Improvements in technology were at the centre of these developments. Among the most important of these improvements were such major inventions as the spinning jenny (James Hargreaves), the steam engine (James Watt), the cotton gin (Eli Whitney), the sewing machine (Elias Howe), the seed drill (Jethro Tull), the steam-driven pump (Thomas Newcomen), the puddling and rolling process (Henry Cort), the flying shuttle (John Kay), the water frame (Richard Arkwright), the spinning mule (Samuel Crompton), and the coke-blasting process (Abraham Darby). Many of these inventions, which were spurred on by the escalating demand for industrial products, appeared between 1700 and 1800, and particularly between 1750 and 1800. Interestingly, they were made by practitioners working in factories and workshops, rather than by scientists and researchers working in laboratories.

These inventions, and particularly the way they clustered together to reinforce one another and trigger other inventions, were so crucial to the realization of the industrial revolution that the prominent Austrian economist Joseph Schumpeter saw them as being the principal reason for the industrial revolution in the first place. Just what a prominent role they played in spawning the industrial revolution can be confirmed by the fact that the number of patents assigned in Britain increased from fewer than 100 in each ten years up to 1760, to several hundred in each of the 1760s, the 1770s, and the 1780s, and then to several thousand in each of the 1820s, the 1830s, and the 1840s (Dean, p. 128). As Dr Samuel Johnson put it, "The age is running mad after innovation."

Many of these inventions occurred first in the cotton textile industry and the iron industry, so much so that these acted as the spearheads of the industrial revolution in Britain, triggering the developments that were needed in other areas to bring the industrial revolution to fruition. Of the two, it is the cotton textile industry that is generally credited with paving the way for the industrial revolution, for two reasons. First, British landlords, financiers, and businessmen had surplus capital, and were looking for a product and an industry where they could invest this capital to dramatically increase their material and monetary wealth. Second, Britain's rapidly expanding population needed clothing that was cheap, strong, and durable enough to cope with the vicissitudes of Britain's difficult climate and geography. This was not provided by woollen clothing, since it was too soft, inconsistent, and prone to unravelling and wearing out.

Unlike wool, for which a domestic supply of raw materials was readily available since Britain possessed a munificent supply of sheep, cotton had to be imported into Britain because a domestic supply did not exist. This meant that the inventions and innovations of Kay, Crompton, Hargreaves, Whitney, Arkwright, and others were necessary if cotton production and a cotton textile industry were to prove viable in Britain. That the British proved more than equal to the challenge is confirmed by the fact that Mahatma Gandhi used cotton and the need for "homespun," rather than dependence on imports from Britain, as his principal device for challenging British rule in India. Despite the fact that Britain needed to import raw materials from abroad, the British were so adept at building up the domestic cotton textile industry that they rapidly captured the world market for cotton products. This produced huge profits for British financiers, industrialists, and capitalists, while simultaneously making other countries and other people heavily dependent on British cotton, British clothing, and the British economy generally.

While the cotton textile industry is usually credited as the industry that spearheaded the industrial revolution, the iron industry was not far behind. Unlike cotton, where Britain did not have a large domestic supply of raw materials, Britain had all the ingredients that were needed to develop a strong and viable domestic iron industry. It had good supplies of coal, coke, and iron ore, as well as a relatively effective system of transportation. It also had the financial resources and commercial acumen to make a domestic iron industry feasible. All that was needed were inventions such as the steam engine, casting, forging, rolling, and the like to produce a continuous supply of finished products. Once these were provided by Watt, Wilkinson, Cort, the Darby family, and others, commercial and financial success was a certainty. What made the iron industry such a key industry in powering the industrial revolution was the fact that there were strong backward and forward linkages between the iron industry and other industries. In order for the iron industry to develop properly numerous raw materials were required. This necessitated backward linkages with the coke, coal and iron ore industries, as well as with transportation, communications, and mining. Once this was achieved and it proved possible to produce high-quality products, iron was in great demand in Britain and elsewhere in Europe for the construction of boats, ships, canals, railroads, and a host of manufactured products. This created a whole series of forward linkages with the consumer industries that acted as the real spur to the British economy.

Just as it is generally agreed that the cotton textile and iron industries spearheaded the industrial revolution, so it is generally agreed that the industrial revolution started in Britain, and spread to other parts of Europe, and to the United States, later on. There are many reasons why the industrial revolution occurred in Britain first. There was, as we have seen, the rapid increase in population, which brought with it significant increases in the demand for all types of consumer goods and durables. Then there was urbanization, which brought with it substantial investment in buildings, lighting, water supplies, sanitation, and street paving. There were also all the improvements that took place in Britain's transportation and communications industries, especially roads, turnpikes, bridges, canals, ocean travel, and railroads. In addition, Britain in general and London in particular were rapidly becoming the financial and commercial centre of the world, with a growing number of banks, financiers, and businessmen ready to supply the capital that was needed to finance economic growth. There were also excellent supplies of such resources as coal, coke, and iron ore, as well as a commercial and political climate highly conducive to industrialization. By the time the industrial revolution was in full swing, in the early part of the nineteenth century, Britain was no longer "a nation of shopkeepers," but rather "the workshop of the world." At least, that was the way it appeared to most authors, raconteurs, and historians writing at the time.

It is impossible to complete this portrait of the industrial revolution in Britain without commenting on the impact that it made on British social life. While output per capita increased in Britain roughly two and a half times between 1750 and 1850, it would be a mistake to conclude that this increase was equally shared by all classes and segments of society. Alongside the portrait of a rapidly expanding economy, with phenomenal increases in production, productivity, industrialization, specialization, technology, and economic growth, must be placed a portrait of squalor, misery, shanty towns, unequal distribution of income and wealth, and high unemployment. Much of this was brought on by developments in technology and the factory system of production, which deprived people of their former jobs, their sources of livelihood, their basic ability to make ends meet. It also produced a large class in society that was at the mercy of powerful producers and had little to sell but its labour, thereby giving rise to a number of social activists and authors, such as Karl Marx, Friedrich Engels, Robert Owen, the Luddites, Charles Dickens, and, later, Sydney and Beatrice Webb, who were quick to point out the shortcomings of the industrial revolution. What they had to say about its social effects filled numerous books, and had a profound effect on economic, social and political thinking in Britain, the rest of Europe, the United States, and elsewhere in the world in the years after 1850.

Next to *The Wealth of Nations*, the industrial revolution had the most powerful effect on the origins of the economic age. It is not difficult to see why. The industrial revolution gave life in Britain and several other European countries a much greater material density and materialistic orientation. Previously, most products had been light and perishable, and technology had been largely non-mechanical in character. This all changed with the industrial revolution. Technology became mechanical and mechanistic in nature, and more and more products became permanent and heavy in character. This was primarily due to developments in the iron and related industries, the factory system of production, the construction of boats, canals, railroads, roads, and other modes of transportation, and the phenomenal increase in the production of manufactured goods. While *The Wealth of Nations* provided the theoretical and practical foundations for the economic age, the industrial revolution provided the physical and material foundations for it. It did so by yielding phenomenal increases in the output of products that were heavy, physical and substantial in nature, as well as giving everything a concrete, quantitative, tangible and material significance. This was to become a key characteristic of the economic age in the nineteenth and twentieth centuries.

Religion and the Rise of Capitalism

The industrial revolution was out in the open for all to see, as the new machines, factories, equipment, consumer goods, steam engines, spinning jennies, hand pumps, flying shuttles, canals, railroads, iron-processing ventures, and manufactured products powered its headlong development. People could also see the shanty towns, the smoke stacks, the poor housing, and the soot and smog that were the inevitable consequences. This makes it comparatively easy to make the case that there was an intimate connection between the industrial revolution and the origins of the economic age, since there is a great deal of visual evidence and factual documentation to support this interpretation of events.

Such is not the case with the relationship between religion and the rise of capitalism, another key factor in accounting for the origins of the economic age. Nevertheless, there was an intimate connection between religion, the rise of capitalism, and the origins of the economic age, even if it was far less visible to the naked eye and there is far less visual or factual evidence to support this contention. Religious and capitalistic changes going on in Britain and elsewhere in Europe at the time progressively loosened and weakened the bonds between church and state, and moved people in a secular rather than a sacred direction.

One of the first scholars to analyze the complex connection between religion and capitalism was the German sociologist Max Weber. In his landmark publication, *The Protestant Ethic and the Spirit of Capitalism* Weber contended that it was the emergence of Protestantism in general, and "the Protestant ethic" in particular, that gave rise to the capitalistic spirit of production, distribution, consumption, and profit that was rapidly emerging in Britain and other parts of the world at the time of the industrial revolution.

It is important to emphasize that it was not capitalism *per se* that Weber linked to the Protestant ethic, but rather "the spirit of capitalism." There is a fundamental difference between the two. Capitalism itself is as old as civilization, if what is meant by capitalism is the creation of capital, the amassing of fortunes, the production of products, and the earning of profits through speculation, money-lending, commercial activities, and the like. However, capitalism as a rational *system* of production, distribution, and consumption, involving the systemic organization and utilization of labour, the creation of capital machinery and equipment, the development of factories, the turning out of a constant supply of products, and, especially, the desire to produce a continuous flow of profits in order to earn even greater profits in the future, was something new.

It was this latter notion of capitalism, and particularly the "spirit of capitalism" that he saw as underlying it, that Weber had in mind. In asserting this connection, Weber contended that it was Protestantism rather the Catholicism that gave rise to "the spirit of capitalism" because Protestantism saw the relationship between God, the church, and the individual in a new light. This was particularly true of Protestant sects such as Calvinism, which extolled the idea of a "calling," of justifying one's existence before God through hard work and excellence in a specific trade or profession. This, according to Weber, resulted in substantial increases in production and productivity because people were anxious to work as hard as possible and produce as much as possible in order to make a success of their calling, justify themselves before God, and gain admission to the Kingdom of Heaven. However, this was not the end of the matter for Weber. It was also necessary for people to abstain from consumption, particularly excessive consumption, if they wanted to justify their existence. In Weber's view, it was the combination of hard work and production, on the one hand, with frugality, thrift, and abstinence, on the other hand, that gave rise to the "spirit of capitalism," and the development of the capitalistic system of production, distribution, and consumption. This was because savings were created that could be ploughed back into more production, more profit generation, and more capital accumulation. John Wesley, one of the founders of Methodism, perhaps said it best when he wrote (quoted by Weber, p. 175; Weber's emphasis):

> religion must necessarily produce both industry and frugality, and these cannot but produce riches . . . We ought not to prevent people from being diligent and frugal; *we must exhort all Christians to gain all they can, and to save all they can; that is, in effect, to grow rich.*

Wesley quickly added that it was also necessary for Christians to donate as much as possible to the church and to good causes, because this was imperative in order to grow in grace and lay up a treasure in Heaven.

For Weber, the person who best epitomized the "Protestant ethic" and the "spirit of capitalism" was Benjamin Franklin, who indeed advocated industry, effort, and honesty combined with parsimony, thrift, saving, and investment. It was Franklin who coined such aphorisms (quoted by Weber, pp. 48–50; Weber's emphases again) as "*time* is money," "*credit* is money," "money is of the prolific, generating nature," "Money can beget money, and its offspring can beget more," and "He that loses five shillings, not only loses that sum, but all the advantage that might be made by turning it in dealing, which by the time that a young man becomes old, will amount to a considerable sum of money."

If Franklin best epitomized the type of individual Weber had in mind when he wrote of the Protestant ethic and the spirit of capitalism, the Protestant countries of northern Europe best epitomized the types of countries Weber had in mind when he made this claim. According to Weber, it was not coincidental that capitalism manifested itself as a system much earlier and more fully in Britain, Belgium, the Netherlands, Sweden, and northern Germany than in France, Spain, Portugal, Italy or southern Germany. Protestantism had progressed much further in the former countries, as had capitalism, and the rational and systematic approach to capitalistic development. According to Weber, Protestants tended to move out of handicrafts and into skilled trades, becoming artisans and manufacturers, whereas Catholics tended to remain in the handicrafts and become masters. The latter were a throwback to the medieval guild system of production, whereas the former were the forerunners of the capitalistic system of production.

It was not long before Weber's theories were being hotly contested as the subject of vigorous debate in the first few decades of the twentieth century (see Tawney, Robertson, Fanfani, and Samuelsson). While most authors and scholars tended to side with Weber, albeit with certain reservations and qualifications, there were several who strongly opposed his views. Talcott Parsons, Eli F. Heckscher, Arthur Lewis, and Gunnar Myrdal, among others, tended to side with Weber, even if they disagreed with specific elements in his theory. Generally speaking, so did the British economic historians William Ashley and R. H. Tawney, and the German economic historian Werner Sombart, although Tawney argued that the prime factor was capitalism, not religion, while Sombart argued that Catholicism as well as Protestantism had fostered a strong capitalistic outlook. However, historians such as Lujo Brentano, H.M. Robertson and Amintore Fanfani disagreed. Brentano argued that many Catholic families were involved in the systematic development of capitalism and exuded the capitalist spirit, not only in Spain, Portugal, and Italy, but also in such northern cities as Amsterdam, Breslau (now Wrocław), Mannheim, Augsburg, or Frankfurt am Main, where Catholic families established banking firms and mercantile houses, and were actively engaged in trade with the colonies. Robertson contended that capitalism and the capitalist spirit existed long before the Reformation. He emphasized that the Italian merchant cities of Venice, Genoa, and Pisa were extremely capitalistic in their commercial operations and trading policies, and were prominent long before Protestantism appeared. He also believed that the idea of "a calling" was not unique to Protestantism in general, or Calvinism or Methodism in particular, but was very much in evidence within Catholicism as well. Fanfani argued that religion was of only minor importance compared to geographical discoveries and the expansion of trade in explaining the rise and spirit of capitalism.

Despite these arguments, Weber's theory concerning the intimate connection between the Protestant ethic and the "spirit of capitalism" has shown a remarkable capacity to endure since it was originally propounded in 1905. Regardless of which side of the controversy one comes down on, one thing is clear. There was a strong connection between religion and the rise of capitalism, a connection that was so strong that it must also be regarded as a key factor in accounting for the origins of the economic age. This is especially true for capitalism as a system, as it has played a pivotal role in driving the development of many countries and the economic age over the past two hundred years and more.

Genesis of the World System

While many other factors contributed to the origins of the economic age, it is clear in retrospect that *The Wealth of Nations*, the industrial revolution, and the interplay of religion and the rise of capitalism contributed the most to setting the economic age in motion, and thus to laying the foundations for the present world system. Of these factors, it is undoubtedly *The Wealth of Nations* that played the quintessential role. In his book Adam Smith focused on the one thing that countries, governments, and people have been increasingly concerned with, and particularly over the past fifty years, namely, the production, distribution, and consumption of material and monetary wealth.

This concern has given rise to the development of the modern world system. It is a system based primarily on economics, economies, and economic growth in general, and specialization, capitalism, capital accumulation, profit maximization, technological development, competition, consumption, international trade, the market, and materialism in particular. This is generally deemed to be the most efficient and effective way to create and augment wealth, increase the supply of goods and services, and make improvements in society. The genesis of this system can be traced back directly to *The Wealth of Nations*. When one looks at the world system today, it is not very different from the one that Smith envisaged, despite the fact that it is infinitely more complex and difficult to manage, and the United States rather than Britain is situated at its core. While the terms used today are different from the ones used in Smith's day, it is still possible to recognize the same basic concerns: the creation and augmentation of wealth, the size of the market, the division of labour and labour specialization, the mobility of labour and capital, international trade, enlightened self-interest, economic and political liberalism, *laissez faire*, the "invisible hand," and the centrality of economics, or what Smith called "political economy," in the overall scheme of things.

This system is the main preoccupation of countries, governments, politicians, planners, corporate officials, international organizations, economists, policy-makers, and development experts in every part of the world. The reason for this is obvious. Without the production, distribution, and consumption of wealth, the prospects for improvements in standards of living and the quality of life are bleak indeed. So are the prospects for social stability and political order. Without the production, distribution, and consumption of wealth, people and countries in every part of the world would be fighting for an economic pie that is shrinking rather than expanding, with all that that would imply for lack of employment and investment opportunities, a great deal of pain and suffering, insufficient opportunities for people to feed themselves and their families, and a great deal of uncertainty and unrest. In such a state of affairs, the potential for violence, conflict, and confrontation would always be close to the surface of society, and much greater than it is today.

If *The Wealth of Nations* played a seminal role in the genesis of the modern world system by focusing attention on the production, distribution, and consumption of wealth, it also played a seminal role in focusing attention on the way in which wealth is defined, measured, compared, and adjusted for changes in price levels. Numerous methods and techniques have been devised for measuring "the wealth of nations," as well as for comparing the wealth of one country with the wealth of other countries. It is thanks in no small part to *The Wealth of Nations* that such well-known forms of measurement and comparison as income per capita, national accounts, consumer price indices, changes in the purchasing power of money, and, particularly, gross domestic product and net domestic product (or, as they are called in *The Wealth of Nations*, "gross revenue" and "neat revenue"), are fundamental elements in the vocabulary and mechanics of the world system today. The notion of "neat revenue" was especially important in Smith's view because it indicated what was left over at the end of one year to be applied to creating and augmenting wealth in the following year (as quoted by Barber, p. 45):

> The gross revenue of all the inhabitants of a great country comprehends the whole annual produce of their land and labour; the neat revenue, what remains free to them after deducting the expense of maintaining; first, their fixed; and, secondly, their circulating capital.

Concern with issues such as these did a great deal to shift attention away from wealth in the form of gold, silver, and other precious metals, which had been central in earlier periods of history, and towards wealth in the form of the "necessaries and conveniences of life," or what today is called gross domestic product. It is on this much more fundamental and tangible way of defining, measuring and comparing wealth that the entire world system of production, distribution, and consumption, with its adjustments for changes in the purchasing power of money, is predicated. Not only are countries compared on the basis of their gross domestic income and gross domestic expenditure, but also changes in gross domestic income and gross domestic expenditure are monitored very carefully to determine whether they are increasing or decreasing, and at what rates.

While much more concern is focused in *The Wealth of Nations* on the production of wealth than on the distribution of wealth, that topic is not neglected, and is indeed fundamental to Smith's view of the world, as indicated above. It is also a fundamental concern of the world system today. While there are more classes and interest groups in society today compared to Smith's time, people and countries in every part of the world are very much concerned about the distribution of wealth among them. In fact, the distribution of wealth has been a consistent concern of economists, politicians, governments, people, and countries ever since Smith's time, resulting in the creation of elaborate theories to explain why different classes and interest groups receive different rates of remuneration for the contributions they make to production and society. The distribution of income and wealth is never far from the front burner of economic and political concern, regardless of whether countries are in an ascending, descending, or stationary state.

The contribution of *The Wealth of Nations* to the genesis of the modern world system does not end here. While this classic publication was concerned largely with the production, distribution, consumption, and measurement of material and monetary wealth, or what economists today call "macroeconomics," it was also concerned to a certain extent with how individuals and institutions function in the economy and the marketplace, or what is called "microeconomics." This gave rise in the nineteenth and twentieth centuries to elaborate theories of consumer and corporate behaviour, the development of corporations and the theory of the firm, the role of "enlightened self-interest" in motivating individuals and institutions to perform in the market, the analysis of consumption patterns and trends, consumerism, and the concepts of labour productivity and productive capacity. Many of the battles that are being waged throughout the world today by labour, management, and governments over labour productivity, and the need to recognize the contributions of health care workers, homemakers, religious leaders, women, service providers, educators, and the like, can be traced back to the distinction made in *The Wealth of Nations* between "productive" and "unproductive" labour.

The Wealth of Nations also contributed substantially to understanding how economies and markets function today. This understanding emanates from the search for laws capable of explaining economic behaviour, the determination of incomes and prices, the circulatory and interdependent nature of the economy and markets, and the need to understand economies and markets as complex entities or "dynamic systems." Governments, corporations, economists, planners, and policy-makers in all parts in the world, as well as international organizations such as the World Bank, the International Monetary Fund, the Organization for Economic Cooperation and Development, the G8, the World Trade Organization, and the World Economic Forum, use this information on a regular basis to develop and plan contemporary economic systems, local, regional, national and international economies, markets, and the world system as a whole.

The Wealth of Nations was not only concerned with how economies and markets *do* function, it was also concerned with how economies and markets *should* function. Adam Smith designated markets as the main vehicles for discharging economic functions, as well as the principal devices for realizing economic and political liberalism, free or freer trade, the unrestricted mobility of labour and capital, and vigorous competition between producers and consumers. This focus on markets is very much alive today, as interest in markets, "market economies," and the market potential of the internet readily confirm. The focus on economic and political liberalism, free or freer trade, the unrestricted mobility of labour and capital, and vigorous competition between producers and consumers has never been greater than it is today, as confirmed by the creation of the European Union, the proposed Free Trade Agreement of the Americas, the World Trade Organization, and the attempt to make the world a "free trade world" predicated on democracy, capitalism, conservatism, competition, and international trade. This is vintage Adam Smith. By arguing in favour of minimum rather than maximum government involvement in the economy and the marketplace, or, as Thomas Carlyle described it, "anarchy plus a constable," Smith set in motion beliefs and convictions about the role of government in economic life that resonate with many people, institutions, countries, and governments today, particularly those concerned with conservatism, capitalism, democracy, and the global economy.

While *The Wealth of Nations* played the pivotal role in the genesis of the present world system, the industrial revolution and the rise of capitalism were not far behind.

The industrial revolution achieved its effects by placing a high priority on industry in general, and industrial development, manufacturing, and commerce in particular. This had the effect of shifting the locus of decision-making from agriculture to industry, from foodstuffs and raw materials to consumer goods and manufactured commodities. While many countries continue to be heavily dependent on agriculture today, particularly in Africa, Asia, Latin America, and the Caribbean, there is no doubt that the large majority of countries lust after industrial development, since they believe, as Adam Smith and the first industrialists believed, that industrial development possesses the potential to expand the economy, and multiply the fruits of economic development, far more than agricultural development does.

Nor is this all. The industrial revolution opened the doors for myriad developments in technological invention and innovation that are still working themselves out today. Thanks in no small part to the industrial revolution, and its heavy reliance on science, scientific achievement, and technical acumen, the world has experienced a continuous outpouring of technological developments, and is currently in the throes of a revolution in communications and information that is every bit as profound and powerful as the industrial and technological revolutions of earlier times.

What is true of the industrial revolution is also true of the connection between religion and capitalism. The phenomenal changes that occurred in religion and capitalism in the sixteenth, seventeenth and eighteenth centuries, whether driven by a "Protestant ethic" or not, have also had a profound effect on the development of the modern world system. There is not a country in the world that does not understand how essential it is to accumulate capital and create a surplus of production over consumption if higher standards of living, and higher levels of income, expenditure, output, and economic growth, are to be achieved. It is clear that more and more countries in the world are moving towards the capitalist system of production, distribution, and consumption in general, and the profit motive and capital accumulation in particular, regardless of whether they are socialist, communist, democratic, dictatorial, liberal or conservative.

In combination, then, these three developments—religion and the rise of capitalism, the industrial revolution, and, above all, *The Wealth of Nations*— laid the foundations for the development of a world system that is predicated primarily on the centrality of economics and economies in general, and markets, profits, specialization, industrialization, capital accumulation, and economic growth in particular. They also laid the foundation for the division of the world into two unequal parts. On the one hand, there were the industrializing and urbanizing countries of western Europe, which rapidly developed their industrial, manufacturing, commercial and technological capabilities, and became highly diversified in their economic output, operations, and economies. On the other hand, there were the countries of Africa, Asia, Latin America, the Caribbean, the Middle East, and (in Smith's day) North America. They quickly became colonial satellites of the leading European countries, and were made to be highly specialized in their economic output, operations, and economies. Their principal function was to provide natural resources and raw materials to those European countries where they could be transformed into finished products, as well as to serve as markets for the rapidly expanding industrial output of these European countries.

This was a very different world from the world of the mercantilists and the great geographical discoveries, which had been based on extending European contact to other parts of the world, and increasing the flow of gold, silver, and other precious metals into Europe. The world of capitalism, the industrial revolution, and *The Wealth of Nations* was increasingly based on colonization, colonialism, and increasing the capacity of colonies to satisfy the economic and political aspirations and interests of their "mother countries." This was accompanied by a shift in the centre of economic gravity in Europe from Spain and Portugal to Britain, France, Germany, and the Netherlands. It was also accompanied by the creation of a whole series of colonial and imperialistic relationships between Europe and the rest of the world that were destined to have a profound effect on economic, social, political and diplomatic developments and relationships throughout the world (see Hobson, Easton, Said, and Asad). While Adam Smith, the capitalists, and the industrialists were excited about colonial development and international trade, they unleashed forces, factions, and divisions that have long dominated the world, and that lie at the heart of many of the pressures, tensions, and hostilities throughout the world today.

2

Evolution of the Economic Age

In the history of economic ideas four major analytical traditions—the classical, Marxian, neoclassical, and Keynesian—stand out. Each was organized around a different set of questions. The circumstances that spurred their formulation have been considerably altered by subsequent events. Nevertheless, many of the central questions on which the pioneer formulators of these "master models" focused are re-asked at later moments in time. When this occurs, we again encounter the theoretical problems with which they wrestled. The study of these systems thus has a perpetual relevance.—William J. Barber (1991), p. 15

The industrial revolution, capitalism, and the theories of Adam Smith proved infectious in the years following the appearance of *The Wealth of Nations* in 1776. In conjunction with many other developments taking place in Europe about the same time—notably, the French Revolution, which espoused liberty, equality, and fraternity, and the Enlightenment, which emphasized reason over passion—this had the effect of generating a rather rosy picture of the future in the minds of many scholars who followed in the footsteps of Adam Smith at the end of the eighteenth century.

One of these scholars was William Godwin, the English political and social philosopher who published *An Enquiry Concerning Political Justice and Its Influence on General Virtue and Happiness* in 1793. In this book Godwin provided a rather glowing account of the future of humanity, despite the fact that his reading of the situation in Britain and the rest of Europe at the time was far more sober. Godwin believed that human beings have a natural inclination to virtue that is corrupted by bad institutions. This inclination would triumph in the end, according to Godwin, thereby making it possible for humanity to create a world free of crime, war, disease, anguish, melancholy, resentment, and bad government, regardless of how far away this might be. Another scholar working in this tradition was the French philosopher, mathematician, and political theorist Marie-Jean-Antoine-Nicolas de Caritat, marquis de Condorcet, whose *Esquisse d'un tableau historique des progrès de l'esprit humain* (*Sketch for a Historical Picture of the Progress of the Human Mind*) appeared in 1795, the year after his death. Condorcet traced human development up to his own time through nine stages, ending with the French Revolution of 1789, and then predicted a "tenth stage" in which, he thought, human perfectibility would be fulfilled. Undoubtedly some of the optimism contained in these and other works can be traced back to Adam Smith and his evocative theories concerning the creation, augmentation, and distribution of wealth.

The only problem with this was that it was not consistent with the type of world that was unfolding in Britain, France, and the rest of Europe at the end of the eighteenth and the beginning of the nineteenth centuries. At the same time as Godwin and Condorcet were predicting a world free of war, vice, violence, and misery, and extolling the perfectibility of humankind, actual conditions were moving in a very different direction. While living standards were improving for landlords, capitalists, and even numerous labourers, a number of negative signs were appearing on the horizon. Most prominent among these signs were the huge concentrations of labourers in highly centralized locations; the intensifying exploitation of labour, particularly child labour; deteriorating social conditions; increases in the cost of living; growing disparities in income and wealth among the three main classes in society; the appearance of slums and shanty towns; and the tendency for increases in population to eat up a large proportion of the gains realized through industrialization, the spread of capitalism, and economic growth.

These signs were seized on in different ways by three very distinguished pioneers of what is now called economics: Thomas Robert Malthus, who was also an Anglican clergyman; David Ricardo, who was also a politician, financier, and landlord; and John Stuart Mill who was also a Utilitarian philosopher, social activist, and humanist. In combination with James Mill (John Stuart's father), Robert Torrens, John Ramsey McCulloch, William Nassau Senior, and others, they comprise what is now seen as the "classical" school of economics, spearheaded by Adam Smith. Since this school was destined to have a profound effect on the evolution of the economic age, particularly in the first half of the nineteenth century, it pays to examine the thoughts of these three remarkable individuals at some length.

Classical Economics

While Malthus, Ricardo, and John Stuart Mill each had their own particular views on a variety of economic, political and social matters, they shared many common convictions concerning the economy, markets, and economic theory. Despite their common debt to Adam Smith, the tone of their writing was distinctly different from that of *The Wealth of Nations*. Whereas Smith was optimistic about the long-term prospects facing humanity, Malthus, Ricardo, and Mill were more pessimistic. Their pessimism sprang from the conviction that a "stationary state" would eventually be reached in human affairs, where little or no economic growth, capital accumulation or wealth creation would take place, largely as a result of the law of diminishing returns. Moreover, whereas Smith visualized a society where there was harmony among all three classes in society—labourers, landlords, and capitalists—as well as rising standards of living for all, Malthus, Ricardo, and Mill visualized a society in which there would be a great deal of conflict among the classes and a rising standard of living for only one, or, under certain conditions, two of these classes. This caused these three writers to direct much of their energy and attention to the way in which wealth is distributed, whereas Smith had directed much of his energy and attention to the way in which wealth is produced.

Despite these differences, Malthus, Ricardo and Mill did share a great deal in common with Smith. For one thing, they believed, as Smith did, that labour is the principal source of all value and wealth. Unlike Smith, however, they were far less optimistic about the possibility of the labouring class benefiting significantly from this fact. They believed that labourers would respond to increases in wealth primarily by having more children, thereby creating a labour force that was too large. This would have the effect of driving wages down to the subsistence level, rather than keeping them above it. This became known in economics as "the iron law of wages," referring to the constant tendency for wages to return to the level of subsistence.

In addition, and more importantly, Malthus, Ricardo and Mill believed that after a certain point was reached "the law of diminishing returns" would cause output to decrease rather than increase, as more and more of the variable factor of production, labour, was added to the fixed factor of production, land. This was because more land would be brought into cultivation to feed an expanding population and this land would be of inferior quality compared to the land already in cultivation. The only exception to this general rule was when technological advances, or improvements in the "state of technique" as the classical economists called it, offset the law of diminishing returns. In this case, diminishing returns could be postponed for a time, but not indefinitely, because sooner or later a limit would be reached where all the land available for cultivation would be exhausted, or the additional land brought into cultivation would be so poor in quality that improvements in the "state of technique" would not be sufficient to offset the law of diminishing returns. This was of great concern in Britain, with its small and fixed land mass, finite resources, limited natural base, and rapidly expanding population.

Malthus was the first person to confront the implications of the complex connection between the quantity, quality, and fixity of land and resources, on the one hand, and population growth, production of the means of subsistence, and the law of diminishing returns, on the other. He did so by attacking the theories of Godwin and Condorcet, particularly those concerned with the perfectibility of humankind and the eventual arrival of a utopian state in human affairs. In fact, according to most authors, Malthus derived much of his passion, or, as some say, venom, for the writing of his *Essay on the Principle of Population as It Affects the Future Improvement of Society, with Remarks on the Speculations of Mister Godwin, Monsieur Condorcet, and Other Writers* (1798) from his desire to expose what he saw as the flaws in their popular ideas. This is how his essay begins (as quoted in Barber, p. 59):

> I think I may fairly make two postulata. First, That food is necessary to the existence
> of man. Secondly, That the passion between the sexes is necessary, and will remain
> nearly in its present state . . . Assuming, then, my postulata as granted, I say, that the
> power of population is indefinitely greater than the power in the earth to produce
> subsistence for man. Population, when unchecked, increases in a geometrical ratio.
> Subsistence only increases in an arithmetical ratio. A slight acquaintance with
> numbers will show the immensity of the first power in comparison with the second.

According to Malthus, population tends to grow at a geometric rate (l, 2, 4, 8, 16, 32 and so on), doubling roughly every twenty-five to thirty years. The means of subsistence, in contrast, tend to grow at an arithmetic rate (1, 2, 3, 4, 5, 6 and so on). He concluded that there is a constant tendency for population growth to outstrip the means of subsistence.

Since this is not possible in fact because people must eat in order to survive, this means that certain "checks" must be brought into play to keep population growth in line with the means of subsistence. These checks were of two types. First, there were "preventive checks": abstaining from sexual relations, late marriage, and, particularly, moral restraint. Second, there were "positive checks": famine, plague, pestilence, disease, starvation, poverty, war, infanticide, and the like. If the preventive checks failed to do the job, the positive checks, whatever their negative effects on individuals, must come into play, because population cannot exceed the means of subsistence.

In raising this issue Malthus put his finger on one of the most difficult and complex problems in economics and human affairs, namely, the relationship between people and population growth, on the one hand, and the means of subsistence and the natural environment, on the other. This brought to the fore both the positive and negative aspects of population growth. On the one hand, population growth acts as a spur to the creation of wealth and to economic growth because it increases the demand for "the necessaries and conveniences of life," as Adam Smith called them. On the other hand, population growth puts considerable strain on natural resources and the natural environment, because of the need to increase the means of subsistence to feed an expanding population. This was especially difficult for Britain in view of its limited domestic supply of natural resources, and its heavy dependence on natural resources and raw materials from abroad, which helps to explain why Britain was so committed to, and dependent on, colonial development and international trade in the eighteenth, nineteenth and twentieth centuries.

Given Malthus's views on this complex and difficult subject, it is easy to see why classical economics took a pessimistic turn after the publication of Malthus's strident polemic. Not only did Malthus believe that there was a constant tendency for population to outstrip the means of subsistence, he was also very pessimistic about the capacity of "preventive checks" to limit population growth, largely because of the inability of the labouring class to control its sexual desires and exercise constraint. Interestingly, this led Malthus to oppose the Poor Law, the English system of state aid to the very poor, because he believed that it discouraged sexual restraint, limited the mobility of labour (since aid was given only to long-term residents of each parish, not to incomers from other parishes), and led to increases in population and deteriorating prospects for the labouring class. He also believed that more and more of the "positive checks" would be brought into play, a prospect that he and others did not relish.

None of this augured well for the types of improvements that Smith wrote about in *The Wealth of Nations*, especially the ability of the economy to produce an expanding supply of goods and services capable of enhancing living standards for all classes in society. In fact, according to Malthus, precisely the opposite could and most likely would be the case. Destructive rather than constructive changes would take place as the population expanded, and more and more pressure was exerted on land and existing resources. This helps to explain why Malthus's views on population in general, and his *Essay on the Principle of Population* in particular, generated a great deal of attention and debate in his day. It also helps to explain why Thomas Carlyle called economics "the dismal science" after reading Malthus's essay.

What made matters worse, in Malthus's view, was the possibility of "market gluts." These could occur when some of the products produced in a given period were not taken off the market because consumers lacked the funds to purchase them. While most of the other classical economists dismissed this possibility, because they believed that "supply creates its own demand" according to the law propounded by the French economist Jean-Baptiste Say, it was clear that Malthus had pinpointed a very serious problem in the functioning of economic systems and markets. This was the possibility of overproduction, underconsumption, market gluts, and business cycles, and whether or not there is a self-regulating and self-correcting mechanism at work in the economy and the market causing things to return to normal when there is a deviation from the norm. Despite this, one hundred years and more were to pass before Malthus's views on this set of issues were recognized and given their due. It was when "market gluts" became a reality during the Great Depression of the 1930s that interest in Malthus's views intensified and it was discovered that in his *Principles of Political Economy* (1820) he had foreseen many of the economic problems encountered at the end of the nineteenth and in the early years of the twentieth centuries.

If classical economics took a pessimistic turn with Malthus's population theory, his views on the Poor Law, and the possibility of market gluts, it took an even more pessimistic turn after the publication of David Ricardo's *Principles of Political Economy and Taxation* in 1817. By then the whole nature and tenor of Britain and the rest of Europe had changed substantially in the wake of the Napoleonic Wars and a series of bad harvests in Britain. Ricardo's classic treatise did a great deal to strengthen the theoretical side of economics, making the case for a more scientific and empirical approach to economic theory, consolidating the classical tradition, and broadening and deepening understanding of the ways in which complex economic systems function. It also did much to reinforce the pessimistic conclusions arrived at by Malthus. As Robert L. Heilbroner has observed (p. 82), whereas Smith had "looked at the world and had seen in it a great concert, Ricardo saw a bitter conflict."

Ricardo followed Smith in one very important respect, in being interested in how production and distribution are handled in complex economic systems. Whereas Smith had been largely concerned with production, however, Ricardo was far more concerned with distribution (as indicated earlier). By the time Ricardo arrived on the scene the rapidly changing conditions in Britain and the rest of Europe were revealing that distribution was not proceeding in a manner consistent with Smith's conviction that all classes would benefit from increases in production and wealth. Indeed, according to Ricardo, only one class was benefiting from the increases in production, the landlord class. To make matters worse, it was benefiting at the expense of the other two classes, the labourers and the capitalists. This caused Ricardo to state in his *Principles* that the interests of the landlord class are opposed to the interests of all other classes in society.

Precisely why this was so Ricardo set out to explain. He did so by creating a hypothetical economic system, similar to the British economic system of his day, which was divided into the three main classes of landlords, labourers, and capitalists. Ricardo then asked what would happen if wealth is increased and economic growth takes place. According to Ricardo, wages, profits, and rents would all increase initially, meaning that all classes would be better off. However, over a longer period of time labourers would respond to the increase in wealth by having larger families, thereby contributing to population growth and driving their own standard of living down rather than up, as they endeavoured to feed, clothe, and house additional members of their families. In response, landlords would bring more land into cultivation to feed the expanding population. Since the land they brought into cultivation was always inferior to the land already in cultivation, and since the price of products is always determined by the costs of production on the last land brought into cultivation, or, in Ricardo's terms, "at the margin," rents would rise on the better land. This would mean that landlords would be better off.

According to Ricardo, capitalists would respond to the increase in population by expanding their output. This would be favourable to the capitalists initially, because their profits would increase rather than decrease, but eventually it would be detrimental because capitalists would be compelled to pay more out of their profits for wages as subsistence costs increased and inferior land was brought into cultivation. Since Ricardo believed that rent is always zero on the last land brought into cultivation, and that price is always determined at the margin, this meant that there had to be an inverse relationship between wages and profits. The higher wages rose to cover the increased costs of subsistence, the lower profits would fall. Ultimately a point would be reached where profits would fall to zero and no capital accumulation would take place. While landlords reaped a double reward from increases in output and prices as more and more land was brought into cultivation, the interests of the labourers, capitalists, and the economy generally deteriorated. For Ricardo this trend amounted to a prescription for social, political and economic disaster. Not only did it possess the potential to produce continuous conflicts between the three main classes in society, but it also rewarded the class that contributed least to the creation of wealth, production, and economic growth. Behind this, of course, was the law of diminishing returns, ever ready to decrease production and productivity, and usher in "a stationary state" whenever technology proved insufficient to meet the limits imposed by fixed amounts of land, scarce resources, and an expanding population.

If this situation disturbed Ricardo a great deal, what particularly irked him was the ability of the landlord class to pass legislation that favoured their interests at the expense of everybody else, thereby reinforcing and perpetuating basic inequalities and injustices in the economic system and society generally. They were able to do this through, for example, the Corn Laws, which kept foreign grain out of Britain when prices for these basic foodstuffs were skyrocketing as a result of the Napoleonic wars and the bad harvests at home. Just how important grain was to Britain at the time can be confirmed by the fact that Ricardo used grain in general and corn in particular, rather than gold, silver, money or precious metals, to demonstrate how the British economy functioned, and how production and distribution were determined in his hypothetical economic model. The reason for this is not difficult to detect. On the one hand, grain was the most important item in the diets both of the labouring class and of the livestock required for agricultural production. On the other hand, grain was the most important output in an economy still heavily dependent on agriculture, despite the fact that the industrial revolution was in full swing and was beginning to assume gigantic proportions. It was logical, then, for Ricardo to use grain to measure and assess the changes that were taking place in the British economy, as well as in prices, incomes, wages, profits, and rents.

This is what made the Corn Laws such a crucial issue for Ricardo. The landlords were able to exploit this staple, turning the trade and consumption of grain to their advantage. They did this by imposing duties and a sliding scale on imports of foreign grain into Britain. The lower the foreign price for grain fell, the higher went the duty. Thus a floor was established that kept low-priced foreign grain permanently out of Britain and also kept domestic prices artificially high. Just how onerous this was for the labouring class can be understood when it is realized that a bushel of wheat cost labourers in Britain twice their weekly wages. This became too much for the labouring class, the capitalists, and the classical economists to accept, particularly when the landlords were lobbying Parliament to raise the duty on foreign grain even higher in order to protect their stranglehold on the domestic market. At this point the capitalists rebelled, organized a powerful lobby, and flooded Parliament with more petitions than it had received on any other issue up to this time. Fortunately, grain prices moved back to more acceptable levels following Napoleon's defeat in 1815. Unfortunately, it took another thirty-one years before the Corn Laws were repealed, in 1846.

There are two additional aspects of Ricardo's economic theory that should be mentioned here because they were destined to have an important impact on the evolution of the economic age, and the development of economic theory and practice. The first is his theory of comparative advantage and international trade, the second his theory of taxation.

Unlike Smith, who believed in the "law of absolute advantage" as it applied to international trade, Ricardo believed in the "law of comparative advantage." A country may possess an absolute advantage in the production of all products over other countries, but it may be able to produce some of these products much more efficiently than others, thereby giving it a comparative advantage in the production of these products (as compared to other products and other countries). Even though Britain had an absolute advantage in the production of all products, it paid Britain to specialize in the production of products for which it had a comparative advantage and let other countries specialize in the production of products for which they had a comparative advantage. In a global sense this would yield an international system where countries specialized in making and exporting products for which they had a comparative advantage, while importing products for which they had a comparative disadvantage. This is pretty much what happened during the nineteenth century, as, in conjunction with the development of the colonies and colonization, Ricardo's views came to be used to justify a whole series of trading policies, practices, and relations among Britain, France, and other countries. These were well-suited to the capitalist class in Britain, which tended to see international trade based on the law of comparative advantage as a powerful tool for increasing exports while simultaneously reducing the cost of imports. They were also well suited to an age in which Britain was rapidly becoming "the workshop of the world." It depended on other countries to provide it with the raw materials, basic staples, and markets that were needed to fuel industrial development, and overcome domestic resource deficiencies through imports from abroad. This had a powerful effect on the division of the world into two unequal parts, "developed" and "developing," that has become a standard feature of the present economic age and the modern world system.

Ricardo's other major contribution to the development of the economic age and classical economic theory was his theory of taxation. Given his commitment to economic and political liberalism, competition, *laissez faire*, and international trade, it is not surprising that he devoted a great deal of time and attention to this subject, and became one of the first economists to delve deeply into matters of fiscal policy and public finance. What concerned Ricardo was not only the incidence of taxation (who actually pays the taxes), but also how taxes affect the three main classes of society, and are shifted from one class to another and from one sector of the economy to another. For example, Ricardo felt that a tax on rent would fall largely on the landlord class and would not be shifted to other classes in society because the landlord class would not be able to increase the price of output at the margin of cultivation. However, other taxes might fall on labourers, consumers or capitalists, depending on specific circumstances. For example, a tax on wages would tend to be borne by capitalists in the form of lower profits because wages were usually at or near the subsistence level and labourers simply could not afford to pay any higher taxes. Taxes on output or land, however, would probably be shifted to labourers and consumers, in the form of higher prices for products.

It is clear from the foregoing that Ricardo's theories on a variety of economic and political matters were destined to have a profound effect on economic theory and practice, and on the development of the economic age. What counted were not only Ricardo's theories themselves—the labour theory of value, the theory of differential rent, the analysis of economic situations at the margin, the law of comparative advantage and international trade, the theory of taxation, and the rest—but also the ways in which the theories were developed and used by others. Unlike Smith, Malthus, and other economists who relied largely on general observation and the inductive method to make their case, Ricardo relied heavily on abstract theorizing and the deductive method to make his case. He was the first economist to use hypothetical models in the search for "scientific laws" capable of explaining economic behaviour. In so doing he set in motion a tradition that has steadily gathered momentum since his time, and has been used to great advantage by economists.

Moreover, and more importantly as far as the evolution of the economic age is concerned, Ricardo was the first economist to advocate looking at problems from a strictly economic point of view, before taking other factors into account. While he had a highly successful career in finance and politics, and was involved in numerous political, commercial, agrarian and governmental affairs, he believed that it was necessary to search for economic solutions to economic problems, develop models that were predicated on economic considerations rather than other considerations, and draw conclusions that were economic in nature. It was only after this rigorous economic process was completed that, Ricardo believed, the political, ethical, philosophical and social implications and consequences of actions and decisions should be taken into account. This conviction too has had a profound impact. It made economics *the* most important discipline in society, thrusting it into a powerful position in society and the political process. This is probably why Ricardo is regarded as "the economist's economist" by the large majority of economists. While Adam Smith played a crucial role in creating the theoretical and practical foundations for the economic age, it was Ricardo who carried the economic age into adulthood. He did so by making economics the highly specialized discipline it is today, as well as an independent rather than dependent factor in society. It is for reasons such as these that Ricardo and Ricardian economics dominated economic thought and practice in Britain and elsewhere in Europe in the middle of the nineteenth century.

John Stuart Mill continued in the Ricardian tradition in virtually all respects, but there is one respect in which he differed somewhat from Ricardo. Whereas Ricardo was pessimistic about the prospects confronting Britain, the rest of Europe, and humanity in general, Mill was more optimistic. He believed that it was possible to separate "the laws governing production" from "the laws governing distribution," which led him to very different conclusions about the distribution of wealth than those reached by Ricardo. He also believed that the "stationary state" could be a universal blessing rather than a diabolical curse, especially if it was understood and dealt with properly.

Mill is much better known today for his social and political writings and activities than for his economic ideas, particularly for his contributions to Utilitarianism, and to both theoretical liberalism and British political Liberalism, as well as for his pioneering writings on women's rights, proportional representation, labour unions, socialism, the education of the poor, and agricultural cooperatives. However, he made many valuable contributions to the advancement of economics as a discipline through his attempts to consolidate and strengthen the classical tradition, and to place economics on a much firmer empirical and scientific foundation.

Some of Mill's most effective writing on economic subjects concerned international trade. In 1829 and 1830, for example, he wrote a series of *Essays on Some Unsettled Questions of Political Economy* that substantially broadened and deepened understanding of the law of comparative advantage advanced by Ricardo. Whereas Ricardo was content to state the law and emphasize its importance, Mill was interested in the ways in which the gains from international trade are shared and distributed among the various trading partners. This led him into such areas as the reciprocal demand for products; the way the terms of trade are determined between countries; the strength and elasticity of demand for international commodities and resources; the effect of tariffs on trading practices and the terms of trade; and how the adjustment mechanism works among countries involved in international trade. As a result, Mill helped to lay the foundations for the modern world's emphasis on international trade, free trade, free trade zones, and globalization, and for the virtually universal commitment to international trade and exchange as a key component in economic growth.

These contributions were enhanced considerably when Mill's landmark publication, *Principles of Political Economy*, was published in 1848. Mill recognized that broadening and deepening understanding of the causes and consequences of production and distribution lay at the heart of classical economics. However, he believed that there are fundamental differences between the laws governing production and those governing distribution. The laws governing production are, in his view, fixed and immutable, because they derive largely from technical and physical factors such as the quantity and quality of land, the application of labour and capital to land, the skill and dexterity of workers, and the operation of the law of diminishing returns. The laws governing distribution, however, are very different. According to Mill, they are not fixed and immutable, but are socially and humanly determined, largely because they are based on such factors as values, value systems, and, especially, the ways in which institutions and societies decide to conduct and regulate their domestic and international affairs. Simply put, Mill's argument was that, once societies have created wealth, they can distribute it in any way they please.

This distinction between the laws governing production and those governing distribution made it possible to reinterpret classical economics in more positive terms. However, this was not possible, in Mill's view, without governments playing a much larger, stronger, and more direct and active role in the economy and markets. Smith, Malthus, and Ricardo had been firmly opposed to state intervention in the free functioning of the economy, but Mill argued that the state should play a "civilizing role" in society, largely by evening out fluctuations in economic activity, making investments in public works, undertaking worthwhile social programmes, and, especially, educating labourers, for Mill believed that their ignorance lay at the root of the distribution problem. Educating labourers would allow society to break the vicious circle created by population growth, the propensity for the labouring class to have more children, the iron law of wages, and the tendency for wages to return to the subsistence level. If the labouring class could be educated to have smaller families when wealth was increased and economic growth took place, their wages would rise above the subsistence level, the pressure of their numbers upon subsistence would be reduced, and the wealth and well-being of all in society, and not just the landlord class, would be improved.

These views were carried over into Mill's interpretation of "the stationary state." While Mill believed, as Malthus and Ricardo had before him, that the stationary state was inevitable, largely because of the law of diminishing returns and the inability of improvements in technology to offset the law in the long run, he was much more optimistic than they had been about what might be achieved once the stationary state was reached (Mill, pp. 748 and 751):

> I cannot, therefore, regard the stationary state of capital and wealth with the unaffected aversion so generally manifested towards it by political economists of the old school. I am inclined to believe that it would be, on the whole, a very considerable improvement on our present condition.
>
> . . . It is scarcely necessary to remark that a stationary condition of capital and population implies no stationary state of human improvement. There would be as much scope as ever for all kinds of mental culture, and moral and social progress; as much room for improving the Art of Living, and much more likelihood of its being improved, when minds ceased to be engrossed by the art of getting on.

It is clear why there was much more enthusiasm and excitement in Britain and elsewhere over Mill's theories than there had been over Malthus's or Ricardo's. Mill provided a way out, an escape from the relentless march of the Malthusian theory of population, the iron law of wages, and the Ricardian theory of rent. Rather than looking forward to a future of poverty, negativity, exploitation, and class tension, Mill was much more encouraging. Through foresight, planning, government involvement in the economy and markets, and, especially, the education of the labouring class, it would be possible to lift the mass of the population out of the economic and social doldrums, and achieve a realistic standard of living and a satisfactory way of life for all. For the first time in more than fifty years, a ray of hope had appeared on the horizon.

This shift towards hopefulness was strengthened by the fact that the stationary state was not emerging in the way the classical economists had predicted. In fact, it was not emerging at all. Technological advances were outstripping the law of diminishing returns, and an international system was evolving that made it possible for Britain and other European countries to overcome their domestic economic deficiencies by drawing on resources, products, materials, and markets in other parts of the world, most notably Canada, the United States, South America, the Caribbean, Asia, Africa, Australia, and New Zealand. While this was to have profound consequences for the evolution of the economic age and the development of the world system, especially through the division of the world into colonized and colonizing countries, dependence on technology to fuel economic growth, and the changing relationship between human beings and the natural environment, these consequences were not fully recognized at the time.

What *was* recognized at the time was that the rapidly changing conditions in Britain and elsewhere in Europe were causing more and more problems for classical economics. A number of economic, social and political thinkers were becoming increasingly uneasy about the highly theoretical nature of classical economics, especially as it was manifested in Ricardian economic theory, even though, for most of them, Mill's more optimistic vision of the future still seemed far-fetched. What is known as the "historical school of economics" came into being, spearheaded by scholars and historians such as John Ingram, Cliffe Leslie, Walter Bagehot, and Richard Jones in Britain, and Friedrich List, Wilhelm Roscher, Bruno Hildebrand, Karl Knies, Gustav von Schmoller, Arthur Spiethoff, and Werner Sombart in central Europe. They believed that economics should be based on history rather than theory, on historical analysis, empirical observation, actual experience, and induction rather than abstraction, theoretical analysis, model-building, and deduction. The "historical economists" did not object to the quest to discover laws capable of explaining economic behaviour, and of guiding public and private policy- and decision-making. What they strenuously objected to were the methods and techniques used to discover these laws. They believed that it was necessary to examine history in great detail before any such laws could be detected and formulated. This was particularly important in view of the fact that public and private policies were predicated on these laws.

While the historical economists failed to generate a great deal of interest in the inductive rather than the deductive approach to economics, except in a few isolated and esoteric cases, John Stuart Mill's vision of the future was coming increasingly into question, despite the enthusiasm and optimism it generated in certain quarters. Most prominent among the rapidly changing conditions that challenged Mill's optimism were the disruptions, dislocations, and transformations that were being experienced as a result of the industrial revolution and the spread of the factory system of production. The industrial revolution was in full swing, reaching its zenith by the middle of the nineteenth century. A much larger proportion of Britain's population was working in manufacturing than in agriculture, resulting in a rapidly burgeoning urban population, huge concentrations of labour and capital in very specific locations, a great deal of monotonous and tedious work, overcrowding, poverty, shanty towns, squalor, misery, and the factory system of production. The pain, suffering, and turmoil caused by this situation were captured by numerous novelists and authors writing at the time. One need only read Charles Dickens's novels *Oliver Twist*, *David Copperfield*, *Bleak House*, *Hard Times* or *Great Expectations* to realize how oppressive economic, social and political conditions were for many people by the middle of the nineteenth century.

With the industrial revolution came greater emphasis on science, technology, industrial development, and materialism. As more and more products poured out of European factories, and as more and more technological inventions and innovations were introduced into the production process, the whole tenor of European life changed. These developments were reinforced by a more scientific view of life, as well as a quantitative rather than qualitative approach to development. This situation was profoundly affected by the appearance of Charles Darwin's *On the Origin of Species* (1859). Not only did Darwin take a highly scientific and empirical approach to the human condition, largely by emphasizing the need to examine situations empirically and delve deeply into the facts of the matter, he also placed a great deal of emphasis on evolution, materialism, competition, and the need to adapt to constantly changing environmental conditions and ecological circumstances. This emphasis was magnified by Darwin's followers, particularly Herbert Spencer, who coined the term "survival of the fittest," which came to epitomize the Darwinian revolution.

Marxian Economics

It was into this highly materialistic, competitive and industrialized world, with all its major social, economic and political problems, inequalities, and dislocations, that Karl Marx stepped in the middle of the nineteenth century. Marx was not, of course, the first scholar to be concerned with the impact of the industrial revolution, and the rapid changes it induced in economic and social conditions, on the labouring class and on society in general. Numerous economic and social thinkers—including Jean-Charles-Léonard de Sismondi, Henri de Saint-Simon, Charles Fourier, and Pierre-Joseph Proudhon in France, Robert Owen and John Francis Bray in Britain, and Karl Robertus in Germany—had expressed concerns about the adverse effects of industrialization, the factory system of production, and massive technological change. Moreover, they were endeavouring to do something concrete and constructive about it in their research, writing, and political activities. With this came questioning of classical economics, as well as the reasons, motives, and objectives behind it. Was classical economics designed to uncover the laws governing economic behaviour and the nature of economic truth? Or was it designed to advance the interests of the rich and privileged classes of society, and to perpetuate the established order? It was questions such as these that Marx, in his turn, set out to address.

While Marx rejected classical economic theory because he believed that it distorted the nature of economic truth and the real character of historical development, he depended heavily on classical economics in most other respects. For example, he adopted "the labour theory of value" propounded by the classical economists, but also claimed that capital is "stored up" or "congealed" labour. This is because capital can be broken into two components, according to Marx: the raw materials used in production, which are given by nature, and the labour required to produce the capital. This made labour the central pillar in Marx's entire economic system. Marx followed in the classical tradition in another very fundamental respect by accepting the basic distinction the classical economists had made between production and distribution. However, Marx believed that it was necessary to analyze these two basic components of the capitalist system together rather than separately, since distribution affects production every bit as much as production affects distribution.

Like Malthus, Ricardo, Mill, and the other classical economists, Marx was also very concerned about the distribution of wealth. The reason for this is not difficult to detect. By the time Marx arrived on the scene the social costs of industrialization were proving to be very substantial, particularly for the labouring class. People were pouring into the newly established urban centres looking for work, social conditions were rapidly deteriorating, pollution was mounting, there was a great deal of poverty and unemployment, labour, particularly child labour, was being exploited unmercifully, and capital was replacing labour at a disturbing rate. This situation troubled Marx very deeply, and caused him to focus attention on who benefits the most and who the least from the creation of wealth within the capitalist mode of production.

By Marx's time capitalists rather than landlords formed the most powerful class in the societies in western Europe that Marx lived in and studied, making it possible for Marx to view society in terms of two classes rather than three. On the one hand, there were the labourers, who had nothing to sell but their labour, despite the fact that they were the real creators of all value and wealth. On the other hand, there were the capitalists, who owned the machinery, the equipment, and, often, the land used by labourers in production. Although the capitalists produced very few products themselves, they had all the advantages in the production process, because they were able to exploit labourers who had nothing to sell but their labour. This in turn made it possible for capitalists to gain "surplus value" on the capital they used in production by compelling labourers to work many more hours for their subsistence than was actually required to produce their subsistence. Whereas it might take labourers two hours a day to produce their subsistence, for instance, they might end up working ten to twelve hours a day for capitalists because the capitalists possessed all the economic advantages. This gave rise to what Marx called "the rate of exploitation" of labour and labourers by capital and capitalists. Whenever and wherever there was a great deal of unemployment in the economy, which was common during the industrial revolution because labour was constantly being replaced by capital, capitalists could increase surplus value and the rate of exploitation by drawing on "the industrial reserve army" caused by technological change and the replacement of labour by capital. This made it possible for capitalists to compel labourers to work even longer hours to produce their means of subsistence.

It was the exploitation of labour and the labouring class by capital and the capitalist class that caused Marx to direct more and more of his time, energy, and attention to understanding "the real nature of capital" and the capitalist system of production (see Sweezy). His views on this subject were set out in *Capital*, his unfinished *magnum opus*. The first volume, the only one completed by Marx himself, appeared in 1867, but the other two volumes, compiled and edited by Marx's collaborator Engels, did not appear until 1884 and 1894, after Marx's death.

According to Marx's analysis in *Capital*, Volume III, there is a tendency inherent in the capitalist mode of production for the rate of profits to fall. This may seem a rather curious conclusion, in view of the fact that capitalists were able to exploit labourers and extract surplus value from them, but it was consistent with the view of most of the classical economists, though they held it for entirely different reasons than Marx. According to Adam Smith, the rate of profits would fall because more and more competition would take place among capitalists, or manufacturers as Smith called them. According to Ricardo, the rate of profits fell because there was an inverse relationship between profits and wages, such that profits would fall as wages rose to cover increases in the cost of living. In Marx's analysis, however, the rate of profits fell because of the composition of capital itself. Since, according to Marx, only *variable* capital generated surplus value, and since profits derive from variable capital rather than from fixed capital, the rate of profits must fall as more variable capital is added to the stock of fixed capital. The only thing that can prevent this is a rise in "the rate of exploitation" as capitalists force workers to work longer hours, use more women and children in production, or increase the productivity of labour. While this was possible to a certain extent, according to Marx, the situation could not be sustained for a long time without the "immiseration of the masses," especially as more and more capital was accumulated, and capitalists tried harder to increase their profits. Eventually, more and more pronounced dislocations, inequalities, and disruptions would take place. As the labouring class became more and more immiserated, there would be more and more unemployment, causing the industrial reserve army to grow. As a result, labourers would have less and less income to purchase the products produced by the capitalist system. This could result in overproduction, underconsumption, and gluts in markets, just as Malthus had predicted, as well as more and more economic fluctuations and instability. This would heighten the conflicts and tensions between the capitalist class and the labouring class.

In *The Communist Manifesto*, written with Engels and published in 1848, Marx argued that this situation could not prevail indefinitely because of the "inherent contradictions in capitalism." These contradictions were numerous for Marx. One resulted from the fact that it was the labourers who were responsible for the creation of all value and wealth, but it was the capitalists who reaped the benefits. Another was due to the fact that the capitalists were able to receive surplus value and exploit labour while, at the same time, there was a tendency for the rate of profits to fall rather than rise in the capitalist system. Still another was due to the fact that, as more and more capital accumulated, the incentive to accumulate capital and increase production was reduced. For Marx, all these factors, and others, would eventually lead to more and more pronounced and erratic disruptions, depressions, and crises in the capitalist system. While international development, imperialism, and colonialism might postpone the collapse of capitalism for a time, they could not postpone it indefinitely. Eventually "the workers of the world" would unite and overthrow the capitalists, and with them, the capitalist system of production. The workers would then abolish the capitalist system and introduce communism. In this state of affairs society and production would be controlled by labourers rather than by capitalists, and would evolve in a manner consistent with the interests and needs of the labouring class rather than the capitalist class. Ultimately, the state would "wither away" because there would no longer be any need for it.

If Marx's views had been confined to an extensive analysis of capitalism, the need for communism, and his impact on economic and political thought and practice, his influence on subsequent events and the evolution of the economic age might well have been far less substantial than it turned out to be. However, Marx's influence does not end with his stinging indictment of capitalism and his prognosis with respect to communism. Marx laid the philosophical and historical foundations for the economic age, just as Adam Smith created the theoretical and practical foundations for it. Marx did this by way of what is often called, perhaps misleadingly, his "economic interpretation of history."

The practice of dividing societies into an economic (or "material") "base" and a non-economic "superstructure" has been evident in the works of most economists, before, during and after Marx's time, whether they belong to the classical, neoclassical, Keynesian, post-Keynesian or development schools of thought. However, these terms have come to be associated with Marx and Marxism in particular. According to Marx, the economic base consists of the material conditions of life and the attendant mode of production in a given society. The arts, ethics, education, religion, philosophy, politics, spirituality and the like form in their turn the superstructure, which depends on the productive base for its existence.

Marx and Engels both emphasized, repeatedly and at length, that there is a reciprocal relationship between base and superstructure, so that changes in one can cause changes in the other. However, many Marxists, and many other interpreters and critics of Marx's ideas, have treated the model as if the base was always and everywhere a "cause," and the superstructure merely the "effect." Thus, while Marx and Engels sought to show how the various elements of the superstructure originated from the base but then developed along their own paths, influencing the base as they did so, it is often assumed that they believed that everything is reducible to economics.

Nevertheless, of all of Marx's ideas, it is the "economic interpretation" of history that has had the most powerful effect, however simplified and misleading some versions of it have been since Marx. In *The German Ideology* (1845), an early philosophical polemic rather than economic analysis, he and Engels boldly asserted that (Gardiner, p. 129):

> Morality, religion, metaphysics, and other ideologies, and their corresponding forms of consciousness . . . have no history, no development; it is men, who, in developing their material production and their material intercourse, change, along with this, their real existence, their thinking and the products of their thinking. Life is not determined by consciousness, but consciousness by life.

In the same work they set out the basis of their programme of research and analysis, again in broadly philosophical terms (Gardiner, p. 126-127):

> The first premise of all human history is, of course, the existence of living human individuals. The first fact to be established, therefore, is the physical constitution of these individuals and their consequent relation to the rest of Nature. . . . Men can be distinguished from animals by consciousness, by religion, or anything one likes. They themselves begin to distinguish themselves from animals as soon as they begin to *produce* their means of subsistence, a step which is determined by their physical constitution. . . . What individuals are, therefore, depends on the material conditions of their production. . . . This conception of history, therefore, rests on the exposition of the real process of production, starting from the simple material production of life. . . . From this starting point, it explains all the different theoretical productions and forms of consciousness, religion, philosophy, ethics, etc., and traces their origins and growth.

By 1859, when Marx wrote his *Preface to a Critique of Political Economy*, his focus was more narrowly on economic issues, and the power of the "mode of production" to "determine" the superstructure (Gardiner, p. 131):

> In the social production which men carry on they enter into definite relations
> that are indispensable and independent of their will; these relations of production
> correspond to a definite stage of development of their material powers of production.
> The totality of these relations of production constitutes the economic structure of
> society—the real foundation, on which legal and political superstructures arise, and
> to which definite forms of social consciousness correspond. The mode of production
> of material life determines the general character of the social, political and spiritual
> processes of life.

However, as many Marxists have pointed out since this was written, human beings live in buildings, not in their foundations. In other words, Marx was concerned to analyze the whole of each "mode of production" (feudal, capitalist, communist or other), comprising both base ("foundation") *and* superstructure, and not just the base. Marxists have also spent years debating exactly what he meant by "determines": does the base merely set limits to what can happen in the superstructure, or does the word have a stronger meaning of causation? It is interesting in this regard that according to Marx the mode of production determines "the *general* character" of other processes, not their specific forms.

Despite these problems of interpretation, Marx's ideas have tended to be adapted to support an ideological view of the centrality of economics and economies, which is by far the most powerful ideology in existence today. It is an ideology based on the conviction that economics and economies should be made the centrepiece of society, and the principal preoccupation of individual, institutional, municipal, regional, national and international development. Economics as a discipline had already been moving in this direction, particularly with Ricardo and Ricardian economics, but since Marx's day it has become so powerful and pervasive that it is the central axiom of the economic age, the cornerstone on which everything else is erected. Its power emanates from its claim to universal validity in space and time, as well as the fact that people desperately need an interpretation of the past in order to comprehend the present and confront the future.

Aside from the ideological impact of the economic interpretation of history, to which Marx contributed at the cost of being misrepresented, Marxian economics comprises a range of ideas and analyses, from the labour theory of value, the division of societies into base and superstructure, the rate of exploitation, and surplus value, to the theory of class conflict and confrontation, the nature of capital, capitalism and capitalist production, the immiseration of the masses, the industrial reserve army, the overthrow of the capitalists, and the introduction of communism. While Marxian economics has taken different forms and directions in different countries and parts of the world, the powerful effect it has had on the world as a whole can be confirmed by the fact that throughout the better part of the twentieth century the entire world was divided along capitalist and communist or, at least in theory and rhetoric, Marxist and non-Marxist lines.

This process commenced when scholars and practitioners in Britain, France, Germany, Austria and elsewhere in Europe began searching for alternatives to Marxian economics and communism that would either strengthen capitalism or provide other socialist alternatives to it. In Britain, a number of socialist thinkers such as Bernard Shaw, Sidney and Beatrice Webb, G. D. H. Cole, and H.G. Wells, all members of the Fabian Society, became deeply committed to the creation of labour unions, the nationalization of key industries, the creation of public enterprises, and the establishment of public utilities to counteract or thwart the advance of Marxism, Marxian economics, and communism. Eventually, however, the entire world became divided along capitalist and communist lines. On the one hand, there was "the communist world" of the Soviet Union, its satellites in central and eastern Europe, China, and a few other countries. On the other hand, there was "the capitalist world" of the United States, western Europe, Canada, Australia, New Zealand, and Japan. Not only was a "Cold War" fought between these two opposing parts of the world throughout the latter part of the twentieth century, particularly between the United States and the Soviet Union, but it is also only recently that interest in communism and Marxian economics has faded in many parts of the world. There are many reasons for this, including the triumph of capitalism and democracy; the inability of communism and Marxian economics to deliver the utopian promise of a classless society with proletarian rule; and, especially, the ability of capitalist countries and capitalism to improve standards of living for labourers as well as capitalists.

While Marx is much better known today for his theories of capitalism and communism than for his economic interpretation of history, it is his economic interpretation of history that, albeit indirectly and in distorted forms, has had the most profound impact on the world, the world system, and the evolution of the economic age. Through the economic interpretation of history Marx plunged the world fully and forcefully into the economic age. This is perhaps understandable in view of the fact that Marx was living at a time when the industrial revolution was at its zenith, and everything was assuming a highly economic and materialistic orientation. In that sense, he reflected the spirit of the age, rather than creating it. Under these circumstances it is easy to understand how and why the economic interpretation of history gripped the entire world.

Neoclassical Economics

We now turn to examine another revolution that was beginning to take shape in economics in the latter part of the nineteenth century, the revolution in price theory, or, as it is called today, the "marginal revolution." It was also destined to have a profound effect on economic theory and practice, and thus on the development of the economic age. Its importance lay in the fact that, as more and more emphasis was placed on economics, economies, and markets, by Marxists *and* non-Marxists alike, economists became less interested in the inherent value or worth of everything, as had been the case for the classical economists as well as for Marx, and more interested in the prices that were paid for goods, services, land, labour, capital, and the like.

This eventually came to be seen as the key to understanding the entire economic system: the buying and selling of products, supply and demand, producers and consumers, and the networks of production, distribution, and consumption. If economists could be successful in unlocking the secret of price, the basic code of the economic system could be broken, and everything would fall naturally and logically into place. Since this eventually gave rise to a preoccupation with markets, the individual as consumer, the power and centrality of corporations, profit maximization and competition, capitalism and the capitalist system of production, distribution, consumption, and many other matters that are standard features of the current economic age, the marginal revolution, and the "neoclassical" economics that gave rise to it, need to be examined in some detail. It is impossible to understand the world we are living in today without doing so.

If expanding the size of the market is the key to increasing wealth, as Adam Smith had contended, then it only made sense to focus attention on how prices are determined in the market, since this is the key to understanding how the market functions. While economists continued to be interested in questions related to the production and distribution of wealth, a new set of questions was beginning to occupy their minds in the last part of the nineteenth century. Foremost among these was the question of price determination. This triggered a series of initiatives aimed at understanding how the economy and the market function in fact, how individuals and institutions behave, how prices are determined in different types of markets, and, especially, how economic systems and markets allocate scarce resources among competing wants through the vehicle of prices.

Most of the neoclassical economists' questions emanated from the fact that the price and value theories of the classical economists and Marx did not stand up to empirical verification or vigorous economic analysis. Those theories were predicated largely on the supply side of the economy and the market, particularly on the amounts of labour embodied or congealed in production and production costs. Yet economists were becoming aware that there were many situations where these were not the main factors in determining prices. While the historical economists referred to earlier had not been successful in their attempts to root economics in history and the inductive method, rather than abstract theory and the deductive method, perhaps they were successful in compelling economists to achieve a reasonable measure of consistency between abstract theories and historical and contemporary realities. If abstract theories did not mesh with historical and contemporary realities, then it was the abstract theories that had to be changed.

Exactly what was it about the price and value theories of the classical economists and Marx that did not mesh with historical and contemporary realities? Surely it was the fact that people were paying prices for products, and that products were selling for prices in the market, that bore little or no relationship to the amount of labour embodied or congealed in production, production costs, and the supply side of the economy. In struggling to find answers to this problem, economists shifted attention from labour, production costs, and the supply side of the economy to utility, marginal utility, and the demand side of the economy. Prices might bear little or no relationship to the amount of labour embodied in them, but instead reflected the *demand* for products. While this observation may appear straightforward and sensible in retrospect, it was revolutionary at the time. It transformed the entire nature of economics as a discipline, and produced the marginal revolution.

Three highly creative individuals—William Stanley Jevons in Britain, Carl Menger in Austria, and Léon Walras in France and, later, Switzerland—were at the forefront of this development. What makes their contributions to the founding of the marginal school of economics and neoclassical economics particularly fascinating is that they worked in comparative isolation from one another, but nevertheless came to very similar conclusions. While each had his own specific ideas and views on a variety of economic matters, they all believed that utility in general, and marginal utility in particular, were the main determinants of price, value, production, distribution, and exchange. This caused the focus in economics to shift abruptly. Whereas the focus of the classical economists and of Marx had been on macroeconomic questions of production, distribution, wealth creation, and economic growth, the focus of the neoclassical economists was on microeconomic questions of prices, markets, scarcity, resource allocation, and individual and corporate behaviour in markets. This caused Joan Robinson, herself a member of the second generation of neoclassical economists, to describe the shift from classical to neoclassical economics as one that replaced bigger and more general questions with smaller and more specific questions, such as "why does an egg cost more than a cup of tea?" (quoted by Barber, p. 165).

In seeking answers to questions of this type, the neoclassical economists were forced to confront the problem of price determination in a totally new way. The first person to tackle this problem in any depth was Jevons (although, unbeknownst to him, Augustin Cournot in France, and Johann Heinrich von Thünen and Hermann Heinrich Gossen in Germany, had been wrestling with the problem of price determination from the standpoint of utility for many years). Jevons was well-suited to the task. He had a strong background in economics, mathematics, science, logic, and statistics, and was steeped in the Utilitarian ideas that were still influential in Britain in his youth (he was born in 1835 and died in 1882). Jeremy Bentham, the consummate Utilitarian theorist and practitioner, had concluded that social life was about achieving "the greatest happiness of the greatest number" by way of endeavours to "maximize pleasure and minimize pain," since pleasure and pain were, in Bentham's view, "the twin sovereign masters" of life. Bentham's concern was with the pleasure, pain, and happiness of human beings in general, rather than with those of specific individuals. It is here that a subtle shift started to take place, away from the political philosophy of Adam Smith, which was based on "enlightened self-interest" and "the invisible hand," towards the political philosophy of acting to secure "the greatest happiness of the greatest number."

Given his background in Benthamite Utilitarianism, it is not surprising that Jevons decided to cut into the problem of price determination through utility, marginal utility, and the demand side of economics. According to Jevons, people will pay more for products than the amount of labour embodied in them and the cost of producing them if the demand for these products is high, and a great deal of utility or satisfaction is derived from purchasing and consuming them. In fact, generally speaking, the greater the utility or satisfaction, the higher the price that people are willing to pay. Conversely, the less the utility or satisfaction, the lower the price that people are willing to pay. It was this fact that caused Jevons to shift attention from the "objective side" of economics to the "subjective side," from society as a whole, the economy, economic growth, and the creation of wealth to the individual and his or her needs and wants in society. Just as beauty is in the eye of the beholder, so the most important factor in determining prices, in Jevons's view, is how much satisfaction or utility individuals get from the products they want, purchase, consume, and possess.

This shift of emphasis led Jevons away from Utilitarianism, with its rather abstract view of general human needs, towards the study of individuals, and the satisfaction of their needs and wants, and propelled him into a systematic study of utility, and especially marginal utility, as it relates to price, value, the demand for products, the economy, and the market. His views on these matters were set out in his *Theory of Political Economy*, which appeared in 1871. Whereas the classical economists and Marx had largely ignored utility and marginal utility as factors in price and value (though Adam Smith had paid a certain amount of attention to these questions), Jevons made utility and marginal utility the centrepieces of his entire theory of price determination. Generally speaking, the value or price of a product is determined by the amount of utility or satisfaction people derive from it. As more and more of a product is offered and consumed, however, the utility that people derive from each successive unit will generally fall because there will be less utility or satisfaction derived from each additional unit. This was the crucial factor for Jevons. While utility is an extremely important factor in determining value and price, it is *marginal* utility that is the most important factor, since it shows how individuals will react as additional units of a product are offered and consumed. This caused Jevons to conclude (as summarized by Spiegel, p. 522): "cost of production determines supply; supply determines final degree of utility; final degree of utility determines value."

To illustrate this point, consider the consumption of food. Food generally provides a great deal of utility or satisfaction, particularly if people are hungry and there is not a lot of food available. As a result, people will usually pay high prices for the initial amounts of food they consume, prices that may be well above the actual cost of producing the food or the amount of labour embodied or congealed in its production. As more and more food is consumed, however, the amount of satisfaction or utility derived from each additional unit will decrease. People will be willing to pay less for each additional unit. Eventually a point will be reached where the consumption of additional units of food yields no satisfaction or utility whatsoever. After this point is reached the consumption of additional units of food may even produce "disutility," or pain, because the consumption of more and more units of food will make people sick. In other words, marginal utility for most products falls progressively as additional units of a product are consumed. After a certain point is reached disutility or dissatisfaction could set in as additional units are consumed.

It was this understanding of utility, and particularly marginal utility, that enabled Jevons to develop a theory of consumer behaviour and demand based on the conviction that the marginal utility for each additional unit of product will decrease as more and more units of a product are consumed. This is the essence of the neoclassical theory of demand, and therefore of price. It was but a short step from here to Jevons's conclusion that people will operate in markets in such a way as to equalize the marginal utilities for all the various products they want, demand, and consume.

What excited Jevons about the theory of marginal utility was not only what he deemed to be its consistency with the way in which prices are determined in reality, but also the possibility of subjecting marginal utility theory to empirical verification and intensive mathematical treatment. On the one hand, Jevons believed that it was possible to derive demand curves for all products by asking people what prices they would be willing to pay for each additional unit of product based on the amount of satisfaction or marginal utility they derive from each successive unit. It is not difficult to see where this leads. It leads to the derivation of demand curves for all products in the consumers' market and the producers' market. On the other hand, Jevons believed that mathematics in general and differential calculus in particular could be used to great advantage because they were capable of dealing with infinitesimal increases and decreases in amounts, thereby making it possible to derive demand curves with exact scientific precision and mathematical accuracy. This strong reliance on mathematics and especially differential calculus eventually led to the development of input-output analysis, and the use of econometrics and econometric models in economics, a standard feature of economic theory, practice, and the economic age today.

As the work of Jevons intensified, a very specific theory of individual behaviour in the market began to take shape. Consistent with the theory of utility and especially marginal utility, it was based on the assumption that people are concerned largely with maximizing their utility, marginal utility, and consumer satisfaction. This gave rise to the concept of "economic man," the individual who is concerned first and foremost with getting as much satisfaction as possible from the consumption of products. According to this view, people will go on purchasing products and adjusting their purchases until the marginal utilities derived from the consumption of the last units of all products are equal. As Jevons put it (quoted by Roll, p. 380), "a person distributes his income in such a way as to equalize the utility of the final increments of all commodities consumed." It is easy to see from this why Jevons was so excited about the use of mathematics and particularly differential calculus in economics. They provided an opportunity to get at the problem of price and price determination with the greatest precision possible.

At the same time that Jevons was researching and writing about these matters in Britain, Carl Menger was studying very similar issues in Austria.

In fact, Menger's *Grundsätze der Volkswirtschaftslehre* (*Principles of Economics*) appeared in 1871, the same year as Jevons's *Theory of Political Economy*. While Menger and Jevons shared a great deal in common, Menger went further than Jevons by applying his utility theory to a broader range of economic situations and problems. For example, Menger applied his theory of utility and especially marginal utility to different types of products, such as lower-order and higher-order products, arguing that people will generally provide for needs that bring them the greatest utility or satisfaction first, such as food, clothing, and shelter, and then turn their attention to other needs. However, they will do this in such a way that all needs are satisfied to an equal degree of satisfaction, fulfilment or marginal utility. In addition, Menger applied his theory of utility and marginal utility not only to products but also to money, arguing that money could be treated very much like products as far as price and value are concerned. This helps to explain why Menger's theories generated a great deal of interest and enthusiasm in Austria and elsewhere in Europe shortly after his book was published, eventually leading to what is called the Austrian school of economics.

This school has made many valuable contributions to economic theory and practice, and the development of the economic age, since it was first founded. These include the theory of utility and marginal utility, the theory of capital and interest rates, monetary and fiscal policy, and the development of capitalism, socialism, liberalism, and democracy. Successive generations of economists followed in the footsteps of Merger, including Friedrich von Wieser, Eugen von Böhm-Bawerk, Ludwig von Mises, Friedrich A. von Hayek, and Joseph Schumpeter. For example, von Wieser and von Böhm-Bawerk made valuable contributions to interest rate theory, and the study of money and banking, signalling the need to examine not only "the real economy" but also "the money economy." Von Mises and von Hayek made valuable contributions to individualism and liberalism, primarily by examining the implications of marginal utility and demand theory in great depth, and making the case for alternatives to Marxism and communism.

It is, however, Schumpeter who, many feel, made the most valuable contributions. He made especially valuable contributions to business cycle theory, the theory of economic development, the analysis of capitalism, socialism and democracy, the study of entrepreneurship, the behaviour of entrepreneurs and entrepreneurial elites, and the nature and importance of technological change. It was Schumpeter who named short, intermediate and long-term business cycles Kitchin, Juglar and Kondratieff cycles, after the scholars who first identified them. Schumpeter was also the first economist to give detailed attention to the roles that entrepreneurs, entrepreneurial elites, and entrepreneurial activity play in economic development. He also predicted the eventual collapse of capitalism, not because of its failures and internal contradictions, as Marx and the Marxists had, but rather because of its successes. According to Schumpeter, capitalism was destined to fail because enterprises would become too large and bureaucratic, innovation would become too depersonalized and institutionalized, and political power would be vested in a business class that was basically unfit to govern. He thus provided important insights into the rise, growth, power, and role of corporations and corporate elites in the economy, the world system, politics, and the economic age in the latter part of the twentieth century.

As important as these contributions were, Schumpeter's greatest contribution was reserved for the nature, role, and importance of technology and technological change in economic development. He contended that technological innovation is "the most important factor in economic development" because it occurs in clusters and triggers other possibilities. This is not far removed from the situation over the past 150 years or so, during which technological innovations in such fields as transportation, communications, industry, advertising, and computers have transformed economic practices and policies in every part of the world and all sectors of society. It is for reasons such as these that Schumpeter's theories on a variety of economic issues are attracting a great deal of attention today among economists, policy-makers, and developmental authorities throughout the world.

Given the evolution and importance of the Austrian school of economics, it is easy to see how important Menger's contributions were to the history of economics and the economic age. Not only did he go further than Jevons in developing marginal utility theory and applying it to a variety of situations, he also triggered a school of economic thought and practice that has had a major impact on economics, and on economic policies and practices, since his own day.

If Menger went further than Jevons, Léon Walras went further than either. Whereas Menger and Jevons were concerned largely with how prices are determined in specific markets and for particular products, Walras was concerned with how prices are determined for all markets, all products, and the economy as a whole. In the market for products, for example, consumers buy products that are produced by businesses and corporations. In the market for productive services consumers sell their productive capabilities to businesses and corporations, and receive incomes or revenue in return. Thus, consumers are buyers in the market for products and sellers in the market for productive services. It was the interrelatedness of markets and of the entire economic system that enabled Walras to conclude that it is possible in theory to develop a set of simultaneous equations showing how equilibrium is determined for all markets, products, and the economy as a whole. In order to do this, it was necessary to make many assumptions about the actions and motives of buyers and sellers, consumers and producers, as well as the general nature of the economy and economic system. On the basis of these assumptions Walras was able to show how it is possible to construct an elaborate "general equilibrium theory," showing how equilibrium prices, values, and resource allocations are determined for all economic activities in society.

Just as Menger's work on utility and marginal utility spawned a school devoted to advancing his work, and exploring its implications for a variety of economic issues and problems, so Walras's work on equilibrium theory and general equilibrium spawned a similar school. In his case, it was the Lausanne school, spearheaded by Walras's principal successor, Vilfredo Pareto. Not only did Pareto build on Walras's general equilibrium theory by showing how it is possible to derive "determinate values" for all unknowns in Walras's set of simultaneous equations, he also advanced Walras's theory of general equilibrium by showing how "optimal distribution" might be achieved for the economy through "perfect competition" and the free mobility of labour, capital, and other factors of production. This possibility, which has become known as Pareto's optimum, strengthened the case for *laissez faire* economics, implying minimal governmental intervention in the economy and the market, making Pareto a champion of economic and political liberalism, and providing an alternative to Marxism. Many neoclassical economists, politicians, corporate executives, and members of wealthy elites have found Pareto's ideas attractive.

Pareto's ideas countered the influence of Marxian economics in one other important respect. Whereas Marx and the Marxists believed that the unequal distribution of income and wealth among the main classes and interest groups in society are inherent in capitalism, Pareto believed that such unequal distribution results from the fact that individuals, institutions, interest groups, and classes are not endowed equally with resources, abilities, opportunities or power, in what has become known as Pareto's law of income distribution. Pareto claimed that this law had been derived from empirical investigations of the distribution of income and wealth in many countries, rather than through abstract theorizing or pure economic analysis. Although there were vigorous attacks on the law, and these attacks were to play an important role in the development of welfare economics, Pareto clung to his convictions on this subject, although softening somewhat later in life. He argued that "aristocratic elites" are always bound to play a crucial role in economic development and in society because this is the inevitable consequence of the unequal distribution of income and wealth. It was Pareto's views on these matters that did a great deal to sanction the policies and practices of ruling elites and the position of capitalists, corporations, and the capitalistic class in society, something that Marxists, but not only Marxists, found abhorrent.

Despite these specific departures from general economic thought and practice, it is not difficult to see what happened as a result of the work of Jevons, Menger, Walras, Pareto, and others of the neoclassical school: economics largely returned to the classical philosophy of *laissez-faire* liberalism, assuming and even demanding minimal state involvement in the economy and the market, following its tumultuous encounter with Marx, Marxism, and Marxian economics. The pendulum had swung one hundred and eighty degrees, from concern with the supply side of the economy, the creation of wealth, and economic growth to the concern with the demand side of the economy, utility, marginal utility, price determination, equilibrium analysis, markets, and consumer and corporate behaviour. Whereas the classical economists put their emphasis on labour and production costs as the most important factors in determining value and price, Jevons, Menger, and Walras put their emphasis on utility, marginal utility, consumer and producer satisfaction, and equilibrium as the most important factors.

It was left to Alfred Marshall, the British economist whom many consider the greatest of the neoclassical economists, to synthesize these two distinct approaches to value and price determination by developing a theory of value and price based on supply and demand, production costs, and utility. His views on this subject and many other matters were set out in his *Principles of Economics*, which first appeared in 1890. Marshall likened the process of price determination to the cutting action of a pair of scissors. It is impossible to determine whether the lower blade or the upper blade does the cutting because both blades play extremely important roles in the process. As Marshall put it (p. 84):

> We might as reasonably dispute whether it is the upper or the under blade of a pair of scissors that cuts a piece of paper, as whether value is governed by utility or cost of production. It is true that when one blade is held still, and the cutting is effected by moving the other, we may say with careless brevity that the cutting is done by the second; but the statement is not strictly accurate, and is to be excused only so long as it claims to be merely a popular and not a strictly scientific account of what happens.
>
> In much the same way, when a thing already made has to be sold, the price which people will be willing to pay for it will be governed by their desire to have it, together with the amount they can afford to spend on it. Their desire to have it depends partly on the chance that, if they do not buy it, they will be able to get another thing like

it at as low a price: this depends on the causes that govern the supply of it, and this again on the cost of production.

Drawing on his conviction that both supply and demand, that is, both production costs and utility, play important roles in determining value and price, Marshall was able to construct supply and demand curves for products, showing how prices are determined through the intersection of the curves. When quantity demanded is depicted on the horizontal axis and price is depicted on the vertical axis, the demand curve for most products will slope down to the right, because consumers will demand more of the products as the price falls, in accordance with utility theory and particularly marginal utility theory. With supply the situation is reversed. When quantity supplied is depicted on the horizontal axis and price is depicted on the vertical axis, the supply curve for the large majority of products will slope up to the right, because producers will have to pay more for the land, labour, and capital used in production, in accordance with the increased cost of wages, profits, and rent, and the law of diminishing returns. It is at the point where the demand and supply curves intersect that the price of products is determined. Marshall called this "the equilibrium price." This, in Marshall's view, is the price that producers, consumers, and the market will always gravitate towards. A price above the equilibrium price will cause producers to bring more products to the market, in order to entice consumers to buy more products. This will cause a decrease in the price and a return to the equilibrium price. A price below the equilibrium price will cause consumers to demand more of the products in the market, causing an increase in the price and a return to the equilibrium price, as producers supply the market with more products. In both cases there is a tendency for prices to gravitate towards the equilibrium price whenever there is a deviation from it.

What is true for consumer products is also true for producer products, according to Marshall, at least in theory if not always in practice. There is always a tendency to restore equilibrium prices once there has been a deviation from them. Whenever there has been a deviation from the equilibrium price, producers and consumers will adjust their actions and practices in such a way that equilibrium tends to be restored. It was but a short step from this to Walras's "theory of general equilibrium" for all products, all markets, and the economy generally. Nevertheless, Marshall did not take this step because he was much more concerned with equilibrium conditions in specific markets, and for particular products and industries, often called partial equilibrium, than he was with general equilibrium in the economy as a whole.

It was the fact that equilibrium theory, regardless of whether it focused on partial equilibrium or general equilibrium, could be applied to producers as well as consumers that eventually gave rise to the development of a theory of corporate behaviour commensurate with the theory of consumer behaviour pioneered by Jevons, Menger, and others. Marshall was in the forefront of this development. He contended that producers will seek to maximize their profits in the market in exactly the same way that consumers seek to maximize their marginal utility and consumer satisfaction. This led Marshall, in conjunction with many others, to develop the theory of the firm, based on the conviction that profit maximization and vigorous competition are the keys to a healthy corporate community and a vigorous economy. This was eventually parlayed into the belief that what is good for corporations is good for the economy and society, an idea that was to play a major role in the development of the economic age in the twentieth century, and has only recently been called into question as a result of corporate scandals and fraudulent accounting practices.

While Marshall believed that there is a tendency in the economy and in markets to yield equilibrium prices for all products and all markets, he also believed that there are numerous exceptions to the general rule. These exceptions resulted from many factors, including increasing and decreasing returns to scale, consumers' and producers' surpluses, the escalating demand for urban land that was occurring in Britain and elsewhere in Europe in his day, and the fact that capitalists must be paid a "quasi-rent" for foregoing present consumption in order to realize potential profits. This led Marshall to differentiate between different types of market situations, such as the market for land, labour, and capital, the producers' market, the consumers' market, the general market, and so forth. It also caused Marshall to distinguish different time frames for markets, including the market period, the short period, and the long period. This made it possible for Marshall to examine the specific conditions and time frames obtaining in different market situations, as these could easily yield cases where the actual prices paid for products deviated from the equilibrium price.

What particularly worried Marshall about all this was the fact that some producers might have advantages over other producers in specific market situations and over particular time frames. Moreover, producers might have advantages over consumers. This would interfere with the smooth functioning of the economy and markets, and therefore with the tendency towards equilibrium and the ability to reward all equally, without the need for much government intervention. This was especially true in the case of increasing returns to scale, in Marshall's view, since this could tip the scales in favour of certain producers over other producers, thereby putting them in a stronger position to exploit other producers as well as consumers. This caused Marshall to conclude that there are specific cases where state intervention is justified, since unregulated markets cannot always be expected to produce socially desirable results.

As neoclassical economics gathered momentum in the latter part of the nineteenth century and the early part of the twentieth, a very specific vision of the ideal economic system began to emerge. It was a system based on the conviction that, generally speaking, equilibrium would be achieved in all markets, and the economy as a whole would function most effectively, when they were left to follow their own course, there was a great deal of competition between producers and consumers, and government involvement was kept to a minimum. Not only would this yield the best possible allocation of scarce resources of land, labour, capital, and entrepreneurship, it would also maximize producer and consumer satisfaction, and do so at or near full employment and on the basis of general equilibrium.

While neoclassical economics shared many similarities with classical economics in this respect, especially the view that markets should be left alone rather than rigidly controlled, except in special cases and specific situations, it was designed to tackle a very different problem than classical economics had been. Classical economics had been designed to tackle the problem of how to create, augment, and distribute wealth among the three main classes of society, particularly in the case of a society characterized by rapid population growth, the pressure of population on the means of subsistence, the operation of the law of diminishing returns, and the ever-present danger of the stationary state. Neoclassical economics was designed to tackle the problem of how equilibrium could be achieved at or near full employment with optimal resource allocation, and the greatest possible producer and consumer satisfaction. It is easy to see from this how neoclassical economics acquired its name. Despite the fact that it focused on a very different problem than the one addressed by classical economics, it followed in the classical tradition in one quintessential respect. Like classical economics, it was based on the conviction that the economy and markets are self-regulating and self-correcting mechanisms, where "an invisible hand" and "enlightened self-interest" ensure that everything turns out for the best. While it might take time for adjustments to work their way out in specific market situations, and in the economy as a whole, these adjustments would be made without the need for government interference, except in the specific and limited cases identified by Marshall and others.

In retrospect, it is clear that neoclassical economics made a number of very valuable and highly original contributions to the evolution of the economic age. For one thing, it focused attention on price determination, the economy, and markets. This led to intensive studies of the nature, functioning, and mechanics of the economy and markets, the relationship between buyers and sellers, supply and demand, different types of markets and market situations, and the determination of prices, value, production, distribution, and consumption, which lie at the core of all economic and market systems. For another thing, it produced a very specific understanding of the ways in which consumers and corporations behave in the economy and in markets, as well as the ways in which they should behave. In order for the economy and markets to function effectively, according to neoclassical theory, consumers should strive to maximize their consumer satisfaction, while corporations should strive to maximize their profits and compete as vigorously as possible because this produces the best possible results for the economy, markets, and society as a whole. This broadened and deepened economic thought and practice considerably by showing how they apply to citizens and corporations, and not just to macroeconomic questions of wealth creation and economic growth. Moreover, it caused a return to the notion that the economy and markets are self-regulating and self-correcting mechanisms, which function most effectively when they are left to their own devices. This signalled a return to the classical conviction that liberalism based on *laissez faire* is the most desirable political philosophy because it produces the most efficient and effective results. It also countered the Marxian conviction that *laissez faire* rewards the rich, perpetuates the status quo, penalizes the poor, exploits workers, and advances the interests of capitalists, capitalism, and the capitalist mode of production at the expense of everybody else.

Despite the contributions made by neoclassical economics to the evolution of the economic age, the economic system visualized by the neoclassical economists did not jibe especially well with the kind of world that was unfolding in the first third of the twentieth century. Cracks and fissures were beginning to appear in the theoretical structure and practical policies of the neoclassical economists. In fact, a number of developments were occurring at the time that directly contradicted the arguments and expectations of the neoclassical economists.

In the first place, it was becoming apparent that imperfect competition rather than perfect competition was the rule rather than the exception in the most advanced economies of the world. While Marshall was very cognizant of this fact and was indeed extremely worried about it, it was exactly the reverse of what the first generation of neoclassical economists had propounded. This caused a number of members of the second generation of neoclassical economists, including Piero Sraffa in Italy, Joan Robinson in Britain, and Frank Knight and E.H. Chamberlin in the United States, to focus their attention on imperfect rather than perfect competition, that is, on competition by a few firms rather than many firms in the marketplace, as well as on the theory of the firm under conditions of imperfect competition. This led to important studies of monopolies, duopolies, oligopolies, and monopolistic competition, situations where some producers enjoy considerable advantages over other producers as well as over consumers. At a time when new corporations were coming into existence, and existing corporations were expanding rapidly in size, stature, power and influence, this led to important changes in the laws governing market behaviour, in order to penalize discriminatory commercial, industrial, corporate, trading and trust practices, although it took a long time for these changes to work their way through into public policies and decision-making.

In the second place, major inequalities were showing up in the distribution of income, wealth and resources, inequalities that were so large they simply could not be ignored. While this was consistent with the findings of Pareto and others, as well as the predictions of Marx and the Marxists, it was not consistent with the theories and system advocated by the large majority of neoclassical economists. Not only did these developments run counter to the belief that a freely functioning economy at or near full employment allocates resources most efficiently and equitably, but it also raised the spectre of Marxism once again. Was Marx right when he said that growing disparities in income, wealth, and resources would eventually spell the death knell for capitalism? In response to this problem, a number of second- and third-generation neoclassical economists, including A. C. Pigou, John Hicks and others, plunged into a protracted study of what became known as "welfare economics." During the course of their studies they identified many cases where there could be major discrepancies and inequalities between the interests of one class and the interests of other classes, as well as between one class or industry and society as a whole. For example, some classes might put a great deal of energy, effort and money into making improvements in their productive capabilities, only to have other classes reap the profits. This often happened in agriculture, where farmers made improvements in their land and equipment, only to see landlords expropriate them and reap the benefits. Also, some producers and industries might cause a great deal of pollution and environmental deterioration, which would then have to cleaned up by others and society as a whole.

Cases such as these, and others, necessitated and indeed justified government intervention in the economy and in markets. They also necessitated achieving much greater understanding of who actually gains and who loses from different types of economic actions and policies, as well as how economic systems can be created that maximize or optimize the welfare and well-being of all classes in society, and not just the rich and privileged class. This provided the theoretical justification that was needed to redistribute wealth, income, and resources on a more equitable basis. Many of these conclusions were bound up in the distinction that Pigou and other welfare economists made between "marginal social net product" and "marginal private net product." This in turn led to the theory of public goods and the public sphere, cost-benefit analysis, the compensation principle, and, in advanced countries such as Britain and Sweden, the welfare state.

Inconsistencies between welfare and *laissez faire*, and between perfect and imperfect competition, were not the only inconsistencies showing up in neoclassical economics between the 1890s and the 1930s. Consumers' behaviour was not evolving in a manner consistent with neoclassical theory either. Rather than being based on rational factors such as utility, marginal utility, and careful calculation, there were many cases where it was based on irrational factors such as whims, fancies, fashion, mass marketing, envy, and emulation. This led to the development of alternative theories of consumption and consumer behaviour, notably the theories developed by Thorstein Veblen and others, who believed that institutional factors were far more important in determining and explaining consumer behaviour and consumption than utility, marginal utility, and careful calculation. These theories had a profound impact on economic thought and practice in the twentieth century, especially when consumption began to loom large as the most important factor in economic growth and development.

Finally, by far the most devastating development as far as neoclassical economics was concerned was the revelation in the late 1920s and the 1930s that there was no self-regulating and self-correcting mechanism at work in the economy and markets, and that they did not tend towards equilibrium at or near full employment once there was a major deviation from it. In fact, precisely the opposite might be the case. The economy could get stuck at equilibrium levels far below full or near-full employment. This proved to be so damaging to neoclassical economics in the end that it provided the impetus for another revolution to take place in economics, a revolution every bit as powerful and pervasive as the Marxian and marginal revolutions of earlier generations.

Keynesian Economics

The British economist John Maynard Keynes spearheaded the revolution in economic thought and practice that bears his name by producing yet another way of looking at the economy, markets, economic theory, and the role of government in public and private life. His was a revolution that was destined to have a profound effect on the economic age and the modern world system by swinging attention away from microeconomics, and its concern with consumer and corporate behaviour, price determination, market equilibrium, and supply and demand analysis, back to macroeconomics, and its concern with monetary and fiscal policy, national income analysis, saving, investment, consumption, economic growth, and, more fundamentally, government involvement in the economy and markets.

What triggered the Keynesian revolution was the Great Depression (1929–39), and the accompanying debate among politicians, bureaucrats, policy-makers, and economists with respect to what, if anything, to do about it. Following the stock market crash of 1929, Europe and North America, and the colonies that depended upon them, plunged into a period of protracted economic crisis and decline. Investment fell, unemployment soared, and national income plummeted, particularly in the United States, where national income fell from 87 billion US dollars in 1930 to 39 billion dollars in 1933 (Heilbroner, pp. 252–53).

More importantly, most of the economies affected showed no signs of recovery. After one hundred years of economic theory and practice, involving concerted efforts by numerous economists to understand the functioning of the economy and the marketplace, US President Franklin D. Roosevelt was forced to accept in the 1930s that little was known about how the economy and markets functioned, or how the US economy could be lifted out of the Depression. All that could be done, in Roosevelt's view, was to try something and, if it worked, try more of it, but, if it did not work, abandon it and try something else. This ran directly counter to the neoclassical economists' belief that there was a self-regulating and self-correcting mechanism at work in the economy, causing a return to full or near-full employment once there was a major deviation. This simply was not happening.

Keynes set out to explain why this was so and, more importantly, what should be done about it. He undertook an intensive study of some of the most important factors in the precipitation of the stock market crash and the Great Depression, including saving, investment, consumption, interest rates, income flows, the propensity to save, invest and consume, the supply of and demand for money, business cycles, and national income analysis. Whereas the neoclassical economists were more interested in "the real economy", by which they meant such matters as the production, distribution, and consumption of goods, services and resources, and the prices paid for them, Keynes was interested in both "the real economy" *and* "the money economy," as well as the intimate relationship between the two. This led Keynes to produce a number of extremely important books, pamphlets, and articles on these matters, including his *Treatise on Money* (1930) and, above all, *The General Theory of Employment, Interest and Money* (1936).

While the classical and neoclassical economists were aware that fluctuations could take place in economic activity because of discrepancies between supply and demand, production and consumption, they believed that long-term overproduction and major gluts in markets were impossible because "supply creates its own demand." As indicated earlier, this common view was known as Say's law because it had been first articulated by the French economist Jean-Baptiste Say. The law was predicated on the conviction that excessive goods would always be taken off the market because prices for excessive goods would fall, thereby increasing the demand for them and causing them to be purchased. The only economists who had expressed reservations about the law were Malthus and Marx. As noted earlier, both Malthus and Marx believed that market gluts and long-term overproduction were possible, and would occur if there was too much unemployment in the economy, or if consumers saved too much and did not return enough of their income to the income stream. However, such views were discounted by Ricardo, Mill, and the neoclassical economists because they believed that unemployment would never reach such high levels and that consumers would never save too much of their income because it was always more advantageous for them to put it to productive use.

Keynes disputed these assertions on the basis of his study of money, which he analyzed as both a store of value and a medium of exchange. Whereas the classical and neoclassical economists saw money largely as a medium of exchange, because of its purchasing power and its command over goods, services, resources, and especially labour, Keynes argued that money functions as a store of value as well, and that there are occasions when consumers and producers prefer to hold on to their money rather than spend it, seeing it as a hedge against poor future prospects, a decline in the value of their capital assets or a possible rise in interest rates. This "liquidity preference," as Keynes called it, could cause more money to be taken out of the income stream in the form of saving than was returned in the form of consumption and investment, thereby causing national income to fall rather than rise. Once this downward process started it could become cumulative as consumers saved more and more of their incomes for precautionary reasons, thereby causing investment and consumption to slow down, and unemployment to increase. This would bring about further reductions in income, saving, investment, and consumption, as well as a great deal more unemployment and underemployment in the economy. This process could go on indefinitely if nothing was done about it. National income could get stuck at an extremely low level and just stay there.

This is exactly what had happened during the early stages of the Great Depression, with the result that at its height consumption, saving, investment, and national income in most countries around the world were at lower levels than they had been for decades. According to neoclassical theory, this should have caused interest rates to fall, thereby drawing savings out, and inducing more investment, consumption, and economic growth. This would eventually reverse the downward spiral and cause the economy to return to full employment equilibrium as a result of the self-regulating and self-correcting mechanism. However, what happened in fact was the opposite. Interest rates fell, but nothing happened. Investment, consumption, income, and saving did not increase significantly, and there were chronically high levels of unemployment and underemployment in most economies.

Keynes argued, quite rightly in retrospect, that, despite significantly lower interest rates, investment could not increase substantially because all the savings had been "squeezed out" of the economy during the downward spiral, as consumers struggled to cope with increased unemployment and reductions in their standard of living. In other words, there was no self-regulating and self-correcting mechanism at work in the economy; equilibrium could just as easily be established with a high level of unemployment as with a low level; and nothing would get better as long as nothing was done about it. In effect, the economic elevator could just as easily get struck in the basement or the ground floor as on the top floor. Keynes was right and the neoclassical economists were wrong.

What, then, was to be done about it? As the Great Depression intensified and dragged on, pressure on governments to do something, anything, increased. According to Keynes, there was really only one thing to be done, once the neoclassical solution of doing nothing, while waiting for equilibrium to be restored at full employment, was rejected. Governments had to step in and "prime the pump" by spending money on a variety of public works projects and welfare programmes, in attempts to induce economic recovery and growth.

Most governments did much that Keynes recommended, and some did so even before his ideas became influential. Roosevelt, for example, introduced the New Deal in 1933, when Keynes was barely heard of in the United States, increasing government spending on public works in order to increase incomes, reduce unemployment, stimulate savings and investment, and put money into the pockets of consumers. Most European governments followed suit. Whether these policies were successful or not is still debated among economists, politicians, government officials, and policy-makers today. While there is no doubt that income, saving, investment, employment, and interest rates increased in most countries from the mid-1930s onwards, a number of economists have contended that it was only when the first new orders for armaments and other war supplies came in that recovery was assured.

In the years following Keynes's death in 1946, economists intensified their efforts to flesh out and refine the Keynesian theory of employment, interest, and money. They did so by examining national income and expenditure, consumption, investment, savings, money, interest rates, and government intervention in the economy and markets in much greater detail. Their work became collectively known as Keynesian economics because it was based on intensive studies of the key economic variables Keynes had drawn attention to, including newly developed statistics of national income and national expenditure, consumption functions, investment functions, the marginal propensity to save, to invest and to consume, the multiplier, the accelerator, actual and anticipated rates of saving and investment, the marginal efficiency of capital, and interest rates. At the root of these studies was the attempt to come to grips with the dynamic, complex, ever-changing, and interrelated nature of the economy and markets, as well as "the real economy," "the money economy," changes in the quantity and value of money, fluctuations in industrial, commercial and financial activity, and business cycles. As their studies intensified Keynesian economists were led into detailed studies of the income stream, and the ways in which it changes over time in response to changes in saving, investment, interest rates, the money supply, and consumption. This made it possible to broaden and deepen understanding of the fundamental links and connections between microeconomics and macroeconomics, by way of the attitudes, expectations, and actions of consumers, savers, investors, corporations, and governments, as well as the complexities of consumption, investment, saving, government expenditure, and the economy as a whole. It also made it possible to produce a much more detailed portrait of the economy and the way it actually functions than had been possible in classical, Marxian or neoclassical economics.

The Keynesians focused on aggregate demand for goods and services as the real engine of economic growth. While consumption formed the principal component of aggregate demand, strategic roles were reserved for saving, investment, and government expenditure. Saving was important because it constituted a withdrawal from the income stream that had to be replaced in some way if economic growth was to be sustained. Investment was important because, while it was highly volatile and unpredictable in nature, it provided the impetus for capital accumulation and economic growth. Saving and investment together were important because they were done by different groups of people, and there was no logical reason why they had to be equal or in balance. Government expenditure was important because it could be adjusted upwards or downwards depending on actual and anticipated conditions in the economy and markets. This in turn provided the justification that was needed for governments to play much stronger, more direct and active roles in the economy.

Before Keynes and the Keynesians became influential the role of governments in most western economies had been, both in theory and in practice, limited in scope and largely political in character, focused on law-making, regulation, governance, and public policy. Economic intervention, where it occurred at all, was usually aimed at regulating monopolies, oligopolies, and imperfect competition, or providing limited amounts of welfare support to the poorest in society. Keynes and the Keynesians, however, contended that governments can and must play a major economic role in society by controlling monetary and fiscal policy, regulating business and industry, managing debts, deficits, and surpluses, stimulating economic growth, dealing with business cycles, and spending public funds to boost the level of aggregate demand, which they deemed to be the key to a healthy economy and vigorous economic life.

According to Keynes, governments should realize budgetary surpluses in times of prosperity, in order to have the funds necessary to spend on economic stimulation and recovery during recessions and depressions. Interestingly, many governments have ignored this sage piece of advice in their haste to activate and accelerate economic growth. As a result, they now find themselves in a situation where they are unable to respond to unfavourable economic conditions and tardy rates of economic growth because they did not realize budgetary surpluses in good times, and are now burdened with debts and deficits.

As the influence of Keynesian economics grew, the role of governments in the economic, commercial, financial, industrial and developmental affairs of nations grew accordingly. Combined with the demand for more government involvement in public affairs, greater control over business and industry, and the need for more social services manifesting themselves at the same time, the stage was set for a dramatic increase in the size and power of governments in many countries. Only in recent years, as governments have been confronted with extremely difficult financial and fiscal problems, and have grown very large and bureaucratic, have questions been raised about the ideal size of governments and their involvement in the economic affairs of nations, especially if, as many economists now argue, this impairs their ability to act objectively, impartially, and in the public interest.

In retrospect, it is easy to see why the Keynesian revolution had such a powerful effect on the development of the economic age. Not only did the pendulum swing from microeconomic concern with individuals and corporations to macroeconomic concern with the economy as a whole, but also opinions on the role of government in society were radically transformed. Whereas the classical and neoclassical economists had expected governments to play a minimal role, the Keynesians expected them to play a central role. Without a great deal more government involvement in the economy and the marketplace, there was the risk that production and consumption would not be optimized, and that economic, industrial, financial, technological, commercial and social conditions would be far from ideal. In fact, they might even be negative and remain there without strong government involvement in the economy. This opened the doors for economic issues and concerns to become public issues and concerns, and not just private issues and concerns. This made them of central importance to governments, politicians, civil servants, and citizens, and not just to corporations, corporate executives, commercial and financial institutions, businesses, and consumers. Without this shift in opinion and attention, economic issues would not attract the media attention, political involvement, and citizen interest they do today.

With the Keynesian revolution and Keynesian economics, all the prerequisites were in place to transport the economic age into full adulthood. Just as Adam Smith and Karl Marx had created the theoretical, practical, philosophical and historical foundations for the economic age, and the neoclassical economists had opened up a commanding place for consumers and corporations within it, so Keynes and the Keynesians drew governments fully into the economic equation. Once governments became actively involved, the economic age became all-inclusive in a way it never had been before. Indeed, governments became so fully immersed in the economic affairs of nations that their primary role came to be seen as economic rather than political, regardless of whether they were right of centre, left of centre, or situated squarely in the middle. All that was required now to complete the supremacy of the economic age was to extend it from western countries to the rest of the world. This happened with the next great epoch in economic thought and practice, development economics.

Development Economics

Keynesian economics proved exceedingly popular after World War II. Economists, civil servants, politicians, statisticians, and policy-makers spent a great deal of time refining the Keynesian system, and fleshing out its various components. It was not long before an idea closely related to Keynesian economics started to attract attention, and begin to dominate economic and political thinking: the idea of "development." Development came to be seen as the principal panacea for many of the world's most difficult and demanding problems, and as the principal means of improving living standards. This was only natural in a world recovering from a severe depression and two major world wars, caught up with Keynesian economics, and preoccupied with macroeconomics and the rate of economic growth.

The origins of the idea of development can be traced back more precisely to the need to bring about post-war recovery in Europe. The main vehicle devised to realize this, apart from the efforts and ingenuity of Europeans themselves, was the US European Recovery Program, better known as the Marshall Plan, initiated in 1947 following the urging of Secretary of State George C. Marshall. It involved billions of dollars of US investment in, and aid to, western Europe from 1947 to 1955.

In 1949, buoyed by the early success of the Marshall Plan, President Harry Truman made "development" the centrepiece of his inaugural speech to Congress, in which he talked about the need for commitment to "development" in order to increase production, achieve prosperity and peace, and bring about fundamental improvements in "the underdeveloped countries of the world" (see the article by Sachs). Development was perceived and defined largely in economic terms, as requiring the building up of the economies of those countries, confirming the centrality of economics, economic growth, and economic issues in public policy, decision-making, and society generally. This had the effect of sustaining the tradition established by the classical, neoclassical and Keynesian schools of economics. It also had the effect of making the "underdeveloped" countries into a battleground, where the conflict between classical, neoclassical, Keynesian, and Marxian views of the nature of "development" was played out.

Two of the first economists to address the theoretical and practical difficulties posed by development were Sir Roy Harrod and Evsey Domar. In the late 1930s and early 1940s they had created the multiplier-accelerator model of economic growth, drawing heavily on both neoclassical and Keynesian economics. According to Harrod and Domar, steady economic growth could be achieved most effectively when intended saving is equal to intended investment, and investment in any one period is equivalent to the change in national income multiplied by the capital-output ratio. While their model of economic growth was designed to address problems in western Europe and North America, especially as they struggled to achieve higher rates of growth after World War II, it had numerous implications for other countries since it focused on the importance of saving, investment, and capital formation as key factors in economic development.

It was not long before economists were asking how development could be achieved in the "underdeveloped" parts of the world, a category generally understood to comprise sub-Saharan Africa, most of Asia, Latin America, the Caribbean, and the Middle East, although some economists also included eastern Europe. Indeed, as early as 1943 Paul N. Rosenstein-Rodan was examining what would be needed to achieve development specifically in eastern and southeastern Europe. He concluded that what was required, more than anything else, was a big push towards industrialization. This quickly became known as the "big push" theory of development, predicated on the conviction that development was needed across a whole range of industries at once, because progress in only one or two industries would not be sufficient to trigger development for the economy as a whole.

Shortly afterwards, economists started to focus their attention on problems in the "underdeveloped" world outside Europe. These turned out to pose a far more formidable challenge than in North America or western Europe, largely because many of these countries lacked the economic, social, political, legal, and capital infrastructure, and the institutional capabilities, that had been built up in North America and western Europe since the seventeenth century. As economists increasingly travelled to these countries, and lived and worked in them for considerable periods of time, they began to study their problems and prospects on the ground, and to deal with the difficulties of development in greater detail. One of the first economists to do this was Ragnar Nurkse. While his theory of "balanced economic growth" was designed to deal with developmental problems and prospects in the underdeveloped parts of the world, it was heavily weighted towards industrialization and capital formation as the keys to development, much as Rosenstein-Rodan's theory had been for eastern and southeastern Europe. According to Nurkse, saving, investment, industrial development, and the introduction of capital-intensive techniques were imperative if these countries were to pull themselves out of the trap of "underdevelopment."

The theories of Nurkse, Rosenstein-Rodan and others posed numerous problems for such countries as India when they actually applied these theories to their own situations, because they focused primarily on manufacturing, and tended to ignore agriculture and the intimate connections between the two sectors. Nevertheless, they opened the doors to much more theorizing about how development might be achieved, by such "development economists" as Albert Hirschman, Gunnar Myrdal, Arthur Lewis, Harvey Leibenstein, and Raúl Prebisch.

According to Hirschman, "unbalanced" rather than "balanced" economic growth was the key, since all industries do not produce final products, and there are many backward and forward linkages that have to be taken into account in the developmental process. This quickly became known as "the lead–lag theory of development," because some industries were seen as leading development and exerting a great deal of pressure on other industries to stop lagging and catch up. It will be recalled that when the industrial revolution occurred in Britain it was the cotton and iron industries that "led development" by creating backward and forward linkages that placed pressure on other industries to follow suit. In contrast to Hirschman's theory of unbalanced growth, the theories proposed by Prebisch, Myrdal, Leibenstein and Lewis put much more emphasis on the dualistic nature of development. This dualism manifested itself in many ways, such as the dichotomies between agriculture and manufacturing, the "modern" sector and the "traditional" sector, export-oriented industries and import-oriented industries, and the domestic economy and the international economy. Development in this case was viewed as a process of breaking down the barriers between the various sectors of the economy and of society.

In 1962, the United Nations formally committed itself to promoting development and published *The Development Decade: Proposals for Action*, which set out the rationale for the first "development decade" (1960–70). The intention was to promote development generally throughout the world, but especially in those parts of the world that were deemed to be "underdeveloped," and to achieve well-defined objectives and priorities for each "development decade." The majority of these objectives and priorities were economic in nature, and were influenced by what the development economists were saying about industrialization, modernization, lack of saving, investment and capital formation, the dichotomous character of "underdeveloped economies" and "underdevelopment" generally, and the problem of decreasing imports and increasing exports in the underdeveloped parts of the world. By this time, the world was increasingly being seen as divided into two very distinct parts: a "developed" world, where higher levels of development, complexity, and sophistication had been achieved, and an "underdeveloped," "less developed" or "developing" world, where a great deal remained to be accomplished. This was the latest manifestation of the trend towards a divided world that had been steadily gathering momentum for hundreds of years.

While the problems of development occupied the attention of economists, political leaders, governments, and international organizations, the Cold War was heating up. As indicated earlier, much of this conflict was waged in Africa, Asia, Latin America, the Caribbean, and the Middle East, and was largely fought over whether the capitalist or the communist economic system and model of development yielded more effective results. The communist approach to development, involving extensive public planning and government intervention in the economy, was well-known by this time, since it had been taking shape in the Soviet Union since the 1920s, and was being expounded by a number of prominent economists and scholars in the West as well. However, there was a dire need to set out a detailed statement of the capitalist approach to development. This occurred in 1960, when Walt Rostow, an American economist and economic historian, produced *The Stages of Economic Growth*. Subtitled *A Non-Communist Manifesto*, this popular publication established the theoretical and practical framework for the capitalist approach to development, as well as the historical justification for it.

Rostow's book came just in time for people in North America and Europe. The United States and the western world were locked in a fierce ideological battle with the Soviet Union and other communist countries over which approach to development produced the best economic, political and social results. According to Rostow, countries had to pass through five well-defined stages if they wanted to become "developed." These stages were "traditional society," "pre-conditions for take-off," "the take-off," "the drive to maturity," and "the age of mass consumption." (Rostow also referred to a possible "sixth stage," which he called "beyond consumption," but he said that it was difficult to visualize and define.) The first stage was seen as presenting major impediments to development because many traditional beliefs and attitudes had to be overcome. Each of the other stages required the realization of very specific economic goals and objectives. For example, in order to "take off," countries had to increase investment from five percent to ten percent of national income, create new industries and expand old industries, reinvest profits, and revitalize and modernize agriculture. What emerges overall is a portrait of countries that increasingly focus attention on the development of their economies and high performance in key economic variables. While Rostow's "capitalist theory of development" contrasted sharply with the "communist theory of development" because it carved out a prominent place for capital rather than labour in the overall scheme of things, it still resorted to "the economic interpretation of history," and assuming the centrality of economics and economies to make its case.

Prompted by Rostow's theory, the theories of numerous developmental economists, the policies of many governments, and the actions of international organizations such as the United Nations, the International Monetary Fund, and the World Bank, the notion of development spread like wildfire throughout the world from the 1960s to the 1980s. Virtually all countries and governments in the world adopted an economic model of development, or some variation on it, as their principal decision-making device and *modus operandi*. They also accepted the conviction of economists, statisticians, and development theorists and practitioners that development could be measured with exact statistical precision. This led to numerous refinements in the theories and models of economic development, as well as the creation of economic indicators capable of measuring and evaluating successful economic performance. Most prominent among these indicators were high rates of economic growth, full or near-full employment, high levels of capital formation and technological development, controlled inflation and price stability, and a healthy balance of payments.

These indicators made it possible to rank countries according to the level, rate, and state of their economic development. They also made it possible to compare one country with another in terms of economic performance. This strengthened the division of the world into two parts. As a result, the challenge facing the world was seen as one of making it possible for the "underdeveloped" or "developing" countries to achieve the same levels, rates, and states of economic development as the "developed" countries.

It was about this time that the dependency theory of development made its appearance on the scene. Advanced by such economic and social thinkers as André Gunder Frank and Samir Amin, the dependency theory was based on the conviction that "developing" countries are poor not because they are incapable of achieving higher rates of saving, investment, and capital formation, or because they are saddled with a large "traditional" sector and a small "modern" sector, but because they have been dependent on developed countries for so long that they cannot break out of the cycle of dependency on these countries. They are dependent on developed countries not only for aid and resources, but also for markets and trade. They must rely on developed countries for manufactured goods, intermediate goods, financial resources, capital, and technology, as well as for markets and trade, so that the prices for their products fluctuate dramatically. The fact that this dependency has been going on for hundreds of years makes the problem chronic, acute and structural, rather than superficial and sporadic, with strong economic, political, social, cultural, psychological, institutional and historical causes and overtones. Frank called this "the development of underdevelopment," the systematic cultivation of dependency through generation after generation of exploitation, colonialism, imperialism, oppression, and structuring of the economies of poor countries to advance the interests of rich countries.

Directly and indirectly, this led to the creation of a number of "structural adjustment" theories, intended to break the dependency of developing countries on developed countries. Many economists and international organizations initially favoured "import substitution" as the best way to achieve this, largely by helping developing countries to build up their own productive capacities and reduce their dependence on imports from abroad through the creation of locally produced products. When this approach failed rather badly to produce the desired results, it gave the dependency theory of development and the need for structural adjustment much more credibility. More recently, and primarily as a result of globalization, the rapidly escalating importance of international trade and free trade, the creation of huge free trade zones, and pressure from the World Bank, the International Monetary Fund, and the World Trade Organization, there has been a tendency to put the emphasis on "export-led development" rather than import substitution as the key to overcoming the structural dependency of developing countries. Many economists and developmental theorists now believe that without the development of a strong export sector and more effective trading capabilities, developing countries will not be able to take advantage of the opportunities offered by globalization, international trade, and trade liberalization. What stands behind this, of course, is the need to develop a strong domestic economy capable of producing the goods, services, and resources that are needed to realize export-led development, as well as the ability of developing countries to sell their agricultural and industrial products in developed countries' markets, and not be put at a competitive disadvantage by the huge subsidies and high protective tariffs of developed countries.

This is largely where matters stand today. Countries in Africa, Asia, Latin America, and the Caribbean claim that it is not possible for them to increase their exports substantially and realize "export-led development" so long as the countries of Europe and North America erect high tariff walls and provide huge subsidies to their own agricultural producers. This practice has become so endemic and commonplace that a group of countries from Africa, Asia, Latin America, and the Caribbean created the G20 at the meetings of the World Trade Organization in Cancun in 2003, the so-called Doha Round, in an attempt to counter the power and influence of the G8 countries. Tired of being shut out of the markets of North America and Europe, they banded together to increase their bargaining power and make the case that things will not change for the better until the countries of North America and Europe reduce or eliminate their agricultural subsidies, lower their tariffs significantly, and eliminate other discriminatory protectionist measures.

The record of development economics over the past 60 years and more is mixed. On the one hand, much has been learned about the process of development that is relevant to every country in the world, particularly as it relates to the pivotal roles played by saving, investment, capital formation, consumption, trade, technology, education, training, the multiplier, entrepreneurship, the interrelatedness of economic systems regardless of whether they are capitalist, socialist or communist in nature, and the use of different methods, tools, and techniques to solve particular problems of development. On the other hand, a great deal remains to be accomplished, particularly as the development problem has worsened in some parts of the world. Clearly, much more needs to be learned about how development can be achieved in Africa, Asia, Latin America, the Caribbean, and the Middle East, particularly when there are such major impediments as adverse historical factors, oppressive institutional, social and political structures, too much dependency on foreign markets, capital and countries, and, especially, an inability to overcome internal shortcomings and deficiencies.

Contemporary Economics

While the economic age has been extended to all parts of the world and interest in development economics continues to be strong everywhere, there is no single body of economic thought and practice that is dominant today, as was the case in earlier periods of history. There are many reasons for this. In the first place, no economic or social thinker of the stature of Adam Smith, Ricardo, John Stuart Mill, Marx or Keynes has emerged over the past 60 years to put his or her stamp on economics, and give it a clear, comprehensive and unequivocal direction. In the second place, no single issue or set of issues has dominated the attention of economists as the theory of production, distribution, and consumption, price determination, general and partial equilibrium, or governmental involvement in the economy did in earlier periods. Finally, many changes have taken place in the world that have affected economic thought and practice in a whole series of diverse, bewildering and often contradictory ways, including the environmental crisis, computerization, commercialization, the creation of the European Union and other regional trading blocs, globalization, the financial turmoil caused by technology stocks and fraudulent accounting practices, the volatility in stock markets and economies, particularly in Southeast Asia and Latin America, the re-emergence of conservative political ideologies, the expansion of multinational corporations, colossal changes in communications, technology, and international relations, the terrorist attacks on the World Trade Center and the Pentagon, and the political and religious upheavals in Iraq, Afghanistan, and elsewhere in the world. This profusion of events, activities, organizations, and developments has caused economists to move in many different directions.

Despite this, it is possible to divide contemporary economics into two fundamental components: mainstream and margin. The mainstream continues to be concerned with the issues and problems raised by the classical, neoclassical, Keynesian and development economists, particularly production, distribution, consumption, saving, investment, income, output, price determination, scarcity, resource allocation, equilibrium, development, and economic growth. The margin is concerned with many new issues and problems that have appeared on the global horizon in recent years, including the environmental crisis, the emergence of the global economy, the need to achieve "development with a human face," the relationship between economics and ethics, and the need to create a very different type of economic system in the future.

As far as the mainstream is concerned, interest in classical, neoclassical and Keynesian economics is still very strong, although not as strong as it was when these systems were created. On the one hand, adherents of classical and neoclassical economics continue to believe that there is a self-regulating and self-correcting mechanism at work in the economy and markets, tending to restore equilibrium once there has been a major deviation from it. On the other hand, adherents of Keynesian economics continue to believe that there is no such mechanism at work, which has profound implications for the role of government, the use of monetary and fiscal policy to solve particular types of economic and social problems, the management of debts, deficits and surpluses, and, especially, the division of politics into "right," "left," and "centre."

In recent years there has been, in particular, a revival of interest in neoclassical economics, with attempts to update it in light of contemporary experiences and present-day realities. This has led to renewed interest in price and value theory, equilibrium analysis under conditions of imperfection and monopolistic competition, and the distribution of income, wealth, and resources among the main classes and interest groups in society. Economists partial to this approach continue to put the emphasis on the need to broaden and deepen understanding of production, distribution, and consumption in markets, buyers and sellers, the unfettered working of the economy to maximize the interests of consumers and corporations, rationality, the choices available to consumers and producers, and Pareto optimums and efficiencies. This has stimulated interest in the work of the Austrian school pioneered by von Mises, Böhm-Bawerk, von Hayek, Schumpeter, and others. In its more contemporary formulation, this approach places greater emphasis on the individual, individualism, freedom from government restraint and control, *laissez-faire* economics, espousal of the market as the main vehicle for discharging economic functions, rejection of quantitative studies and public policies, and emphasis on both the supply side and the demand side of the economy. It is an approach that meshes well with many developments that took place in the world in the closing years of the twentieth century and first few years of the twenty-first, especially the revival of conservatism, globalization, commercialization, free trade, computerization, international trade, and the promotion of democracy and capitalism throughout the world.

The same holds true for the Chicago school of economics, spearheaded by Milton Friedman. Like the Austrian school, the Chicago school places a great deal of emphasis on the individual, individualism, maximizing consumer satisfaction and choice, utility, consumer and corporate sovereignty, independence from government regulation, and reliance on the market to clear surplus commodities and restore equilibrium. Strongly opposed to Keynesian economics and increased government intervention, the Chicago school recommends relying almost entirely on monetary policy rather than fiscal policy to bring about changes in the economy. Being advocates of the quantity theory of money, members of the Chicago school believe that monetary changes have profound effects on economic activity and conditions, and that price changes generally reflect changes in the quantity of money. Consequently, central banks have a strategic and vital role to play. Through their ability to manage and control the money supply and monetary policies, they can affect all the main economic aggregates, whether investment, consumption, saving, interest rates, the velocity of money, capital accumulation or technological development. This is why many contend that "the Fed" (the US Federal Reserve Board) possesses more power and authority than the US government.

The situation with respect to Keynesian economics, the other principal element in the mainstream of contemporary economics, is more difficult to pin down and explain. In recent years there has been a tendency for Keynesian economists to subdivide into three main groups: conventional Keynesians, pure Keynesians, and post-Keynesians. Much of the distinction between the first two groups revolves around how Keynes's general theory is interpreted, as well as whether a static or a dynamic approach is taken to the theory. This has important implications for the amount of emphasis placed on the real economy as opposed to the money economy, and therefore on fiscal policy compared to monetary policy. Of greater interest is the work of the post-Keynesian economists. Spearheaded by the research and writings of Joan Robinson, Nicholas Kaldor, Michal Kalecki and others, and, like Keynes himself, largely though not exclusively based at the University of Cambridge, post-Keynesian economics is based on the belief that the capitalist system is inherently unstable, operates at far less than full capacity or full employment, is characterized by imperfect rather than perfect competition, is prone to unequal distribution of income, wealth, and resources, produces high levels of unemployment and underemployment, and has a built-in inflationary tendency. As a result, post-Keynesian economists tend to be very sceptical about the ability of markets and the economy to generate steady economic growth, and about the likelihood that individual and corporate actions in the producers' and consumers' markets will necessarily yield socially desirable results. The solution, in their view, is for governments to play a much more substantial, active and direct role in the economy and the marketplace, a role that would be even more extensive than was recommended by the first generation of Keynesian economists. They argue that this is necessary in order to counteract the power of large corporations and financial and commercial elites, and to redistribute income, wealth, and resources on a more equitable basis. This takes economics out of the realm of theory and places it squarely into the realm of "political economy," political practice, and welfare economics. As a result, there is much more emphasis on reallocative monetary and fiscal policies, increased government expenditure on health, education, welfare, and social assistance, and improvements in labour productivity and wages.

Much of the debate going on in the western world at present revolves around whether governments should use actual and projected budgetary surpluses, if and when these occur, to increase expenditure on social programmes, as opposed to cutting taxes for citizens and corporations. Proponents of the first line of action favour the post-Keynesian approach, whereas proponents of the second line of action favour the Chicago school's approach. Regardless of the approaches favoured by economists, politicians, political parties or governments, however, there is no doubt that all have been strongly affected by the terrorist attacks on the World Trade Center and the Pentagon, the wars in Afghanistan and Iraq, and the war on terrorism. This may well favour the Keynesian approach to economics in the years ahead, since governments will probably be compelled to play a much larger, more direct and assertive role in society through the prevention of terrorism, the provision of numerous safety and security measures, and the protection of citizens from terrorist attacks. This will result in much more expenditure on defence, the rooting out of terrorists and terrorist organizations, the firming up and protection of borders, and a host of new policies on immigration and security.

While the majority of economists continue to be interested in mainstream economics, and therefore in the real economy, the money economy, and the intimate connections between the two, there is growing interest in some of the new issues and problems that have arisen over the past few years to challenge orthodox economic thought and practice. The most obvious example of this is the environmental crisis. What has forced this crisis to the forefront of attention is the rapid deterioration of the natural environment, as well as the phenomenal growth of the world's population compared to the finite carrying capacity of the Earth. This is having an important effect on economic thought and practice in every part of the world, affecting not only the problems that economists and development theorists are wrestling with at present, but also the problems they are likely to have to wrestle with in the future.

Focused interest in the environment by economists started in the 1960s and 1970s with the appearance of a number of influential books and articles, including seminal publications by Paul Ehrlich and the Club of Rome. These twentieth-century updatings of Malthus's theory of population signalled a return to the central problem of population growth as it relates to the means of subsistence and the finite carrying capacity of the Earth. Clearly, there are limits to the carrying capacity of the planet that must be taken fully into account in the formulation and implementation of all future economic, demographic and political policies, practices, strategies, and systems. By focusing on five key variables affecting people and countries in every part of the world—population, resources, industrial output per capita, food per capita, and pollution—the authors of the Club of Rome's *Limits to Growth* (1972) constructed a dynamic model that, they claimed, demonstrated in scientific, statistical and quantitative terms how crucial it is to achieve "global equilibrium" among the five key variables if human welfare and environmental well-being are to be assured in the future. While there have been claims that the model was too simplistic and flawed to produce reliable results, the authors concluded that the future of humankind will be adversely affected if this situation is not addressed successfully in the future. Without the ability to keep population growth in check and to limit the pressure of human numbers on the finite carrying capacity of the Earth, the future of humanity is, in their view, bleak.

This conclusion, however pessimistic, simplistic or flawed it might be, forced people and countries in every part of the world to become much more aware of the extent to which human numbers, and consumption demands and expectations, are exerting enormous pressure on renewable and non-renewable resources, and the globe's fragile ecosystem. This subject was taken up in earnest when the World Commission on Environment and Development released its report, *Our Common Future*, in 1987. Chaired by Gro Harlem Brundtland, former Prime Minister of Norway, the Commission emphasized the need to make a strong commitment to "sustainable development," development that takes the natural environment and future generations into account, in all future economic planning and decision-making. Since that time, public and private institutions in most if not all parts of the world have been paying much more attention to the need to contain economic growth within carefully controlled and well-defined limits, rather than allow it to take on a life and character all its own. This may well have an important impact on economic thought and practice in the future, as economists, statisticians, and development theorists delve much more deeply into the complex connections between economics and the natural environment, and how the environment might be incorporated into economic thought and practice. One consequence of this may be that economists will put an economic value on the natural environment and give natural resources specific monetary prices. This could have profound implications for economic thought and practice, with recognition of the fact that natural resources are exceedingly limited in supply and cannot be taken for granted or treated as given in economic theory. This would cause a severe break with the traditional practice of treating natural resources as "free goods" that stand outside the realm of economics and economies.

If coming to grips with the environmental crisis is one direction in which economics is moving at present, achieving "development with a human face" is another. What is sometimes called "the alternative economics movement" places a great deal of emphasis on "economics as if people mattered," to use E. F. Schumacher's evocative phrase. According to proponents of this movement, there is a need to protect social and public spaces in modern economic systems, many of which cannot be described in economic terms but are nevertheless exceedingly important to the functioning of the economy, markets, and society generally. This movement views economics as an extremely important part, but only one part, of a vast social and human undertaking that includes ethics, morality, ecology, cosmology, humanism, and many other activities (see, for example, Daly, Townsend, Etizoni, Henderson, Schumacher, and Hunt). At the root of this movement is concern for civil society, and the need to ensure that people are able to participate actively and fully in the public and private policy- and decision-making processes affecting their lives.

Yet another development in contemporary economics is the concern for "the new economy," "the global economy," "economic security," and the possible emergence of an entirely different type of economic system in the future. This is because economics and economies are being radically transformed as a result of colossal developments in technology, communications, information, information systems, globalization, commerce, finance, terrorism, and trade. Rather than being based on machinery, equipment, industry, products, and factories, the "new economy" will be based on knowledge, information, ideas, the internet, cyberspace, a variety of protective measures, and increased volatility and uncertainty. For those who subscribe to this view, the electronic revolution going on in the world today is every bit as powerful and pervasive as the agricultural and industrial revolutions of earlier times, and is causing humanity to switch from depending on animals and machines to depending on electricity and electronic forms of communications. Many believe that developments in this area will eventually make traditional approaches to economics, as well as the methods, models, and techniques devised by past generations of economists, obsolete.

While it is still too early to say which direction the "new economy" will move in, there is no doubt that economics will move in some very different directions in the future. Despite this, many of these directions may hark back to issues and problems encountered by economists in earlier periods: dramatic fluctuations in economic activity, business cycles, shortcomings in economic growth, recessions, depressions, economic volatility, and instability. Developments as dynamic as these are so complicated and diffuse that it will take an economist of the stature of Adam Smith, Ricardo, John Stuart Mill, Marx or Keynes to pull them all together into a coherent and comprehensive system of thought and practice. Nevertheless, this does not alter the fact that we are living in an economic age. Regardless of whether it is powered by electronics, information, ideas, technology, products, machines or the internet, this age is driven by the belief that economics and economies in general, and economic growth and development in particular, constitute, and *should* constitute, the centrepiece of society, and the principal preoccupation of municipal, regional, national and international development. This belief, which has progressively broadened, deepened and intensified as a result of a whole series of theoretical and practical developments since the industrial revolution began, plays the dominant role in the world, and keeps the economic age functioning and intact.

3
Mechanics of the Economic Age

The economic ideology, the dominant intellectual framework in the world today, has reduced practically every human value to the categories of economics: production and consumption, basic needs and satisfiers, human rights, scarcity, nature, energy, systems, Cartesian time and space, the assumption that all things are measurable and comparable. One example is the expression "Third World," now used in an exclusively economic sense, which overlooks all the other significant differences between the industrialized world and the alternatives to it.
—Susan Hunt (1989), p. 3

Now that the origins and evolution of the economic age have been examined, it is possible to turn to the mechanics of the economic age. How does the economic age function? What worldview underlies it? What model of development drives it? What forces dominate it? How does it shape the character of the present world system?

The Economic Worldview

Like every age, the economic age is predicated on a very specific way of looking at the world, acting in the world, and valuing things in the world. It is based primarily, if not exclusively, on economics, which yields an "economic worldview" that is by far the most powerful worldview in existence today. This worldview is based on the conviction that satisfaction of people's needs and wants *in all areas of life* can be attended to most effectively by making economics and economies the centrepiece of society, and the principal preoccupation of individual, institutional, municipal, regional, national and international development. Through commitment to this conviction, it is believed that wealth can be increased most effectively, the supply and demand for goods and services can be satisfied most efficiently, living standards and the quality of life can be improved most fully, population growth can be curtailed most judiciously, poverty can be reduced if not eliminated, and the natural environment can be managed and turned to humanity's advantage.

Not all individuals, institutions, countries or governments share these convictions, but enough of them share it to make the economic worldview the most powerful worldview in existence today. It is this worldview that people and countries in virtually all parts of the world have become accustomed to, as a result of the triumph of economic thought and practice, globalization, computerization, commercialization, the operation of the mass media, and the diffusion of information about the policies and practices of the most powerful institutions and countries. As a result, the economic worldview is now so powerful and pervasive that it provides the foundation for the modern era. It is accepted without reservation or qualification by the large majority of institutions, countries, and governments in the world. Everywhere it is assumed, either implicitly or explicitly, that as economics, economies, and economic growth go, so goes the world. It is a way of looking at the world, acting in the world, and valuing things in the world that is based on seeing things in economic terms.

Like the economic age itself, the economic worldview did not suddenly vault onto the global scene. It took several hundred years, and the efforts of countless individuals, institutions, countries, and governments, to create the economic worldview and coalesce it into the powerful force it is today. The story of how this worldview unfolded sheds a great deal of light on how the world system functions in fact, as well as on how it influences people, institutions, governments, and countries.

The origins of the economic worldview are buried deep in the Judeo-Christian tradition. Nevertheless, it did not really begin to take concrete form until the decline of the Middle Ages, and their preoccupation with religion and religious institutions. The great geographical explorations of the sixteenth, seventeenth and eighteenth centuries, the rise of nation states, and the wealth-oriented policies of the mercantilists played pivotal roles in this process. The explorations had the effect of orienting the leading European countries outwards as well as inwards, as they became committed to tapping land, wealth, resources, and trade in other parts of the world as well as at home. The rise of nation states had the effect of making economic and political power the principal preoccupation of governments, both in foreign policy and in domestic affairs. The wealth-oriented policies of the mercantilists had the effect of building up the financial, commercial and manufacturing capabilities of countries, since goods had to be produced at home before they could be exported and exchanged for goods, resources, and raw materials abroad. As noted earlier, the object was always to increase exports and decrease imports, since this would cause more gold, silver, and other precious metals to flow into a country than out of a country, thereby enlarging its national wealth, and enhancing its power and prestige in the world.

As important as these developments were, it was Adam Smith who, as we have seen, laid the practical and theoretical foundations for the emergence of the economic worldview. He did so by making the development of economics and economies the key to expanding "the necessaries and conveniences of life," and to "making improvements in society." Little else could be accomplished until this was accomplished, and this was primarily, if not exclusively, an economic requirement, according to Smith. Smith's beliefs were so powerful in this area that they have dominated economic, political, social and developmental thinking ever since. This is confirmed by the fact that the large majority of economists, politicians, and social and developmental thinkers since his time have been content to work within the ideological framework that he created, rather than question its basic assumptions or his fundamental beliefs. Even as revolutionary a thinker as Marx was greatly influenced by Smith's dictum concerning the centrality of economics and economies.

By the end of the nineteenth century, the economic worldview had become part of the conventional wisdom, making it possible for economists to devote most of their time, energy, and attention to fleshing out the economic worldview in areas where it was deficient, rather than questioning its theoretical and practical foundations, or its historical and philosophical justifications. As we have seen, the neoclassical economists did this by extending the economic worldview into the realm of individuals and institutions in general and consumers and corporations in particular, the Keynesians and post-Keynesians did it by extending the economic worldview into the realm of government, politics, and the political process, and the development economists did it by defining development in economic terms, and contending that economic growth and development are the keys to overcoming developmental problems in all countries, but particularly in the "underdeveloped" countries of sub-Saharan Africa, Asia, Latin America, the Caribbean and the Middle East. As a result of these initiatives, and others, it is now generally accepted that the central role of governments is to facilitate as much economic growth and development as possible, primarily by controlling monetary and fiscal policy, participating in a variety of economic causes and concerns, creating a climate conducive to corporate, commercial, financial, industrial and technological development, and spending public funds to influence the level of aggregate demand.

So powerful has the economic worldview become that it dominates thinking about how countries should develop in both a domestic and international sense, in every conceivable area of life. In domestic terms, this is confirmed by the belief that economies should be made the centrepiece of municipal, regional and national development because this is the most effective way to increase material and monetary wealth, and to satisfy people's economic and non-economic needs. In international terms, it is confirmed by the belief that countries engage in international relations largely for the purpose of advancing their economic interests and objectives. Relations in other areas, such as the arts, education, athletics, social affairs and the like, are regarded as important, but primarily as facilitators for commercial, industrial, financial and technological relations, rather than in their own right.

While the development and promulgation of the economic worldview have produced countless benefits for people and countries in every part of the world, and for the world as a whole, it is clear that the economic worldview colours the ways in which people, institutions, countries, and governments view the world, behave in the world, value things in the world, and think about the world. The most obvious example of this is the relationship between human beings and the natural environment. It has proved to be almost impossible to make economics and economies the centrepiece of society without viewing the natural environment as an economic resource, to be used primarily for the purpose of advancing commercial, industrial, financial and technological interests. In effect, the natural environment is seen as an extension of the economy, since it provides the sustenance that is necessary to increase the supply of goods and services, and to generate material and monetary wealth. It is a resource that economists generally regard as a "free good," a good that has no monetary value because it is provided free by nature. Only now, as environmentalists have caused people to turn their attention to the enormous importance of the natural environment, and to the ways in which natural resources are being consumed, contaminated, depleted and exploited at an exponential rate, have economists been compelled to consider putting a financial or monetary value on the natural environment and natural resources. This is essential if the natural environment and natural resources are to be preserved and protected for future generations as among the most valuable assets of all.

What is true for the natural environment and natural resources is equally true for life and living. This area has also been strongly influenced by the economic worldview, as confirmed by such concepts as "economic man," citizens as consumers, the theory of the firm, the centrality of corporations, the role of government in economic life, "the new economy," "the global economy," and "the consumer society." Here too the economic worldview has had a powerful impact on public and private policy- and decision-making, and thus on people's lives, particularly in relation to getting as much consumer satisfaction as possible from the economy, spending as much money as possible to stimulate economic growth, expanding the level of aggregate demand, maximizing corporate profits, and promoting economic expansion and development. These factors play a crucial role in shaping the behaviour and attitudes of individuals, institutions, governments, countries, and international organizations.

Even the arts, sports, education, communications, and other activities are drawn into the economic worldview and given precise monetary values. For example, there has been a discernible trend over the last few decades to treat artistic, athletic, educational and communications activities as means to economic ends rather than as ends in themselves, and they have come to be seen as having powerful effects, yielding substantial economic, commercial and financial benefits. In respect of the arts, for example, numerous studies have been conducted to show how the arts can have a "multiplier effect" on the economies of communities and countries, largely through their capacity to generate additional rounds of expenditure on transportation, communications, tourism, clothes, hotels, motels, and restaurants, to affect the physical location of businesses and industries, and to stimulate a great deal of consumption, investment, income, employment, and tourist activity (see, for example, the publications by the Canada Council, Hillman-Chartrand, and Myerscough).

In sports, similar claims are made for professional sports events and such events as the Olympic Games, which explains why these activities have been so commercialized in recent years, as cities, regions, and nations compete vigorously to attract them in order to reap the economic rewards and spin-off effects. In education and communications, comparable justifications are made for the economic impact of educational and media institutions and activities on the economies of cities, regions, and countries.

Eventually, almost everything is drawn into the orbit of the economic worldview, and given a precise monetary value, price, and justification. As this happens, economics and economies are treated more and more as if they stand for the whole of human activity. From this perspective, social, aesthetic, spiritual and human goals and objectives increasingly become synonymous with, and subordinated to, economic goals and objectives.

While certain individuals, institutions, and countries have vested interests in promoting the economic worldview, and promulgating it throughout the world, this is not the real reason for the power and prevalence of the economic worldview. That has much more to do with the belief that this is the most effective way to address people's needs in all areas of life, to make improvements in society, and to increase "the wealth of nations." It is this, far more than greed, lust for power, or any other factor, that accounts for the popularity and pervasiveness of the economic worldview, and its perpetuation and promulgation throughout the world. This is the worldview that the world's most powerful individuals, institutions, countries, and governments deem to be essential in order to satisfy people's economic and non-economic needs, and to solve humanity's most debilitating, demanding and difficult problems.

The Economic Model of Development

Just how pervasive the economic worldview has become can be gleaned from the fact that the large majority of countries and governments use an economic model of development, or have one in mind, when they make decisions about a variety of economic and non-economic matters. This model derives directly from the economic worldview. While it takes different forms in different countries, it is predicated on ideological beliefs and convictions that can be traced back to Adam Smith, Ricardo, John Stuart Mill, Marx, Marshall, Keynes, and a host of other economic thinkers and practitioners. Most prominent among these ideological beliefs is the belief that development is primarily, if not exclusively, an economic, material and quantitative matter. As illustrated in Chapter 2, this belief is deeply rooted in the history of economic thought and practice, which gave rise to the "economic interpretation of history," as well as the conviction that economics is concerned primarily with the production, distribution, and consumption of material and monetary wealth and goods and services.

The corollary is a division of human needs into economic and non-economic components. Economic needs are deemed to be of principal importance because they comprise people's requirements for food, clothing, shelter, jobs, income, employment, and survival. Non-economic needs are deemed to be of secondary importance because they comprise people's requirements for education, artistic, religious and spiritual fulfilment, recreation, social interaction, and political stability. It is this division that makes it possible to think of societies in terms of economic bases and non-economic superstructures, a habit of thought that is shared by the large majority of political, corporate and international leaders throughout the world. This helps to explain why economies are given the highest priority in public policy- and decision-making by most countries, governments, and international organizations. On this view, the economy creates a surplus of production over consumption that can be ploughed back into more economic growth and development, or can be used in other ways. Thus commercial, industrial, business, agricultural, financial and technological activities are seen as forming the foundations of society, because they create the wealth that is needed to facilitate developments in other areas. "Growing the economy" is seen as the key to everything else.

This conviction is most prevalent in the corporate community, but it is also prevalent in the political community. Regardless of whether governments or political parties are "right," "left" or "centre," and irrespective of whether they are capitalist, socialist or communist in their rhetoric, the vast majority of them share the conviction that "growing the economy," and strengthening the commercial, industrial, business, agricultural, financial and technological foundations of society, are what is most essential. Ultimately this is what social development and the political process are all about in the thinking, policies, and practices of most corporate and political leaders and institutions.

This conviction is strengthened whenever governments and political parties depend on individuals and institutions in the private sector to provide them with the financial support they need to finance their electoral campaigns and maintain their political power. Discussions of "values," "value systems," and "value changes" in this context mean making decisions that are consistent with the ideological framework provided by the economic model of development and the economic worldview, rather than contesting or changing it. This explains why political parties such as the Green Party are always frustrated with governments and the political process. There is seldom if ever much willingness, or opportunity, to consider worldviews or models of development that provide alternatives, since all discussion and debate takes place within the framework provided by the economic worldview and the economic model of development.

Viewed from this perspective, non-economic activities may be treated as if they play important roles in society, as we have seen above, but they are never regarded as having primary roles. This leads to the marginalization of these activities and the conclusion that they can be expanded only when the economic base is expanded, and must be cut back the moment the economic base is jeopardized. This is consistent with the conviction that non-economic activities owe their very existence to the economy, and makes it possible to incorporate them into the economic model of development by subordinating them to economic ends, thereby reinforcing the notion that they are marginal rather than mainstream activities.

It is this way of thinking about and looking at development that is provided in the graphic representation of the economic model of development to follow. While the model is a theoretical abstraction that has been greatly simplified and stripped to its essence to facilitate analysis, illustrate basic principles, and shed light on the way decisions are made in the public sector and the private sector, it encapsulates the understanding of development that has evolved over the last two centuries and particularly over the last fifty years.

What is most conspicuous about the model is the economic base on which everything is predicated. Since the economic base is deemed to create the material and monetary wealth that is necessary to fuel all activities in society, it is given priority over everything else in the model. It is this fact that has led to the conclusion that the most important factor in a country's development is the economy, and with it, the development of activities like commerce, finance, industry, agriculture, business and technology that are deeply imbedded in the economy and the economic base. These activities tend to be seen as the "productive" activities in society because they result in the creation of tangible products and the creation of things of "lasting value." It is this view of development — more than any other — that has led to the conclusion that if the development of a country's economy or economic base can be attended to properly, everything else will fall naturally and logically into place.

Since the economic base is assumed to create the wealth that is needed to fuel all developments in society, it is deemed to "drive" society and the non-economic superstructure of society. This conviction can be traced back directly to the economic interpretation of history, where it came to be assumed that

Figure 1. The Economic Model of Development

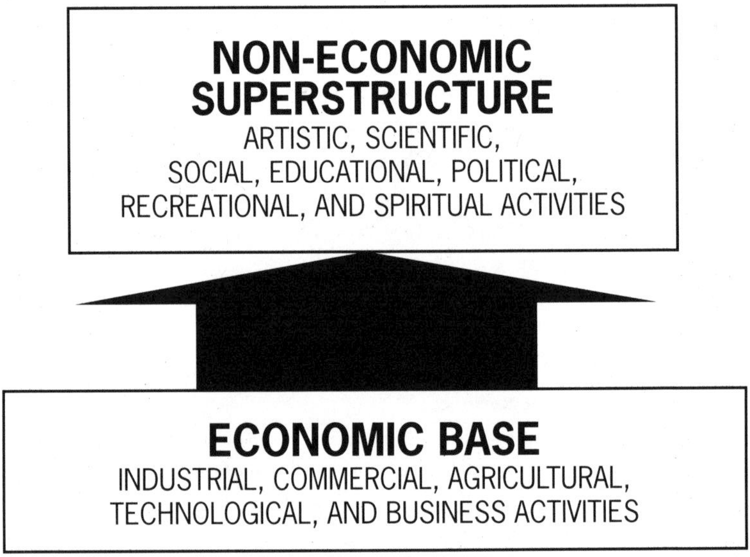

NON-ECONOMIC SUPERSTRUCTURE
ARTISTIC, SCIENTIFIC, SOCIAL, EDUCATIONAL, POLITICAL, RECREATIONAL, AND SPIRITUAL ACTIVITIES

ECONOMIC BASE
INDUSTRIAL, COMMERCIAL, AGRICULTURAL, TECHNOLOGICAL, AND BUSINESS ACTIVITIES

there is a unilateral relationship between the economic base and the non-economic superstructure: changes in the economic base cause changes in the non-economic superstructure, *but not the reverse*. This is why a one-way arrow has been used to depict the relationship between the economic base and the non-economic superstructure. It is consistent with the conviction that the economic base is "cause," and everything else is "effect," despite the objections to this that were discussed earlier.

Whereas the economic base is concerned with commercial, financial, industrial, business, agricultural and technological activities, the non-economic superstructure is concerned with artistic, social, ethical, spiritual, educational, recreational, political, and religious activities. Just as there is a tendency to assume that the economic base is concerned with the "productive" activities in society, so there is a tendency to assume that the non-economic superstructure is concerned with the "non-productive" — or "less productive" — activities in society. While this view lacks credibility in many circles today, it continues to linger on in the minds of numerous people, countries, institutions, and governments. This is apparent in the distinction that is often made between "hard" and "soft" disciplines and activities. Hard disciplines and activities, such as business, commerce, finance, industry, technology and so forth, are associated with the economic base and therefore the "productive sectors" of society. Soft disciplines and activities, such as the arts, humanities, education, religion, social affairs, recreation, spirituality and the like, are associated with the non-economic superstructure and the "non-productive" or "less productive" sectors of society.

According to this view, the only way there can really be an expansion in the non-economic superstructure of society as indicated earlier is if there has been a previous expansion in the economic base. The conclusion that is drawn from this is that the economic base must be given priority over everything else. If people want more artistic, social, educational, religious, spiritual, recreational and other amenities, the only way they can get these amenities is to expand commercial, industrial, agricultural, business, financial and technological activities and increase economic growth, since it is assumed this is where the wherewithal is created that makes the expansion of non-economic or superstructural activities possible. This reinforces the priority that is given to the economic base because everything is believed to derive from it or be traceable back to it.

Just as the economic worldview colours everything it comes into contact with, so the economic model of development does likewise. Individuals execute their responsibilities most effectively in the model when they maximize their consumer satisfaction in the market and spend as much money as possible, because this contributes to the expansion of the economy and therefore to the satisfaction of both economic *and* non-economic needs. Corporations execute their responsibilities most effectively in the model when they maximize profits and compete as vigorously as possible, because this fuels economic growth and ensures the most desirable situation for producers, consumers, the economy, and society as a whole. Governments execute their responsibilities most effectively in the model when they stimulate as much economic growth and development as possible, because this increases the aggregate demand for goods and services, and provides an additional stimulus for the satisfaction of economic and non-economic needs. Countries execute their responsibilities most effectively in the model when their economies grow as rapidly as possible, because this advances their economic interests in both a domestic and an international sense, and provides the greatest possible incentive for the economic development of all countries.

What is most striking about the model is that the natural environment is missing from it. This is because the natural environment was treated "as a given," and was not a major concern when the theoretical, practical, historical and philosophical foundations were being laid for the economic age.

The population of the world was much smaller then than it is today, and it was assumed that it would always be possible for countries with domestic resource deficiencies to draw on natural resources available in other parts of the world. This situation has changed drastically in recent years. The population of the world is substantially larger than it was even in the middle of the twentieth century, let alone as compared to the situation in the eighteenth or nineteenth centuries. Moreover, the "developing" countries are no longer willing to allow their natural resources to be exploited in the name of international progress and economic growth. This signals the need for an entirely new model of development in the future, a model that can deal fully and effectively with the natural environment and the complex associations that people have with it. Without this, it will not be possible to come to grips with the environmental crisis, or with the need for an approach to development that puts the natural environment at the very centre of the development process, and ensures human survival and ecological progress in the future.

Dominant Forces in Society

An age predicated on the economic model of development and the economic worldview is bound to place a high priority on certain forces that then become the dominant forces in society. These forces are specialization; products and production; capital accumulation; profits, the profit motive, and profit maximization; competition; technology; the processes of centralization, urbanization, and mechanization; consumption; materialism; the market; globalization; trade; and monetarization. It pays to examine these forces in turn, since it helps to expand our understanding of the ways in which the economic age functions. It is not the intention here to comment on the desirability or undesirability of any of these forces, but rather to identify them, to demonstrate how they function in the economic age, and to show how they are the inevitable consequences of an age predicated on economics, economies, and economic growth.

Specialization is the most dominant force in the economic age. Ever since Adam Smith made specialization the centrepiece of his entire economic system, because he was convinced that it was the key to increasing material and monetary wealth, and making improvements in society, specialization has spread like wildfire throughout the world. Individuals, institutions, and countries in every part of the world are encouraged to specialize in the execution of very specific production functions, since this increases productivity, output, income, and wealth most effectively.

In Smith's day, specialization was limited largely to agriculture and the newly emerging industrial and commercial ventures, but by the time Ricardo was writing on economics, specialization had been extended to other areas of life, most notably international trade. It will be recalled that Ricardo believed that countries should specialize in the production of products for which they have a comparative advantage and import products for which they have a comparative disadvantage. So powerful was the logic behind this argument that it gave rise to the development of an international system based primarily on countries specializing in the production of a narrow range of products which they then exchanged for products produced by other countries. By the end of the nineteenth century, specialization had worked its way into many other areas of public and private life. Educational institutions, for example, specialized because this increased knowledge and understanding of specific subjects and disciplines. As a result of these developments, and others, specialization is no longer confined to particular professions, disciplines, organizations, or parts of the world, but is evident in each and every sector of society. One consequence of this is that everything is broken down into parts, and subjected to detailed analysis and scientific examination. Although this has caused people and countries to lose sight of the big picture, it has yielded countless benefits by increasing output and wealth considerably, and expanding knowledge and understanding in every domain of public and private life. One need only think of the prodigious achievements in science, medicine, technology, business, education, agriculture, politics, the arts, and every other field of human endeavour to confirm this.

In the economic age, a high priority is also placed on *products and production*. There is an intimate connection between these forces and specialization, of course, since specialization enhances the capacity to produce products and expand production. This is why Adam Smith made specialization the centrepiece of his economic system. Production has increased exponentially throughout the world since the early years of the twentieth century. Not only are more products being produced than ever before, but humanity is capable of producing more products in every domain of human life. Even with many industries operating at far less than full capacity, the production of food, clothing, shelter, and a host of other items, whether durable or perishable, has increased beyond the wildest dreams of classical, Marxist, neoclassical, Keynesian and post-Keynesian economists.

Specialization is not the only thing that has made this increased production possible. It has also been made possible through *capital accumulation*, yet another dominant force in the economic age. With capital accumulation, production and output can be increased substantially, even astronomically. Without it, they cannot be increased significantly. This is why capital accumulation is awarded a prominent position in all the economic literature. It increases production, productivity, output, wealth, and income in ways that could only have been dreamt of at the beginning of the economic age. While it is possible for people to increase their production and productivity without capital accumulation, particularly when they are trained to do so, this process is very much enhanced when capital is available to cooperate with labour in production. The more capital is available, the greater the potential for production and productivity. One need only think of the automobile industry to confirm this. Think of how much production and productivity is increased when capital equipment is available to assist labour in the production of automobiles. What is true for the production of automobiles is equally true for virtually all other products. Production, productivity, and output are enhanced considerably by capital accumulation.

As it is for products, so it is for countries. Countries that consume all they produce in a given year are always starting from zero the following year because there is no capital accumulation to devote to production. Conversely, countries that consume less than they produce in a given year always start above zero the following year because capital accumulation is available to contribute to production. The more capital accumulation is available, the more countries are able to reap the benefits. This makes capital accumulation one of the most important factors in development in the economic age.

In the modern world, capital accumulation takes many different forms. In the material and technological sense it takes the form of all the machinery, equipment, methods, techniques, and expertise that are available to assist labour in specializing more, producing more, and expanding the supply of goods and services more. In the monetary and financial sense it takes the form of the savings, investment, stocks, bonds, and other financial instruments that individuals and institutions have to apply to production and the creation of material and monetary wealth. In recent years, a great deal of attention has been paid to "human capital," a key aspect of capital accumulation in general. While it is essential to invest in machinery, equipment, technology, and monetary and financial assets, it is even more essential to invest in people. Since it is people who create the aforementioned assets through their ideas, insights, inventions, and innovations, investments in people increase the skill, dexterity, and creativity of workers, and their ability to contribute to production and productivity. This is particularly important in the modern era where economies have become much more knowledge-based and information-oriented in character. As a result, more of the actual physical labour is done by machines and other equipment, above all by computers, and more of the creative thinking and application of knowledge, information, and ideas is done by people. This is why investments in education and training are so imperative, to ensure that people are enabled to compete in economies that depend much less on physical skill and dexterity, and much more on intellectual capacity, ideas, and creativity.

If capital accumulation in all its diverse forms is so essential, what is it that generates capital accumulation? Surely it is *profits and the profit motive*. Whether it is people earning interest on the money they put into banks and other financial institutions, or invest in stocks and bonds, or corporations earning profits on the investments they make in production and the productive process, people and corporations are willing to forgo consumption only if it is profitable for them to do so. An actual or expected return on money invested is imperative if people and corporations are to be enticed to forgo consumption in order to invest in capital accumulation. It is clear from this why economists, corporate executives, politicians, and governments are always so worried about the level and rate of profits. Without significant and expanding profits, real and anticipated, economies are unable to expand, and countries are unable to make advances in improving material standards of living or generating production, productivity, specialization, capital accumulation, and economic growth.

While the gains that individuals make from saving and investing are important, it is corporate profits that are deemed to be the most essential of all. Corporate profits drive the economy, in the view of most economic and corporate leaders, because they provide the incentives that are needed for capital accumulation, the production of goods and services, and the generation of material and monetary wealth. Small corporate profits and a low rate of return on money invested can cause serious problems for economies and countries, because everything slows down and little or no economic growth takes place. Conversely, large profits and a high rate of return on money invested can solve many problems for economies and countries, because everything is speeded up and a great deal of economic growth takes place.

While this explains why economic and corporate leaders are committed to profit generation, it does not explain why they are committed to *profit maximization*. While many people see profit maximization as a form of greed or lust for power, influence, and wealth on the part of corporate executives and shareholders, this does not explain why corporate leaders and shareholders are so concerned, indeed, some would say, obsessed with it. The real reason has much more to do with the belief that is prevalent among economists, corporate executives, and shareholders that profit maximization is the key to realizing the ideal economic situation, because economic growth is maximized and prices are the best for producers and consumers. The entire neoclassical economic system was predicated on the conviction that consumers should pay attention to marginal utility and that producers should maximize their profits, because together these activities would yield the ideal state of affairs.

It is impossible to place a great deal of emphasis on profits and the profit motive in general, or profit maximization in particular, without placing a great deal of emphasis on *competition*, yet another dominant force in the economic age. Without competition there is a constant danger that some producers will gain the upper hand over other producers and be in a position to exploit consumers by driving those other producers out of the market. This is why virtually all economists extol the virtues of competition, especially "perfect competition" or competition by numerous corporations or firms, rather than monopoly, duopoly or oligopoly (domination by one, two or a few corporations or firms). Competition yields the ideal economic situation, according to economic theory (especially neoclassical economic theory), because it provides the best prices for consumers and prevents excessive profits for producers. Not coincidentally, and equally important in terms of explaining why competition is such a powerful force in the economic age, it meshes well with "social Darwinism," the idea, adapted by Herbert Spencer and others in the late nineteenth century from Darwin's theory of evolution, that human beings in society, like living species in nature, must compete to survive because resources are scarce. There is no doubt that the crude notion of "survival of the fittest" (a phrase coined by Spencer, not Darwin) has had a profound impact on economic theory and practice, making competition one of the most conspicuous forces in the economic age.

It is impossible to examine forces as powerful as competition, the profit motive, capital accumulation, and specialization without examining another dominant force in the economic age, namely *technology*, the force that makes it possible to produce more products, as well as better, newer, and more efficient products. It also makes it possible to produce "waves of economic expansion," and upheavals in social and economic practices, such as the agricultural revolution, the industrial revolution, and the computer revolution. These upheavals have been colossal in size, scope, and influence, and have produced phenomenal results. Each new wave of expansion and innovation has brought with it substantial changes in the way life is lived in every part of the world. One need only think of the impact that trains, aircraft, telegraphy and telephones, radio and television, and computers have made to confirm this.

Technology has also played an essential role in bringing other dominant forces to the fore, most notably *centralization*, *urbanization*, and *mechanization*, which have been evident from the earliest days of the industrial revolution. It is not coincidental that London, Paris, New York, Shanghai, Tokyo, Hong Kong, Mexico City, Rio de Janeiro, Mumbai, Lagos, and other cities have grown astronomically in size, scope, and influence, or that an increasing proportion of the world's population now lives in towns, cities, and other forms of urban agglomeration. Eventually everything is compelled to move to, or emanate from, established centres of technological, commercial and financial activity. This has compelled societies to become increasingly mechanized in character, particularly as labour is replaced by capital, and must find other suitable outlets and possibilities for its application. This fact, which has been very much in evidence since the beginning of the industrial revolution, is still very much in evidence today.

Thus far, we have been examining forces that emanate from the supply side of economies, and the need to produce goods and services. Now the time has come to look at forces that emanate from the demand side, and the need to consume goods and services. The most obvious example of this is *consumption* itself. Whereas classical, Marxist and development economists focused attention primarily on the supply side of the economy, because they were interested in how production could be increased, neoclassical and Keynesian economists focused attention largely on the demand side of the economy, because they were interested in how consumption could be increased and how prices were determined. The two are related, of course, because the primary objective of all production is consumption. Just how important consumption is in the economic age is revealed by the fact that Keynes made consumption the most important factor in his economic system. The higher consumption is, the higher the level of aggregate demand and the greater the incentive for economic growth. Conversely, the lower consumption is, the lower the level of aggregate demand and the less incentive there is for economic growth. This is why economists, corporations, politicians, and governments are always so concerned about the direction consumption is moving in the economy. Like saving, investment, and economic growth, consumption can move upward or downward and be cumulative in nature.

Moreover, consumption can change rapidly depending on what is going on in the economy and in consumers' minds. When consumers lose confidence in the economy, as they did during the Great Depression and still do whenever there is a major recession, depression or downturn, their consumption decreases, bringing about adverse economic conditions that are not easy to correct. What particularly bothers economists and politicians about all this is the fact that consumption can be influenced by psychological and social factors beyond their control, including fads, fashions, marketing tactics, terrorist attacks, international tensions, global hostilities, and the like. Following the terrorist attacks on the United States in 2001, for example, consumption fell dramatically, particularly consumption related to travel, tourism, hotels and restaurants, despite the urgings of President George W. Bush and of Rudy Giuliani, then Mayor of New York, to return to "business as usual."

It was not until Thorstein Veblen started to examine consumption practices and consumer behaviour, in the 1890s, that economists realized why it is that consumption is such a powerful force in the economy. Most economists had believed that production was the most important activity, and that consumers were passive recipients of goods and services. "Supply creates its own demand" was how Jean-Baptiste Say had expressed the perceived tendency for production to lead and consumption to lag. Veblen, however, uncovered many cases where consumption actually leads production, and shed light on the motives, desires, interests and needs behind consumption, in his classic study *The Theory of the Leisure Class* (1899). Veblen identified two major motives that drive consumption and help to increase overall demand: "pecuniary emulation" and "conspicuous consumption." Pecuniary emulation results when the lower classes emulate the consumption practices and preferences of the upper class. Conspicuous consumption results when people increase their consumption in order to be seen to be keeping up with, or even going beyond, the practices and preferences of their neighbours, friends, colleagues, and peers. Veblen deployed these concepts to explain the uniformity that exists in consumer habits, behaviour, and tastes: consumers tend to want the same or very similar things, because their choices are constantly influenced by those of others. Veblen also contributed to understanding of the phenomenal increases that have taken place in consumption over the past one hundred years, and particularly over the past fifty years. People have both economic needs and economic wants, and once their needs have been satisfied, their wants can be increased without limit. Much depends on marketing, advertising, and publicity, how creative and imaginative it is, and how much is invested in developing and using such techniques. In the United States, for example, Madison Avenue is at least as well-known as Wall Street because of the enormous investment in the marketing, advertising and publicity activities associated with that particular thoroughfare in New York City.

The phenomenal increase in consumption explains, in turn, why *materialism* has become such a dominant force in the economic age. It is impossible to increase consumption substantially without placing a great deal of emphasis on materialism. As consumers' needs and wants have increased and diversified, more and more varied products have been produced to satisfy them. In today's world many of these products have extremely short lifespans: they wear out quickly and are often not very reliable. This increases materialism even more, since more products have to be produced to keep up with the exponential increases in consumer demand. This is facilitated by placing more emphasis on obsolescence than on permanence, as well as on replacing products rather than repairing them. This adds significantly to the high levels of materialism that are evident throughout the world today, though particularly the Western world, as well as the mounting problems associated with the management and elimination of waste.

Of all the forces of the economic age, *the market* is the most obvious, being the point where consumption and production, supply and demand, and buyers and sellers come together and interact. As the main vehicle for discharging economic functions since human beings began to truck, barter, and exchange, the market can be traced back to the earliest times. It has changed radically over the centuries, and particularly over the past one hundred years or so, yet it can still be seen in something close to its original form in most parts of the world, wherever farmers bring in fresh produce and livestock to be sold, or hucksters peddle their wares on city streets. The enjoyment that people derive from markets is as conspicuous as it is contagious, whether in chance encounters and discoveries, haggling over prices, hunting for bargains, engaging in social interaction or finding a sense of accomplishment.

Despite all this, it was not until the nineteenth century that the market became one of the most dominant institutions in society. The process whereby this came about was captured in brilliant fashion by the social critic and historian Karl Polanyi in his book *The Great Transformation: The Political and Economic Origins of Our Time* (1944). Polanyi documents how the market achieved prominence as a result of its capacity to extend itself around virtually everything else. So powerful did the market become that the entire economic system was transformed into a "market system," or "market economy," in which everything was seen as being actually or potentially shaped and influenced by, and subordinated to, the market (p. 68):

> A market economy is an economic system controlled, regulated, and directed by markets alone; order in the production and distribution of goods is entrusted to this self-regulating mechanism. An economy of this kind derives from the expectation that human beings behave in such a way as to achieve maximum money gains. It assumes markets in which the supply of goods (including services) available at a definite price will equal the demand at that price. It assumes the presence of money, which functions as purchasing power in the hands of its owners. Production will then be controlled by prices, for the profits of those who direct production will depend upon them; the distribution of the goods also will depend upon prices, for prices form incomes, and it is with the help of these incomes that the goods produced are distributed amongst the members of society. Under these assumptions order in the production and distribution of goods is ensured by prices alone.

Polanyi also describes how the various factors in production, distribution, and consumption eventually became subjected to the interests of the market. Labour became subordinated to, and dependent on, the labour market, natural resources and the environment became subordinated to, and dependent on, the land or real estate market, and capital became subordinated to, and dependent on, the money and stock markets. In this way, the market system and the market economy transformed society into a "market society," in which "the market" in general and specialized, segmented markets in particular determine all values, prices, and decisions. In Polanyi's view this was not, on the whole, a desirable development. In the process of asserting priority over everything else, the market in general, and the markets for land, labour, and capital in particular, revolutionized every aspect of public and private life, destroying the social fabric, and eroding the sense of community, solidarity, and public space required for people to function effectively, and to experience fulfilment and happiness in life. In the contemporary world, the market is colossal in size, ubiquitous in character, continuous rather than periodic, and omnipresent rather than sporadic. It is filled with products from every conceivable part of the world, and in recent years it has been extended well beyond physical locations with the development of the internet. It is becoming increasingly electronic in character, capable of uniting buyers and sellers from every part of the world, and moving goods and services quickly from one part of the world to another, without the need for physical proximity or contact. The market occupies a central position in the economic age, and therefore in the life of every individual, institution, community, region, country, and continent.

Focusing attention on the market helps to shine the spotlight on another dominant force in the economic age, namely, *globalization*. While much has been made of globalization in recent years, it is not a new phenomenon, but, as many writers have pointed out, has been going on and steadily gathering momentum for centuries. Wherever and whenever individuals, institutions or countries have manifested a desire to reach beyond themselves and their immediate surroundings to explore and exploit other parts of the world, there globalization is to be found. The earliest bands of humans, scouring the Earth in search of food, resources, and favourable conditions for life led the way, to be followed not only by such military leaders as Alexander the Great, Attila the Hun or Genghis Khan, but also by international travellers such as Ibn Batuta or Marco Polo, and the explorers of the fifteenth, sixteenth, seventeenth and eighteenth centuries. The transportation advances of the nineteenth century, which made it possible for people, products, ideas, and information to be moved long distances in shorter and shorter periods of time, built on their discoveries, showing that the drive to globalize has been much in evidence long before the contemporary debates about globalization began. That drive has since manifested itself in the establishment of multinational corporations, phenomenal advances in the aerospace, aircraft and satellite communications industries, the creation of international institutions to deal with global problems, colossal developments in banking, commerce, finance, marketing, and trade, and the creation of huge trading blocs such as the European Union and the North American Free Trade Agreement. Finally, and perhaps most importantly, it has manifested itself in the phenomenal developments in communications technology that have played key roles in converting the world into "a global village," as Marshall McLuhan once put it. As a result of these developments, and many more, information, ideas, people, resources, capital, and products are moving around the world in volumes and at speeds hitherto unknown in history.

At the beginning of the twentieth century, it was still possible for individuals, institutions, and even countries to remain relatively isolated from one another, and from other parts of the world, but by the end of the century this was no longer possible. Globalization is now a force that people in every part of the world must reckon with on a daily basis. It promises to make an even more powerful impact in the future, affecting not only the ways in which people view the world and relate to the world, but also the ways in which they conduct their affairs and position themselves in the world. This is a trend that may eventually end up in the creation of a single worldwide financial, judicial and trade system, a world police force, possibly even a world government. These would be institutions in a world very different from the world of the present, with its battery of nation states, international organizations, and multinational corporations. What makes globalization such an important force is the fact that it is contributing to the extension of the economic age into every area of public and private life in every part of the world. The economic age is no longer a Western phenomenon, but has become a global phenomenon.

As important as transportation, communications, and other factors have been in accounting for globalization, the most important factor is *trade*, yet another dominant force in the economic age. With the popularity of political and economic conservatism in many parts of the world in recent years, trade, especially free trade, has come to be seen as one of the most essential devices for increasing material and monetary wealth, and improving living standards. This can be traced back to the kind of world visualized by the classical economists, particularly Ricardo and John Stuart Mill, who believed that the global system should be structured in a manner consistent with the law of comparative advantage, and the free movement of labour and capital in response to opportunities to be employed to best advantage. This is not substantially different from the kind of world that many political, economic and corporate leaders are anxious to see come to fruition today, in which corporations would be free to move their productive facilities and capabilities from one country to another without constraints, while countries would be able to enjoy free trade with other countries that share their interests and objectives. It is this kind of world that has moved the World Trade Organization (WTO), the recently founded successor to the old General Agreement on Trade and Tariffs, from the wings to centre stage. Its principal objective is to create the legal and institutional mechanisms, and promote the technical and political infrastructure, that are needed to foster liberalization of trade throughout the world, through the elimination or substantial reduction of barriers to trade in goods, services, and investments of all kinds. The WTO has experienced resistance to its initiatives from protest groups that believe it is failing to address poverty, disease, homelessness, unemployment, environmental degeneration, and other social and ecological consequences of free trade, but the WTO continues to emphasize "export-led development" as the most promising solution to the problems of the less developed countries, even if this results in fundamental changes in traditional ways of life.

There is one final force that should be examined before we turn our attention to the functioning of the modern world system: *monetarization*, the tendency to turn every activity into an activity with a monetary value and price. The impetus for monetarization emanates from all the other dominant forces of the economic age. Given their pervasiveness, it is understandable that eventually everything gets drawn into the economic system and given a precise monetary value. This is necessary in order to determine the economic worth of everything, as well as to make it possible to assess and compare everything in terms of the amount of money spent on it or the price paid for it. It also makes it possible to include as many transactions as possible in the calculation of gross domestic product ("the wealth of nations") and taxable incomes. However, while money plays an important role as a medium of exchange, it plays an even greater role as a measure of value. Not only are all things measured in terms of money, but everything is valued in terms of money, as evidenced in the colossal movements of money and capital between countries, dramatic changes in the prices of stocks and other financial assets, the volatility of financial, technological, capital and futures markets, competition among individuals for higher incomes, and the fact that voluntary activities are dying out in many parts of the world because no price is paid for them and no money is spent on them. Whereas, at the beginning of the economic age, the value and worth of products was determined by the amount of labour embodied in production, at least according to the labour theory of value favoured by Adam Smith and other classical economists, as well as by Marx, today the value and worth of goods and services are determined by the prices paid for them, and if no price is paid for them, it is widely assumed that they have no value or worth.

The Modern World System

Of all the developments that have taken place over the past one hundred years or so, none is more important or more pertinent to people in every part of the world than the development of the world system. While the genesis of this system can be traced back to Adam Smith and *The Wealth of Nations*, it has only been since the early twentieth century, and more particularly since the end of World War II, that the world system has evolved into the powerful and pervasive system it is today. Developments taking place in transportation and communications began to make the world all of a piece, in a way it never had been before, and then the two world wars compelled people and governments in every part of the world to interact on a more frequent, intense and systematic basis. In addition, there was the establishment of many international organizations, most notably the United Nations and its various agencies, as well as the World Bank and the International Monetary Fund, all intended to address worldwide problems and issues rather than local, regional or national ones, and then the intensified development of globalization, as outlined in the previous section.

What stands out most clearly when the world system is looked at in its totality and stripped to its essence is its economic character and orientation. In the most fundamental structural sense the world system is designed to foster the economic development of the various countries of the world, and to facilitate as many commercial, financial, industrial and technological relationships among them as possible. Many other types of relationships take place in this system, including political, social, scientific, artistic, educational, recreational, religious and spiritual relationships (see, for example, Clough), but the principal objectives of the world system are to build up the various economies of the world, and to increase the monetary and material wealth of countries and of the world as a whole.

This is confirmed by the fact that all the countries in the world are ranked according to gross domestic product, rate of economic growth, volume of consumption, saving, and investment, income per capita, and extent of capital accumulation and technological development, despite attempts by the United Nations and other organizations to rank countries on a broader set of social, educational, demographic and economic variables. Countries that have achieved high levels and rates of economic development are considered to be developed, while countries that have not are considered to be developing, creating a pecking order in the world that is based primarily on financial, commercial, industrial, technological and military power. The most obvious example of this is the central importance of the G8, formerly the G7, the group of highly industrialized countries (the United States, Germany, France, Britain, Japan, Italy, Canada, and, most recently, Russia).

Superimposed on the network of developed and developing countries is the "global economy," the aggregate of all the national economies of the world, which in turn are the aggregates of all the municipal and regional economies. Detailed statistics are kept for all these economies and their various components, recording changes in the global economy and allowing evaluations of its overall performance from year to year. This in turn makes it possible to determine whether consumption, investment, saving, employment, and economic growth are increasing or decreasing for the global economy as a whole, as well as for municipal, regional and national economies. Increases in these indicators are taken as signs that an economy is getting stronger, decreases as signs that it is weakening.

International institutions play an extremely important role in this system. Together with the major corporations of the world and the governments of the "developed" countries, they are the most powerful institutions in the world. Their principal, though not their only, function is to help in building up the various economies of the world, and in facilitating as many financial, industrial, commercial and technological transactions among them as possible. They provide the international infrastructure, and the legal and institutional mechanisms, that are needed to promote economic growth and development, as well as to achieve economic, political and social stability. The World Bank and the International Monetary Fund, for example, provide countries, particularly "developing" countries, with the loans, technical assistance, monetary capabilities, currency stabilization, and balance of payments support they need to develop their economies and promote growth. The WTO, as mentioned above, works out the rules and procedures that are necessary to increase trade among the various countries of the world. The World Economic Forum provides opportunities for economic, corporate, political and intellectual leaders to meet and discuss major trends in development throughout the world, and to plan effective strategies for the future. Meanwhile, such regional organizations as the African Union, Asian Pacific Economic Council, or the Organization of American States promote specific economic objectives, and promote peace and security within their respective regions.

The goals and objectives of the United Nations and its various specialized agencies are more general and diverse, as their function is to assist countries with the growth and development of their societies as well as their economies. This takes the United Nations into the realm of political and social development, the promotion of peace and peacekeeping throughout the world, security arrangements, developments in the arts, education, culture, and the sciences, the welfare of children, the elimination of racism, and numerous other issues. Just how onerous this task is can be realized when consideration is given to all the social, educational, political, military and racial problems that exist in the world today.

Situated squarely in the middle of the modern world system is the United States. As the most powerful country in the world today, commercially, financially, politically, militarily and technologically, the United States plays a dominant role in the functioning of the world system. On the one hand, it provides much of the impetus that is required to fuel growth and development, largely by providing many of the goods, services, incentives, creative stimulation, technological innovation, entrepreneurship, consumption, investment and marketing that are needed. On the other hand, it provides the markets and trade opportunities that are needed for other countries to earn foreign exchange, expand their domestic output, and pay for essential economic, social and political services. This is why the United States has been seen as the epitome of the economic age ever since President Calvin Coolidge said that "the chief business of Americans is business." Globalization is a natural consequence of this world system with the United States at its centre, highlighting the interdependence of the various elements in the system. Events are not only happening at lightning speed, but are inexorably and intimately interrelated. It is impossible to have a major event taking place in one part of the world today, be it a terrorist attack, a crash in the value of technology stocks, an oil spill, a hurricane, a flood or a rash of forest fires, without affecting people in many other parts of the world.

Not everyone is in favour of this modern world system, with its high priority on economics and economic growth in general, and on the US economy, globalization, corporations, commercialism, consumerism, and international trade in particular. In fact, in recent years there has been growing opposition to it. This opposition has taken many forms.

In some cases, it takes the form of outright rebellion against the modern world system, particularly as it manifests itself in the creation of huge trading zones, the establishment of powerful economic and political "superstates" such as the United States or the European Union, and the concentration of financial, corporate and technological power in fewer and fewer hands. The reactions to meetings of the WTO, the World Bank, and the G8 in Seattle, Quebec City, Gothenburg, Genoa, Cancun, and elsewhere have demonstrated that these developments are having a disorienting and unsettling effect. In other cases, opposition takes the form of countervailing movements aimed at restoring people's sense of empowerment and control over the decision-making processes affecting their lives, whether through the quest for sovereignty, "sovereignty association," independence or autonomy, or through the resurfacing of interest in neighbourhoods, communities, towns, cities, and regions. The consequences of this are everywhere much the same: the more pressure is exerted towards globalization, "Americanization," and the creation of a single, homogeneous world system, the more people draw into themselves and institute countervailing measures aimed at providing greater control over their destinies and decisions. Finally, and most conspicuously, opposition takes the form of terrorist attacks on the major symbols of economic, commercial, financial and military power.

Specific countries and groups of countries are beginning to exert a more powerful influence over the areas in which they are situated, either as a result of their desire to capitalize on the benefits of globalization and international trade, or as a result of their desire to break with the dominance of the United States and the constraints of a unipolar world. The most obvious examples are the developments that are taking place in the Islamic countries, which are becoming a much more powerful force as a result of the emphasis on religious fundamentalism and the desire to assert Islamic influence in the world; the rise of China and India, which are exerting powerful influences over significant parts of Asia and the world as a whole as a result of their huge populations, their gigantic market potential, and their rapid development; the drive in

Europe, with its strong historical traditions, to overcome social and political differences through the creation of the European Union; and the beginning of movements in North, Central, and South America, as well as the Caribbean, towards the creation of a free trade zone centred on the United States, although there is considerable resistance to this in South America and Canada. These developments suggest that the world of the future could be much more diverse, complex, and multipolar than it is today.

It is unlikely that the modern world system would be as powerful and pervasive as it is today without the vision that underlies it. It is a vision based on the belief that eventually it will be possible for people in every part of the world to enjoy high standards of living and a great deal of leisure. While it has always been recognized that this ideal state of affairs will be exceedingly difficult to achieve in sub-Saharan Africa, Asia, Latin America, the Caribbean, and parts of the Middle East, largely because of the pressure of human numbers on land and resources in these areas of the world, it has always been assumed that it will eventually be possible to achieve a high level of affluence and a great deal of leisure in these regions too, through commitment to the economic age, the economic worldview, and the economic model of development.

There is one final matter that must be addressed if justice is to be done to the economic age and the way it functions in fact: that is the way in which the economic age is extended in space and in time. The economic age is extended in space through the promotion and dissemination of the economic worldview to more and more countries. At the beginning of the economic age, only a few countries, such as Britain and France, were directly affected, but today virtually every country in the world is affected by it, and affected by it all the time as a result of the developments in communications, finance, transportation, technology, and trade. While there may be a few parts of the world still unaffected by the economic age, they are now the exception rather than the rule. With globalization, computerization, commercialism, and urbanization occurring at phenomenal rates, virtually every country in the world is affected by the economic age.

Just as the economic age is extended in space, so it is extended in time. This results from two powerful developments. In the first place, there is no comprehensive system of thought and practice in existence anywhere in the world today to rival the system of thought and practice on which the economic age is based. This is because, as indicated earlier, most of the time, energy, and effort over the past two hundred years or so has gone into building up the system of thought and practice on which the economic age is based, and fleshing it out in areas where it is deficient, rather than questioning its fundamental beliefs and assumptions, or creating a viable alternative to it. As a result the economic age has enormous staying power: there is simply no other system available.

In the second place, there are always economic problems to be solved. And since economic problems are never really solved, this makes it possible to perpetuate the economic age in time as well as in space. No sooner is an employment problem solved than an inflation problem appears to take its place. No sooner is this problem solved than a deficit problem, a fiscal problem or a growth problem emerges. No sooner are these problems solved, if they ever really are, than a stock market problem, a trade problem, a balance of payments problem, or a recessionary problem occurs. The consequence is that other problems and possibilities are almost always put on the back burner as long as there are economic problems to be solved. This has the effect of perpetuating the economic age in a temporal as well as a spatial sense.

This, combined with the fact that more and more people, institutions, and countries rely on the economic age for their income, consumption, employment, and profits, and that the US and world economies are going through a period of readjustment and change, explains why the economic age is carried forward from one generation to the next, despite the fact that there are exceedingly dangerous and potentially life-threatening storm clouds gathering on the global horizon. If it turns out that it is unwise or inadvisable to perpetuate the economic age, what must be kept in mind is that the biggest obstacle to the realization of a different kind of age may not be the inability to visualize a different kind of age, or even to create it, but rather the inability to transcend the economic age, because of its capacity to reinvent itself and perpetuate itself in space and time.

4
Assessment of the Economic Age

There is . . . one difficult exercise to which we may accustom ourselves as we become increasingly culture-conscious. We may train ourselves to pass judgement upon the dominant traits of our own civilization. It is difficult enough for anyone brought up under their power to recognize them. It is still more difficult to discount, upon necessity, our predilection for them. They are as familiar as an old loved homestead. Any world in which they do not appear seems to us cheerless and untenable. Yet it is these very traits which by the operation of a fundamental cultural process are most often carried to extremes. They overreach themselves, and more than any other traits they are likely to get out of hand. Just at the very point where there is greatest likelihood of the need of criticism, we are bound to be least critical.—Ruth Benedict (1963), p. 179

Now that the mechanics of the economic age have been dealt with, it is possible to turn our attention to the task of assessing the economic age. This is surely the most difficult task of all, because it is difficult not only to find the right perspective from which to view the economic age, but also to overcome basic biases and fundamental beliefs. It is this that the distinguished anthropologist Ruth Benedict had in mind when she wrote about the difficulty of making an objective assessment of contemporary civilization. Yet, despite this difficulty, it is essential to persevere with this task. Logic and common sense demand it; concern for humanity, and the welfare of people all over the world, compel it.

Numerous problems have loomed up on the global horizon in recent years that make assessment of the economic age imperative, most prominently the environmental crisis, involving global warming and consumption of the world's renewable and non-renewable resources at alarming rates; the large disparities in income, wealth, and resources between the rich and poor countries, giving rise to unacceptable levels of poverty, hunger, and unemployment in the latter; rapid rates of population growth (in absolute if not relative terms); escalating violence and terrorism, along with the constant threat of nuclear, biological and chemical warfare; and growing tensions between the diverse religions, cultures, and civilizations of the world. Given the severity of these problems and their implications for the future, it is tempting to plunge directly into an assessment of the shortcomings of the economic age, in view of the many concerns and reservations that have been expressed about it. Such a temptation must be resisted, however, at least until time has been taken to assess the strengths of the economic age. If the economic age has its shortcomings, it also has its strengths.

Strengths of the Economic Age

Most of the strengths of the economic age have to do with the enormous advances that have been realized in production, productivity, and productive capacity over the past two hundred years or so. These advances would not have been possible without the economic age and its commitment to economics, economies and economic growth, the economic worldview, and the economic model of development. One need only walk through any market, mall, shopping centre or store to confirm this. Not only has production been increased substantially, it has been increased in every domain of life, whether agriculture, industry, business, government, education, social affairs, the arts, science, religion, politics or technology. More of everything is being produced than at any other time in history. The fact that many people are badly off rather than well off has much more to do with problems in the distribution of goods, services, and wealth than it does with problems in production.

What is true of production is also true of productivity, which has risen dramatically during the economic age, largely because of specialization, capital accumulation, improvements in labour-management relations, education and training, and increases in the size of markets. While conditions are far from ideal in most parts of the world, workers in virtually every country can now produce more per capita than was possible even a few decades ago.

As a result of the phenomenal increases that have occurred in production and productivity, productive capacity is greater than ever before, despite the fact that many companies are operating at far less than full capacity. Just as the problem is much more one of distribution than of production, so it is much more one of demand than of supply. Whenever there is enough effective demand, meaning demand backed up by the money to pay for it, supply increases to take advantage of it. This is actually a reversal of Say's Law, since in this case demand creates its own supply.

These phenomenal increases would not have been possible without phenomenal advances in science and technology, which have been crucial to the development of the economic age. Not only have they proved capable of outstripping the law of diminishing returns and warding off the stationary state, they have also made life far less physically demanding and strenuous for many people. In agriculture, production, productivity and productive capacity have all increased tremendously as a result of technological and scientific achievements. The entire way in which manufacturing is conceived and practised today, from automation to the management and organization of industrial life, has been fundamentally changed as a result of improvements in "the state of technique," as the classical economists called it. Numerous advances have also been recorded in disease control and prevention, sanitation, health care, delivery systems, life expectancy, birth rates, and death rates. In transportation and communications, the most conspicuous field for technological and scientific invention and innovation, there have been enormous advances too, as mentioned in the previous chapter. The benefits of these scientific and technological advances are by no means accessible to everyone, but few would deny that they have contributed to improvements in living for millions of people throughout the world.

In the first place, these momentous accomplishments of the economic age have expanded the realm of choice and made many more products available, from new forms of food, clothing, and shelter to cars, television sets, stereos, household appliances, and other consumer durables. In addition, there are many more opportunities for education and training, particularly advanced education and training, as well as for tourism, travel, recreation, and entertainment. There have also been substantial improvements in health care and medical systems that have made it possible for people, at least in some parts of the world, to live longer and enjoy their lives more. They have also made it possible for people to live with a great deal more confidence that their lives will not be snuffed out as a result of medical emergencies or uncontrollable events (although of course floods, hurricanes, avalanches, forest fires, wars, terrorism, and infectious disease can still erupt, and with devastating consequences).

For those who are fortunate enough to enjoy these opportunities and benefits, life is no longer, as Thomas Hobbes called it 350 years ago, "nasty, brutish, and short." On the contrary, it is more enjoyable, more fulfilling and longer-lasting than in previous generations, which is why people in every part of the world are anxious to enjoy the fruits of the economic age. While some lament the passing away of bygone eras, few would exchange their present situation for shorter lives, higher mortality rates (especially infant mortality rates), premature death, destitution, a great deal more poverty and disease, sixty to eighty hours at work each week, and a great deal of squalor, misery, starvation, and deprivation. Nor would they want to return to the past if it meant eating the same food three times a day, or having no holidays or vacations, few opportunities for education, training or entertainment, and no central heating or air-conditioning. Life in previous centuries was demanding, strenuous, and brief for many even in the most developed countries, much as it still is in many parts of sub-Saharan Africa, Asia, Latin America, the Caribbean, and the Middle East.

While the benefits and opportunities of living in the economic age are worthy of a great deal of reflection and respect, these are not its only strengths. One of its greatest strengths has been its capacity to confront the various challenges and problems that have loomed in its path.

When, for example, the preoccupation with production was getting out of hand, in the early part of the nineteenth century, Malthus, Ricardo, John Stuart Mill, and especially Marx shifted attention from production to distribution. While this did not solve the distribution problem, it did help to achieve a better balance between production and distribution, and it signalled how dangerous it is to focus exclusively on production if insufficient consideration is given to the ways in which the fruits of production are distributed among the various classes and interest groups of society. This same responsive capacity was evident in the middle years of the twentieth century, when the preoccupation with economic growth and *laissez faire* economics was getting out of hand. In this case, welfare economics, aiming to take into account the needs and interests of all classes and interest groups, not just those of the rich and privileged, grew and spread rapidly. Spurred on by theoretical contributions from A. C. Pigou, John Hicks, Gunnar Myrdal, John Kenneth Galbraith, and others, as well as practical measures such as medicare, workers' compensation, pension plans, progressive taxation, the spread of labour unions and better labour relations, and a variety of redistribution schemes, the economic age demonstrated a similar capacity to respond to the problems it was confronted with at this time. More recently, with the increasing recognition of the environmental crisis has come the concept of "sustainable development," development that takes the needs and interests of the natural environment, other species and future generations into account. While the capacity of the economic age to respond has not solved the crisis and, indeed, most would argue that it is worse than ever before, it has certainly helped to mitigate its worst effects. The environmental crisis would be far worse today than it is if economic growth had been allowed to run rampant over the past fifty years and the concept of sustainable development had not been developed and applied in attempts to counteract environmental excesses and deficiencies.

This responsive capacity of the economic age has been matched by numerous advances in the capacities of planners, policy experts, decision-makers, politicians, and governments to manage complex economic systems and local, regional and national economies. This ability should never be overestimated or taken for granted, since forces capable of having devastating effects can hit at any time, as has been shown repeatedly from the stock market crash of 1929 to the financial crisis in East Asia in the 1990s and the events of 9/11. However, economic, corporate, government, and financial authorities now have a better understanding of how complex economic systems function, and how they can be managed effectively, than they did before the economic age began. They also have a much better understanding of how to use all the various monetary and fiscal tools and techniques at their disposal to control fluctuations in economic activity, and to address economic, commercial, and financial problems. Many of these advances grow out of the experience of the Great Depression, including "New Deal" economics, management of business cycles, Keynesian economics, refinements in economic science, and advances in monetary and fiscal policy.

Another strength of the economic age is that, while it has contributed to population growth throughout the world as a result of the impact it has had on birth rates, death rates, and life expectancy, it has also helped to alleviate population growth. Although it is difficult to determine which is cause and which is effect, there is no doubt that there is a high correlation between improvements in living standards, production, productivity, productive capacity, and economic growth, on the one hand, and reductions in the rate of population growth, on the other hand. People who enjoy higher standards of living and higher levels of affluence need fewer children to provide for them in old age. They also need more income and wealth to educate their children and grandchildren, and are thereby prone to limiting the number of children they have. As a result, population growth has slowed significantly in those parts of the world where economic growth and development have been most rapid, particularly in Europe, North America, Australia, New Zealand, and Japan, presenting the only effective alternative to direct government control of population growth, as in China. While population growth is still increasing at an alarming rate in absolute terms, there has been a significant improvement in the relative rate of population growth in recent years.

There is one final matter that must be addressed if the strengths of the economic age are to be assessed properly, and that is the creation of a set of goals and objectives that people and countries can identify with, work towards, and strive to achieve. There can be no doubt that most people and countries share the conviction that the highest priority should be given to increasing rates of economic growth, high standards of material living, and making economics and economies the centrepiece of society and principal preoccupation of municipal, regional, national and international development. This conviction has been extremely valuable in providing a common bond among numerous people and countries, and in yielding a great deal of stability and order in the world system. Without it, there would be a great deal more instability, disorder, and conflict, as people and countries pursued different courses of action or aspired to goals and objectives that were divergent rather than convergent.

While all these strengths of the economic age represent substantial achievements for global development and human welfare, they should not be allowed to obscure the fact that there are some fundamental shortcomings to the economic age. These too must be taken into account in any assessment of this age.

Shortcomings of the Economic Age

The most obvious shortcoming of the economic age is the devastating effect this age is having on the natural environment. As economic demands and expectations escalate at an alarming rate, more and more damage is being done to the natural environment, including other species. This is contributing to the numerous problems that have loomed up on the global horizon in recent years, particularly global warming, floods, droughts, hurricanes, forest fires, earthquakes, the spread of greenhouse gases and toxic substances, and pollution. So pronounced have these problems become that many contend that the global ecosystem could collapse if aggressive action is not taken to prevent it. As the economist and environmentalist Barbara Ward pointed out in 1979 (p. 266):

> so delicate is much of the environment, so precarious are its balances, that human
> actions and interactions (especially now that they are armed with the forces of
> modern science) can have vast, potentially catastrophic and even irreversible effects.

What lies at the root of these problems is that, as we have seen, the natural environment is taken for granted and treated as a given in the economic age. It has long been deemed to stand outside the realm of economics, particularly economics as it was evolving in the eighteenth, nineteenth and twentieth centuries, and seen as the concern of environmentalists or ecologists, rather than of economists or others concerned with economic growth. While certain economists have been and are very sensitive to environmental problems, and are working hard to develop the theories, policies, practices, and insights that are needed to take the natural environment fully into account in economic planning and decision-making, the profession as a whole continues to view these problems and their solutions as "externalities." Indeed, many economists contend that the preoccupation with environmental issues is having a debilitating effect on economic growth and making it difficult for people to earn a decent living. On the other side of the argument, environmentalists contend that most economists are so preoccupied with economic growth that they are oblivious to the environmental consequences of their theories.

What is disturbing about this situation is that the positions of the two groups have become so polarized and entrenched that there appears to be little hope of finding any common ground between them. Yet, in a world of increasing pressures on resources, and of increasing tensions between resource-rich and resource-poor countries, discovering and applying viable solutions to problems that are both environmental *and* economic is imperative for human survival and environmental well-being.

If devastation of the natural environment is one shortcoming of the economic age, promotion of a highly materialistic way of life is another. The two are intimately connected, of course, because materialism has a negative rather than a positive impact on the natural environment, making colossal demands on scarce renewable and non-renewable resources, the global ecosystem, and the lives of other species. This is inevitable, since the modern world system is based on the centrality of economics and economies, and therefore on the production, distribution, and consumption of material goods and commodities. The origins of this highly materialistic way of life can be traced back to the rise of the western countries as the most dominant countries in the world, as well as the economic interpretation of history, the propensity for defining "wealth" in material and monetary terms, and the promotion of consumption as the main component in economic growth. The creation of more and more wealth and material goods, which had largely been an ideal in the eighteenth century, became an ideology in the nineteenth and early twentieth centuries, and an obsession in the later twentieth and early twenty-first centuries. People in many parts of the world now revere wealth as never before.

One consequence is that living and development have become so deeply rooted in, and dependent on, the production, distribution, and consumption of material wealth that it is difficult to see or think about anything else. With this has come a rapid expansion of the demand for goods and services that are

high in material inputs and outputs, which exerts even more pressure on the
carrying capacity of the Earth, by causing consumption of wood, coal, land,
gas, oil, electricity, water, fish, livestock, minerals, and other resources to rise
to disturbingly high levels. Meanwhile, the population of the planet is growing
rapidly (in absolute terms) and a major proportion of that population lacks
the resources it needs for survival. For example, the World Commission on
Water for the Twenty-first Century, established by the World Water Council,
estimated in 2000 that the use of water would increase by 40 percent between
that year and 2020 (see Keung). This was especially disturbing in light of the
fact that 1.5 billion people, one quarter of the world's population, still lacked
access to safe water and that 2.4 million children were dying every year from
water-borne diseases (see Crane 1999).

Rapid consumption of the world's resources is not the only problem associated
with a highly materialistic way of life. Materialism has become so dominant in
such parts of the world as the United States, Canada, Europe, and Japan that it
is causing a great deal of hostility, resentment, and alienation in those parts of
sub-Saharan Africa, Asia, Latin America, the Caribbean, and the Middle East
where people live without the basic material necessities of life and countries
that have not achieved the high levels of material development. Arguably, the
use of yardsticks to measure developmental progress and performance, such as
gross domestic product, level of capital formation or rate of economic growth,
that are themselves materialistic and economic in nature, fans the flames of
resentment, because it demeans many countries and people, condemning them
to an inferior status, and robbing them of their dignity, identity, and sense of
self-worth.

Nor are these the only shortcomings of the economic age. There are others,
the most prominent being: major inequalities in the distribution of income,
wealth, and resources among the diverse peoples and countries of the world;
unacceptable levels of poverty, hunger, and unemployment; the division of the
world into two unequal parts; and the rise of violence and terrorism in the
world. While the various attacks that have been launched on these problems
have helped to alleviate some of them, others are worse than before. When one
quarter of the world's population owns or controls approximately three quarters
of the world's income and wealth, the prospects for the larger proportion of the
world's population are bleak.

Fortunately, some impressive gains have been recorded in reducing disparities
in income and wealth throughout the world in recent years, thereby lessening
some of the tensions that exist between rich and poor countries and rich and
poor people. Due to developments in the global economy and international
trade, commitment to the United Nations' millennium goals, and rapid rates

of economic growth in China, India, Brazil, and other countries in Africa, Asia, and Latin America, the World Bank predicted in its *Global Economic Prospects Report* for 2007 that the number of people living below $2 a day will be reduced from 1.9 billion in 2005 to 1.1 billion in 2030, and that the share of "developing countries" in global output will increase from one-fifth to one-third over the same period, provided that population increases, income inequalities, and global warming do not jeopardize or interfere with this.

Nevertheless, some very troubling problems remain. The average income of people living in the richest countries is still more than twenty times greater than the average income of people living in the poorest countries, indebtedness among the low-income countries continues to be very high, more than ten per cent of the world's population still lives on less than $1 a day, and aid from the richest countries to the poorest countries declined over much of the last two decades, despite the fact that it has stabilized or risen slightly over the last few years (see *Equitable Growth* for example). Not only do these problems confirm the fact that the economic age is much more effective in dealing with production problems than distribution problems, but it also explains why a significant percentage of the world's population is living without a great deal of hope for improvements in their situation in the future. While this is not, of course, the only cause of violence and terrorism, it is certainly a contributing factor.

A related problem is the human cost of production, productivity, productive capacity, wealth, and materialism. While increases in these capabilities are recognized as a real strength of the economic age, they are not without their problems. It has been argued that these increases would not have been possible without the exploitation of sub-Saharan Africa, Asia, Latin American, and the Caribbean in the form of low wages, deplorable working conditions, the creation of giant sweat shops, and the exploitation of labour, especially child labour. Multinational corporations no longer engage in selling products, but rather logos, brand names and lifestyles (see, for example, Klein), realized through mass advertising, marketing and media techniques, as well as contracting out production to companies that use unfair labour practices, make phenomenal demands on their employees, pay very low wages, provide few social benefits, and exploit women and children. This too is contributing to the explosive situation that exists throughout the world at present. In the developing parts of the world, there is animosity over exploitation, injustice, indifference, neglect, and colonization, while in the developed parts of the world, there are tighter and tighter security measures to protect income, wealth, and resources, including gated communities, border patrols, elaborate military installations, and sophisticated defence systems. These trends are heightening a situation that is close to the breaking point.

One of the most serious shortcomings of the economic age is the priority that is placed on products, profits, profit maximization, capital accumulation, and the market, as opposed to human welfare and well-being. While this was not the intention when the economic age began, or as it evolved, it is a conspicuous feature of the economic age today, with profound consequences for every part of the world. For example, athletic events such as the Olympic Games are valued far more for generating millions of dollars in revenue for owners and promoters than for promoting athletic prowess, ideals and capabilities; space programmes are valued more for generating financial returns from trips to space stations than for advancing new frontiers in scientific knowledge; and artistic activities are prized far more for generating economic impact and multiplier effects than for artistic inspiration. To these examples should be added the inflation of stock prices and the distortion of financial information to keep prices and profits artificially high, sustain the ideological commitment to profit maximization, and exploit commercial and consumer opportunities. While this has always been a cause for concern in the economic age, not to mention the capitalist system of production, distribution, and consumption, it has reached alarming proportions recently as a result of the falsification of accounting records and financial statements, and the manipulation of stock prices and transactions by such companies as Enron and WorldCom. So scandalous have these activities become that they are threatening to undermine the entire ethical foundation of the economic age and the capitalist system.

The upshot of these developments is that people are treated more and more as commodities and objects rather than as persons and subjects. This has been particularly evident since the introduction of the concept of "economic man." By focusing attention on the way in which the abstract individual functions in the economy and the market, the economic age has turned people into consumers whose principal function, if not their sole function, is to maximize satisfaction by purchasing products. This is making it difficult, if not impossible, for people to realize their full potential, because their potential is defined primarily in economic, commercial, and financial terms. This in turn has led to what is often called the crisis of maldevelopment, or spiritual poverty in the midst of plenty. People in the developed parts of the world are discovering that high levels of income, wealth, consumption, and materialism are not necessarily guarantees of spiritual fulfilment and happiness in life. In fact, the more consumer goods and material possessions people possess, and the more they participate in the economic system, the more they may discover that they are unfulfilled, and lacking in the spiritual, intellectual, emotional and religious requirements for a happy and healthy existence. They have become like the cynic, who, in Oscar Wilde's words, "knows the price of everything and the value of nothing." While this attitude may be starting to change, it is clear that people in the more developed parts of the world will have to change their ways of life quite substantially if they want to capitalize on Wilde's remarkable insight. Meanwhile, so much time and attention are focused on business, financial, industrial, commercial, corporate, and technological matters that little time and attention are left for focusing on artistic, educational, humanistic, social, and spiritual matters. This tends to downplay or disregard the valuable contributions that numerous groups make to social progress and human welfare, including educators, artists, health care workers, social and environmental activists, homemakers, and spiritual leaders.

A related problem is the high level of stress and anxiety that many people experience as a result of the economic age. For some people, this is because contemporary economic systems are depriving them of their jobs, incomes, and sources of livelihood, largely as a result of the rapidity and pervasiveness of technological change, accompanied by a great deal of corporate and commercial downsizing. This is contributing to the high levels of unemployment and underemployment that exist throughout the world, as well as a global unemployment rate that has been estimated to exceed one billion. For others, it is because the economic age is destroying their traditions, customs, identities, cultures, and ways of life, as well as eroding such key institutions as families, neighbourhoods, communities, and religious bodies. For still others, it is because life has been drastically speeded up, making it impossible to escape the economic system, or fulfil the need for rest and relaxation from the relentlessness of contemporary economic change. While it would be a mistake to blame the economic age for all of this, there is no doubt it has been a major contributor to it. The social and human bonds, recreational practices, and therapeutic and recuperative measures have not be created that are required to counteract major transformations in the character of economic life.

This brings us to a final shortcoming of the economic age, the tendency to destroy the social fabric of society and sense of community that binds people, institutions, groups, countries and cultures together. Karl Polanyi focused attention on this when he described the transition that took place in the nineteenth century from the market economy to the market society. Through the progressive development of markets for land, labour, capital, and commodities everything eventually became highly individualized and atomized, severing the bonds between people and the various collectivities they had created. This is what is being experienced by many people, institutions, groups, countries, cultures, and civilizations throughout the world today. Economic growth and development are destroying organic collectivities and, with them, the ability of people to trust and rely on one another in times of adversity and hardship.

When all these shortcomings are added up and compared with the strengths of the economic age, it is possible to compose a balance sheet, and to reach some very definite and specific conclusions about the costs and benefits of the economic age, and the requirements for the future.

A Balance Sheet on the Economic Age

When the balance sheet is composed on the economic age, two undeniable but highly contradictory facts stand out above all else. First, the economic age has produced countless benefits for people and countries in many if not all parts of the world, and for the world as a whole. Production, productivity, productive capacity, wealth, and living standards have increased substantially, particularly as compared to where they were in the late eighteenth century when the economic age began. This has brought with it significant improvements in the quality of life on many different fronts, social, political, educational, artistic, scientific, economic, industrial, financial, commercial, and technological. While this is much truer of people and countries in the global North than in the global South, even people and countries in the latter have benefited from the economic age, despite the large disparities in income, wealth, and resources. Second, and almost diametrically opposed to the first, there are real dangers and risks ahead for humanity if the economic age is perpetuated. Material demands will be created that are beyond the capacity of the natural environment to fulfil, and substantial disparities will be experienced in income, wealth, and resources between the rich and poor countries and people of the world. This will cause significant hardships as resources are increasingly used up.

These dangers and risks did not exist when the economic age began, in the late eighteenth century, or as it developed in the nineteenth and twentieth centuries. The population of the world was substantially smaller than it is today, and the disparities in income, wealth, and resources, though they certainly existed, were arguably not as pronounced or as life-threatening as they are today. Moreover, as we have seen, it was always possible for countries with domestic resource deficiencies to draw on resources in other parts of the world. Since this possibility no longer exists to any significant degree, this makes recognizing the risks and dangers that could easily result from perpetuating the economic age a categorical imperative. The longer it is ignored, the more severe the consequences will be.

Clearly, the environmental crisis will not be resolved as long as the economic age is perpetuated. The economic age is predicated on the production, distribution, and consumption of goods and services, rather than on an intimate relationship between people and the natural environment. The more economic growth takes place, the more damage will be done to the natural environment and the carrying capacity of the Earth, the more resources will be consumed and contaminated, and the less will be available for future generations. This will result in even more rapid depletion of scarce renewable and non-renewable resources, as well as a great deal more pollution, global warming, the spread of toxic substances, the extinction of many species, far more environmental damage, and growing shortages and higher prices for strategic resources such as wood, water, gas, oil, coal, electricity, fish, precious metals, and arable land. These problems will be exacerbated whenever consumer demands and expectations are created that are high in material inputs and outputs, as they are in various parts of the world.

The problem here is that no distinction is made between consumer needs and consumer wants in the economic age, because both contribute to economic growth and development. Nevertheless, since consumer wants have a way of multiplying indefinitely, if the experience of the western countries is any guide, this will aggravate even more an ecological situation that is close to the breaking point.

The gap between rich and poor people and rich and poor countries could also widen if the economic age is perpetuated. Income, wealth, resources, and power may well be concentrated in fewer and fewer hands, with more and more emphasis on globalization, commercialism, capitalism, trade liberalization, and the market. Even with the most aggressive redistribution policies possible, there is an inherent tendency in highly developed economic systems to produce substantial disparities between rich and poor people, classes, and countries. This could result in a great deal more violence, terrorism, conflict, and confrontation, a chilling prospect in view of the state of the world at present.

There is also the very real possibility that there will be more unemployment, underemployment, financial insecurity, inflation, and economic instability in many countries, and in the world system as a whole, if the economic age is perpetuated. This will be aggravated wherever companies engage in downsizing, cost-cutting, capital transfers, profit maximization, globalization, mergers, and promotion of their financial and commercial interests. This could result in a worsening of the economic situation for many people and countries throughout the world.

The world is also likely to become more dehumanized and impersonal as more emphasis is placed on products, profits, production, consumption, capitalism, competition, and the market than on people and matters of human welfare. It will also deepen the crisis of maldevelopment, thereby making it difficult for people to find real fulfilment and happiness in life, realize their full potential, and achieve a healthy balance between material and non-material needs.

Finally, and perhaps most importantly, the global ecosystem could collapse as a result of the colossal demands and expectations made on it. Surely wars over resources, a great deal of poverty and famine, and further deterioration of the natural environment are inevitable if humanity does not curb its economic, materialistic and consumption excesses, and bring its environmental demands and expectations under control. This is especially true now that the world's population is six billion and growing rapidly, while the carrying capacity of the Earth is severely limited.

Many believe that technology is capable of solving these problems and others that may loom up on the global horizon. They contend that technology has been so successful in warding off the law of diminishing returns, thwarting the stationary state, keeping the Malthusian spectre at bay, and increasing production, productivity, and wealth that it can overcome any problems humanity is confronted with now and in the future. However, while it is true that technology has been successful in alleviating many of the problems that humanity has been confronted with so far, it is not capable of overcoming the problems humanity is confronted with today or may be confronted with in the future. These problems are much more chronic, pronounced, life-threatening, and explosive than they have ever been in the past, largely because humanity's dependence on "Spaceship Earth" has increased substantially in recent years. While technology may be successful in alleviating certain types of problems, by reducing dependence on fossil fuels or paper, for example, or creating better and longer-lasting products, it will not solve the biggest threat to human survival and well-being, the relentless march of human numbers compared to the finite capacity of the Earth.

Anyone who doubts this need only reflect on the following statistics. The world's population was 771 million in 1750, 2.5 billion in 1950, 5.3 billion in 1990, and more than six billion in 2000, and it is expected to increase to somewhere between eight and ten billion by 2030 (Robbins, p. 148). Meanwhile, the carrying capacity of the Earth will not have increased and, if anything, it will have been reduced, as more and more demands are made on it, and more ecological deterioration, contamination, and loss of arable land take place. While technological advances may help in alleviating these problems, they will not overcome them. Severe shortages of, and higher prices for, renewable and non-renewable resources, global resource wars, and excesses, imbalances and deficiencies in the world system are inevitable if this situation is not addressed.

While some people put their faith in technology, others prefer to look to improvements in the economic age, especially the body of thought and practice, and the world system, that underpin it. They contend that the problems humanity is confronted with can be solved by developing further the theoretical ideas and practical policies that are required to deal with these problems effectively. However, while making such improvements is imperative, they will not make it possible to come to grips with the demanding and debilitating problems that have loomed up on the global horizon in recent years. The economic age is based on theoretical, practical, historical and philosophical foundations that aggravate these problems more than alleviate them. Take the environmental crisis, for example: it is not possible to incorporate the natural environment into the economic age after the fact. Clearly what is needed now, more than ever, is a body of thought and practice, a world system, and an age that open up a commanding place for the natural environment and for the intimate relationship that people have with it at its very core.

Likewise, making improvements in the economic age, far from closing the gap between rich and poor countries and rich and poor people, will not prevent further divisions as economic growth and development take place. What started out with Adam Smith as a commitment to creating wealth in order to make improvements in society has long since become a commitment to creating wealth in order to increase the incomes of the richest people and countries of the world. Not only are they getting richer, they also seem unprepared to share a great deal of their income, wealth or resources with poor people and poor countries, despite such highly publicized events as the Live-8 concerts in 2005. In combination with Pareto's law of income distribution, which states that there is an inherent tendency in complex economic systems to increase rather than decrease disparities in income, wealth, and resources between the different classes and interest groups in society, this means that conditions could get worse rather than better for a substantial portion of the world's population if the economic age is perpetuated.

It follows that what is needed is a different body of thought and practice, and a different world system. Clearly, a much higher priority will have to be placed on equality of income, resources, and wealth, and on a united world, rather than on products, profits, inequality, and a divided world. This cannot be accomplished by the economic age because it is not designed to do this. The economic age makes it impossible to achieve balanced, harmonious and equitable relationships between the economic part of human activities and other activities because everything is reduced to economics, economies, and materialism, and made dependent on them. It also makes it impossible to deal with major excesses, imbalances, and deficiencies in the world system and in people's lives because the emphasis is on means—production, distribution, consumption, profits, products, the market—rather than ends, such as a healthy environment, people, human welfare, sustainable communities, cities, countries and societies, and real fulfilment and happiness in life. While it would be foolhardy to suggest that economics, economies, and materialism will ever cease to play extremely important roles in the world and people's lives, they do not cause everything in society or constitute the basis of everything. This is the fundamental flaw in the economic age.

This is why perpetuation of the economic age into the future is so dangerous and potentially life-threatening. People will not sit idly by while their environments are devastated, higher and higher prices are charged for increasingly scarce resources, living standards are reduced, and life takes on negative rather than positive connotations. This is a recipe for revolution and for global disaster. This acts as an early warning signal that violent outcomes are in store if the problems confronting humanity are not dealt with successfully. We cannot allow ourselves to reach the point where, as Ruth Benedict put it (1963, p. 179):

> Revision comes, but it comes by way of revolution or of breakdown. The possibility of orderly progress is shut off because the generation in question could not make any appraisal of its overgrown institutions. It could not cast them up in terms of profit and loss because it had lost its power to look at them objectively. The situation had to reach a breaking point before relief was possible.

Given the fact that more and more countries possess nuclear weapons and are capable of conducting warfare, reaching such a breaking point, and thus precipitating a revolution or breakdown, is too frightening to contemplate. It need not happen. By learning the lessons that must be learned from an assessment of the economic age, we can identify the changes that are required in the human condition, the world system, and people's lives in order to set things right. These changes necessitate a renaissance rather than a revolution in global development and human affairs, through visualizing and interpreting the world, acting in the world, and valuing things in the world in a new way.

This renaissance is best realized by incorporating the economic age, and a great deal more, into a broader, deeper, and more fundamental way of looking at living, reality, history, and the human condition, rather than by rejecting the economic age The world needs strong economies and the strengths of the economic age if improvements are to be made in material living standards and people's lives, but it needs them to be counterbalanced and constrained by powerful social, artistic, educational, scientific, spiritual, and human activities. This is precisely why undertaking an assessment of the economic age and composing a balance sheet on it are so essential. Exposing the shortcomings as well as the strengths of the economic age signals the changes that are needed. This is as it should be. A good balance sheet should shed light on the existing situation, and identify those developments and directions that are most needed for the future.

Surely the most important of these is the creation of a new theoretical, practical, historical and philosophical framework for the world of the future. The key to this lies in placing the priority on the whole rather than on a part of the whole, and on ends as well as means. There are always problems when priority is given to one activity over other activities, because this creates excesses, imbalances and deficiencies. Secondly, a very high priority will have to be placed on dealing with the intimate relationship between people and the natural environment. Failure to deal effectively and fully with the environmental crisis will cause severe hardships in every part of the world, as well as even more conflict, confrontation, hostility, and violence. Thirdly, a much higher priority will have to be placed on people and matters of human welfare than on products, profits, and the market, in order to create the sensitivities and sensibilities that are required to open up many more opportunities for people to live creative, constructive and fulfilling lives, as well as to participate fully, actively, and freely in the public and private decisions that affect their lives. Finally, a much more effective balance will have to be achieved between consumption and conservation, competition and cooperation, scientism, aestheticism and humanism, economics and ethics, and spiritualism and materialism. This is imperative if nature, and other species, are to be treated with the dignity and respect they deserve, if people are to be provided with opportunities to realize their full potential, and if humanity is to go fruitfully into the future.

With these developments and directions in mind, what can be said in conclusion about the economic age that is relevant to a future age? Surely this, while the economic age has made countless contributions to global development and human affairs, it is not capable of carrying humanity forward into the next great epoch in human history. For this a different type of age is required. This age must flow from a different set of foundations, principles, practices, policies, and priorities, as well as a different worldview, value system, and model of development. The key to this age lies in the realm of culture rather than in the realm of economics.

Part II

The Age of Culture

5

Signs of a Cultural Age

Culture in the future is the crux of the future.
—Eleonora Barbieri Masini (1991), Vol. I, p. 6

If there were signs that an economic age was dawning towards the end of the eighteenth century, there are signs that a cultural age is dawning today. While these signs cannot be traced to a single year, such as 1776, or a specific event, such as the publication of *The Wealth of Nations*, as was the case with the economic age, they are signs nonetheless that a cultural age is slowly but surely taking shape in the world.

One sign is the holistic transformation that is going on in the world today. Another is the environmental movement. Still others are the encounter with human needs; the quest for quality of life; the struggle for equality; the necessity of identity; and the focus on creativity. Since these signs may hold the key to the ways in which living, development, and human affairs are dealt with in the future, it is important to identify these signs and interpret them correctly. This is achieved most effectively by analysing each sign separately and showing how it is intimately connected to culture or deeply rooted in culture. When this process has been completed for all the signs, it is possible to understand why culture is emerging as a crucial force in the world, as well as why it contains valuable clues and ideas about the future.

The Holistic Transformation

After two hundred years and more of preoccupation with specialization and a specific part of the whole, namely economics and economies, there are strong indications that attention is being shifted to the whole, and to the complex relationships that exist between the parts and the whole. This holistic transformation is extremely important because focusing attention on the whole is the most pressing requirement for a cultural age.

While the holistic transformation is going on in many areas, it is perhaps most conspicuous in the field of medicine. After several centuries of focusing on the individual parts of the human body, more attention is being focused by some medical practitioners on the human body as a whole (see, for example, Weil). In their view, medical knowledge confirms that the human body is a whole composed of many interrelated parts, all of which constantly affect one another and interact with one another. They believe that it is impossible to deal with many types of illnesses and diseases, psychological as well as physiological, without dealing with the human body as a whole. Their goal is to focus attention on primary causes rather than secondary symptoms, primary causes that they say can be attended to properly only by dealing with the human body in holistic rather than partial or specialized terms. Finally, and perhaps most importantly, there is growing interest in "holistic medicine," naturopathy and homeopathy. All these approaches emphasize the need to understand how all the various parts of the body combine to form the total person. Their view is that the key to good health lies in achieving harmony and balance between the physical, mental, emotional, spiritual and intellectual parts of the body.

A holistic transformation is also going on in education. After many years of preoccupation with individual subjects and specific disciplines, some educators have concluded that a holistic rather than specialized approach is needed in order to help students to understand the complex connections and relationships among the different disciplines, and to come to grips with the underlying threads and unifying themes that link all the disciplines together. These developments are manifested in interdisciplinary and multidisciplinary studies as well as in "holistic education" (see, for example, Miller, as well as the collection edited by Bloom).

Then there is development, which has long been dealt with in fragmented, compartmentalized, partial and partisan ways, with the focus on economic, commercial, technological, corporate or financial development. Now development is being dealt with in a more all-encompassing and all-inclusive way. It is now generally accepted that development is also social, political, environmental, artistic, scientific, recreational and spiritual, and that there is a holistic quality to development that cannot be denied. This was confirmed in 1982, when delegates at the Second World Conference on Cultural Policies, in Mexico City, defined development (UNESCO 1994, p. 7) in the following terms:

> a complex, comprehensive and multidimensional process which extends beyond mere economic growth to incorporate all dimensions of life and all the energies of a community, all of whose members are called upon to make a contribution and expect to share in the benefits.

This much more all-encompassing concept of development has been manifested in the policies and practices of many international organizations, as well as numerous governments and other political institutions throughout the world, following from the recognition that development should be dealt with comprehensively and inclusively, and in a spirit of egalitarianism.

The holistic transformation is also affecting some areas of science, and the ways in which some scientists view the cosmos, the world, human beings, and evolution. The Human Genome Project has been presented as an example of what can result when, after many years of breaking the human body up into specialized parts in order to study the parts in detail, efforts are made to reconnect them in order to provide a comprehensive understanding of the human body as a whole. This is producing a blueprint or code that sheds a great deal of light on how DNA forms human beings as members of a complex and dynamic species.

The emphasis on interpreting the world as a whole composed of many interacting and interdependent parts also influences political thinking and action. It is not possible to understand developments taking place in one part of the world without understanding those taking place in other parts of the world, and in the world as a whole. The world was long seen as, and indeed effectively was, a smorgasbord of separate and individual parts, but today it is a dynamic whole in a way that it never was before, due largely to globalization, and to the numerous developments in trade, transportation, technology, communications, and computerization.

What is true of the world is also true of the universe, following the phenomenal developments in quantum physics, quantum mechanics, and cosmology from the early twentieth century onwards. Albert Einstein was only the first of the many physicists who have attempted to expound a post-Newtonian "theory of everything" that would uncover the underlying laws that explain how the universe functions as a dynamic whole, largely by linking the subatomic and the cosmic realms of matter, and attempting to make sense of everything from quarks to supermassive black holes. At present, the laws governing quantum mechanics describe the behaviour of elementary particles, while separate laws governing relativity describe the behaviour of vast forces such as black holes, but physicists hope that eventually it will be possible to unify them.

While it is necessary to be aware of the myriad parts that comprise a given whole, regardless of whether we are discussing individuals, families, institutions, communities, ethnic groups, regions, countries, the world, the world system, the natural environment or the universe, it is equally necessary to understand that the parts are always bound together in specific combinations and arrangements to form those wholes. Despite the long-established practice of breaking wholes down into parts in order to study the parts in detail, the fact remains that all these entities *are* wholes, and not just random assortments of disconnected and unrelated parts. They represent the basic building blocks of a cultural age because they relate fundamentally to what the human condition is all about.

Anyone who doubts this need only reflect on the character of his or her life. While much attention has been paid to birth, adolescence, adulthood and death, work and leisure, education and training, spiritual and religious life, recreation, survival, and other component parts of people's lives, every person's life is a whole comprised of many parts. Failure to recognize this and to deal with its consequences can cause serious problems, making it difficult for people to meld the parts of their lives together to form a coherent and comprehensive whole. What is true of individuals is also true of the other wholes we have mentioned here. Every family, for example, needs to be understood as a whole, as a set of separate and different individuals, and as a set of relationships among them.

The holistic transformation is coming at a very propitious time in history. Preoccupation with specialization and the parts of the whole has caused humanity to lose sight of the whole, and wholes, and of the underlying interrelatedness and interconnectedness of things. This is most apparent in the case of the natural environment and its intimate relationship with human beings, but it is equally apparent in all the other cases mentioned here. When attention is focused on the parts of the whole rather than the whole, the whole is lost sight of. In contrast, the holistic transformation focuses attention on "the big picture," and with it, the intimate relationships among its component parts. Understanding and coming to grips with these relationships is of vital importance if the world is to be a better and safer place for all, if the environmental crisis is to be addressed successfully, if sensible and sustainable decisions are to be made about the future course of planetary civilization, and if basic inequalities, injustices, and excesses are to be dealt with effectively.

Another benefit of the holistic transformation is the ability to see things in context rather than in isolation. This is imperative in the modern world, where the preoccupation with specialization and the parts of the whole has caused a situation where decisions are often made without sufficient consideration of the context in which things are located. The most obvious example of this is, again, the environmental crisis and the failure to realize that all human activities take place in an environmental context, but it is equally true with respect to the inability to realize that all commercial, economic, and technological activities take place in a broader, deeper, and more fundamental cultural container.

A third benefit of the holistic transformation is that it focuses attention on the total ways of life of people and countries, and, with this, on the worldviews, values, and value systems that people and countries use in different parts of the world to link all the activities in which they are engaged together to form wholes that are greater than the parts and the sum of the parts. This is essential if cultural understanding is to be enhanced in the world, and people and countries everywhere in the world are to live in peace and harmony rather than conflict and confrontation.

What makes the holistic transformation especially relevant to the dawning of a cultural age is the fact that cultural scholars have been concerned with holism ever since Edward Burnett Tylor, one of the world's first anthropologists, broke with the long tradition of defining culture in terms of the parts and started defining culture in terms of the whole. This occurred in 1871, when Tylor defined culture formally (Tylor, Vol. I, p. 1) as "that complex whole which includes knowledge, belief, art, morals, law, custom, and any other capabilities and habits acquired by man as a member of society." Since that time, as the US anthropologist Marvin Harris put it (1968, p. 63): "Many cultural anthropologists have proposed that the distinctive feature of the anthropological approach is its holistic framework, that is, the point of view which attempts to describe the parts of a system by reference to the whole." The holistic transformation is deeply rooted in the work of anthropologists, as well as the work of sociologists and cultural historians, who have been writing from a holistic perspective for more than one hundred years. Culture, more than any subject, holds the key to capitalizing on the holistic transformation and realizing its full potential.

The Environmental Movement

If the holistic transformation is one sign that a cultural age is slowly but surely developing, the environmental movement is another. Growing awareness of the present and prospective state of the natural environment is causing people and countries in every part of the world to realize that human needs are not fulfilled in a vacuum, but in very specific ecological settings. Failure to recognize this, and to come to grips with its implications, could have serious consequences.

The environmental movement is the result of numerous developments throughout the world over the past forty years. One outstanding contributory factor was the Stockholm Conference on the Human Environment and the creation of the United Nations Environment Programme (UNEP) in 1972. Another was the publication of the first *State of the World Report* by the Worldwatch Institute in 1984. Still others were the publication of *Our Common Future* by the World Commission on Environment and Development in 1987; the *Exxon Valdez* oil spill of 1989; the Earth Summit in Rio de Janeiro in 1992; the Kyoto Protocol of 1997; and the activities of organizations such as Greenpeace, Friends of the Earth, and the Sierra Club. More recently, the environmental movement has received a major boost in public consciousness from Al Gore's film *An Inconvenient Truth* and the publication of the United Nations Intergovernmental Panel on Climate Change's report: *Climate Change 2007: the Physical Science Basis.* The roots of the movement, however, can be traced back to such publications as Henry David Thoreau's *Walden* (1854), Darwin's *On the Origin of Species* (1859), George Perkins Marsh's *Man and Nature* (1864), and the creation of the Sierra Club in 1892.

It was Rachel Carson, however, who first riveted public attention on the natural environment and the damage that people were doing to it in her book *Silent Spring* (1962). Carson argued that human beings were destroying the natural environment at a rapid rate through insensitivity to its fragility and to their own interdependence with it. Carson contended that it is not possible to release pollutants and chemicals such as DDT into one part of the natural environment without them eventually ending up in other parts of the natural environment. What was particularly disturbing for Carson was the fact that much of the damage being done seemed to be irreversible. For example, pesticides designed to kill some insects may seep into the soil and kill other insects, as well as other species, without ever disappearing. The result, she argued, was the steady deterioration of the environment.

The environmental movement has been gathering momentum ever since. It is divided into three main groups at present. In the first place, there are those who believe that the emphasis should be on regulation, control, and protection in order to curb emissions, prohibit pollution, reduce the spread of toxic substances, prevent or reduce global warming, and clean up the environment. It is this group that often finds itself pitted against people who contend that the environmental movement is depriving them of their jobs, incomes, and sources of livelihood. Second, there are those who believe that the emphasis should be placed on "sustainable development," development that takes the natural environment, other species, and future generations fully into account in all planning and decision-making. This was the approach taken by the World Commission on Environment and Development, chaired by Gro Harlem Brundtland in its report. Third, there are those who believe that the emphasis should be on what they call "deep ecology," or treating the environment as a spiritual reality and mystical experience. They assert that it will not be possible to address the environmental crisis successfully until people evolve an entirely new understanding of the environment and their relationship with it. This is the stance taken by many environmental, spiritual and religious leaders such as Arne Naess, Fritjof Capra, George Sessions, Thomas Berry, Brian Swimme, and James Lovelock.

As a result of the lobbying efforts and activities of these three groups, as well as countless other people, institutions, and groups throughout the world, a great deal of progress has been made in addressing environmental concerns. Nevertheless, environmental problems continue to grow at an astounding rate. Pollutants and toxic substances continue to be released, causing unprecedented damage, and environmental destruction continues at an unacceptable pace, as do global warming and other ecological disasters. It follows from this that a new environmental reality is imperative if the environmental crisis is to be addressed successfully, especially now that the world's population is six billion and growing rapidly in absolute if not relative terms, renewable and non-renewable resources are being consumed and contaminated at disturbing rates, and the carrying capacity of the Earth remains severely limited. Not only is this one of the most pressing priorities for a cultural age, it will also fundamentally change the way we understand and deal with development and the human condition.

Just as the holistic transformation is intimately connected with culture, so too is the environmental movement. Concern with the intimate relationship between the natural environment and human cultures can be traced back to the German poet and philosopher Johann Gottfried von Herder, whose writings helped to launch the unending debate over the respective roles of "nature" and "nurture" in human development. Similar themes have been explored in the pioneering work of contemporary cultural anthropologists and ecologists such as Julian Steward and Gregory Bateson. Clearly, cultures that ignore the environmental consequences of their activities run the risk of overextending themselves and collapsing entirely. This has happened numerous times throughout history. While environmental clean-ups are imperative after the fact, and while every precaution must be taken to protect the natural environment whenever and wherever possible, ultimately it will be through changes in cultures that the environmental crisis will be solved, if it is to be solved at all.

Without fundamental changes in the ways in which people perceive the natural environment, interact with it, and live their lives, the environmental crisis will broaden, deepen, and intensify. It is by no means coincidental in this regard that the World Commission on Culture and Development followed closely on the heels of the World Commission on Environment and Development.

In particular, cultural changes may well come through the shift from a mechanistic view of the world and the universe to an organic view as a result of the environmental movement and the holistic transformation. The mechanistic view was expressed most succinctly by one of the fictional speakers in David Hume's *Dialogues Concerning Natural Religion* (See Spiegel, p. 222):

> Look around the world: contemplate the whole and every part of it: You will find it to be nothing but one great machine, subdivided into an infinite number of lesser machines, which again admit of subdivisions, to a degree beyond what human senses and faculties can trace and explain. All these various machines, and even their most minute parts, are adjusted to each other with an accuracy, which ravishes into admiration all men, who have ever contemplated them.

The mechanistic view had a profound effect on scientific and economic thinking from the seventeenth century down to the first half of the twentieth century. Economies were seen and treated as mechanistic systems in which the challenge was to understand how they functioned as systems, and how a change in one part of the system affected other parts of the system and the system as a whole. This view, which dominated the thinking of many of the classical, neoclassical, Marxian, and Keynesian economists alike, has started to give way to a more "organic" view of economics in recent years. The environmental movement and the holistic transformation have together had a major influence on this trend.

The Encounter with Human Needs

Over the past fifty years or so a great deal of attention has been focused on the ways in which human needs are understood, defined, and dealt with. In this encounter with human needs it is possible to detect an intimate connection with culture, since the fulfilment of human needs is what culture is all about.

Indeed, more than eighty years ago, the cultural anthropologist Bronislaw Malinowski identified seven "basic human needs" following his intensive studies of many cultures throughout the world, most famously that of the Trobriand Islanders of eastern New Guinea. These needs he identified as nutrition, reproduction, bodily comforts, safety, relaxation, movement, and human growth. In retrospect, it is clear that Malinowski's pioneering work on this subject did a great deal to pave the way for subsequent scholars to address the question of human needs.

Nevertheless, it continued to be commonplace to view human needs in economic terms, until numerous problems were encountered with this approach. In sub-Saharan Africa, Asia, Latin America, and the Caribbean in particular it was revealed that people have many "non-economic" needs, such as for fresh water, clean air, medical facilities and health care, educational opportunities and recreation, which must also be satisfied if they are to survive and function effectively in society. In the developed world, meanwhile, it was discovered that even when people's economic needs have been satisfied, they can still have a great deal of difficulty functioning in society if their religious, aesthetic, social and spiritual needs are not met. It was this problem that gave rise to the notion of "maldevelopment," sometimes expressed as "spiritual poverty in the midst of plenty."

The combined effect of these discoveries was that developmental theorists and practitioners started to look at human needs in a much more concentrated and detailed way in the latter part of the twentieth century. This resulted in a more systematic, comprehensive and egalitarian approach to human needs than had been taken previously. As a result, it is now generally accepted that people have a broad spectrum of needs that must be satisfied if they are to function effectively in society, live creative, constructive and fulfilling lives, and survive. These needs give rise to a complex constellation of social, scientific, economic, artistic, educational, spiritual, technological, political, environmental, commercial, and health requirements. How these requirements are dealt with in specific situations and particular parts of the world constitutes the essence of culture, cultures, and cultural development. What does it mean, for example, to satisfy people's economic needs if there is so much violence, terrorism, and conflict that people's lives can be ended at any time and without notice? What does it mean to satisfy people's economic needs if their psychological, social and spiritual problems are so acute that life takes on negative rather than positive connotations? Problems such as these gave rise to attempts to identify and define a set of "basic human needs" that all people in the world share in common, regardless of age, gender, education, class, economic, social or political circumstances, or geographical location. Initially, basic human needs were defined primarily in economic terms, but they are now defined in a more comprehensive, integrated and egalitarian way.

One of the first people to tackle the problem of human needs in a sustained, systematic and sophisticated way was the Pakistani developmental theorist and practitioner Mahbub ul Haq. He did so by taking a holistic and "people-centred" approach to human needs. According to ul Haq, the challenge of development is to enlarge the realm of choice in as many different directions and areas as possible. In his seminal publication *Reflections on Human Development* (1995) ul Haq wrote (p. 14):

> The basic purpose of development is to enlarge people's choices. In principle, these choices can be infinite and can change over time. People often value achievements that do not show up at all, or not immediately, in income or growth figures: greater access to knowledge, better nutrition and health services, more secure livelihoods, security against crime and physical violence, satisfying leisure hours, political and cultural freedoms and a sense of participation in community activities. The objective of development is to create an enabling environment for people to enjoy long, healthy, and creative lives.

Mahbub ul Haq's efforts led him to focus on four key factors in the fulfilment and development of human needs: equity, sustainability, productivity, and empowerment. This led him to create the Human Development Index (HDI) as an alternative to gross national product (GNP) for measuring overall standards of living. Whereas GNP is based on exclusively economic indicators, the HDI includes longevity and knowledge in addition to income. For the purposes of the HDI longevity is defined in terms of life expectancy at birth, and knowledge is defined in terms of adult literacy and mean years of schooling. Today the HDI is used by more and more international organizations to assess standards of living and rank countries according to their ability to satisfy people's needs.

Along with these initiatives have come attempts to define more precisely what is meant by "basic human needs." The peace activist and social theorist Johan Galtung has proposed the following set of basic human needs as a working hypothesis (see Coate and Rosati, p.136): security or survival needs (individual and collective protection against crime, violence, terrorism, and so forth); welfare or sufficiency needs (water, air, food, sleep, protection against climate and disease, and so forth); identity or "closeness" needs (self-expression, self-actuation, roots, support systems, partnerships with nature, purpose in life, and so forth); and freedom or "choice" needs (choice of location, occupation, way of life, and so forth). For Galtung these needs form a constellation rather than a pyramid, hierarchy or ladder, with the economic needs spread out across the lowest rung. He does not deny that there is a "rock bottom of material needs" that is necessary for survival, but he is strongly opposed to using this as a device for asserting the priority of economic needs over all other needs, since this makes it possible for economic needs to dominate all other needs and yield excessive economic, commercial, technological, and materialistic practices.

While Galtung's views on this subject are not consistent with the economic model of development, they are consistent with historical experience and most of the contemporary evidence. Although Galtung accepts the fact that human beings have crucial economic, technological, commercial, financial and material needs that must be met, and that these needs occupy an important position in the total spectrum of human needs, he contends that people have a diversity of needs that must be attended to if they are to survive and function effectively in society. Many of these needs must be addressed simultaneously rather than sequentially, which explains why it is essential to take a holistic, comprehensive and egalitarian approach to human needs rather than a partial, piecemeal, and partisan approach.

This is the principal lesson to be learned from the encounter with human needs in general and basic human needs in particular. It is a lesson that has profound implications for a cultural age because it means that much more attention will have to be paid to inclusiveness and equality in the fulfilment of human needs. Concern for human needs and matters of human welfare are imperative in a cultural age. Moreover, it is impossible to define culture in holistic terms, as Tylor and countless others have, without taking a comprehensive, egalitarian and integrated approach to human needs. Viewed from this perspective, economic, commercial, technological, and material opportunities must be carefully blended with, and complemented and counterbalanced by, social, aesthetic, educational and spiritual opportunities if human welfare is to be assured.

The Quest for Quality of Life

It is impossible to deal with human needs in all their diverse forms and manifestations without encountering the quest for quality of life, though the question of what quality of life is has confounded philosophers, and many others, in every part of the world from the beginning of human history. Clearly, there can be no quality of life without sufficient food, clothing, shelter, and security to ensure survival. However, from these needs onwards, quality of life takes on many different meanings. For some people, it means producing a great deal of income and wealth. For others, it means possessing a great deal of power. For still others it means acquiring many material possessions. For others again, it means having numerous artistic, educational and recreational possibilities. It all depends on what brings people real fulfilment and happiness in life.

Just as the historical encounter with human needs sheds a great deal of light on the nature and meaning of human needs in general, and basic human needs in particular, so it sheds a great deal of light on the quality of life. While income, power, material possessions, and creative possibilities are important determinants of quality of life, so are health, freedom, security, independence, spirituality, and the like. As wealthy, powerful and materially well-to-do people are discovering, income, power, and material possessions do not guarantee quality of life if physical health is lacking, freedom is non-existent, security is absent or spiritual fulfilment is unattainable. Nor do they guarantee quality of life if the environment is so polluted and disease is so prevalent that medical problems run rampant.

Mahbub ul Haq was surely right when he said that the challenge is to enlarge the realm of choice in as many directions and areas as possible. However, more is required if quality of life is to be achieved. There must be a great deal of knowledge, wisdom, and understanding with respect to how all the diverse facets of life are blended together to form a comprehensive, coherent and meaningful whole. For people who are unable to weave all the diverse fragments of life together in this sense, life may take on negative rather than positive connotations. The key lies in achieving a harmonious balance between the material and non-material, or the quantitative and qualitative, dimensions of life. In parts of the world where there are major deficiencies in the quantitative or material dimensions of life, such as in many parts of sub-Saharan Africa, Asia, Latin America and the Caribbean, historical and contemporary experience indicates that there are so few quantitative and material resources that a reasonable quality of life is denied to the large majority of people. In parts of the world where there is abundance in the quantitative or material dimensions of life, especially North America, western Europe, Australia, New Zealand, and Japan, historical and contemporary experience suggests that too many quantitative and material possibilities may produce a great deal of stress, anxiety, alienation, frustration, and lack of fulfilment. This is because many of these possibilities bring only fleeting rather than lasting happiness, thereby making it impossible to achieve real happiness and satisfaction in life.

Just as it is possible to detect a fundamental connection between culture and the holistic transformation, the environmental movement, and the encounter with human needs, so it is possible to detect a fundamental connection between culture and quality of life. Culture has been concerned with quality of life for hundreds of years, as evidenced by the greatest artistic, scholarly, and scientific accomplishments, and the entire cultural heritage of humankind. In fact, many would contend that realization of a better quality of life is what culture is most concerned with, since it is concerned with elevating and enriching people's lives well beyond their basic physiological, biological and material requirements. For people who share this conviction, culture is the thing that separates human beings from other species, since it is directed towards the realization of higher and higher forms of accomplishment. It is culture that makes it possible for people to achieve a judicious blending of the quantitative or material dimensions of life with its qualitative or spiritual dimensions, largely by focusing on the whole, as well as on the need to achieve balanced and synergistic relationships between the parts and the whole. This is why people in the cultural field have been concerned with the education and development of the whole person ever since the British poet and social critic Matthew Arnold made the case, in 1869, for the "harmonious expansion of all the powers that comprise human nature."

What is true of people is also true of countries and cultures. Countries and cultures that are unable to provide their citizens with opportunities to attend to the harmonious development of all the powers that comprise human nature are unable to provide the means that are required to ensure a reasonable quality of life and to enable people to realize their full potential. These necessitate the full complement of resources, not just economic and material resources.

The Struggle for Equality

After hundreds of years of colonialism the countries of Asia, sub-Saharan Africa, Latin America, the Caribbean, and the Middle East are endeavouring to achieve equality with Europe, North America, Australia, New Zealand, and Japan. This is having a powerful effect on development policies and practices everywhere in the world, as it is fuelling demands for a level playing field for all countries. Much the same process is going on within countries. Marginalized peoples and ethnic minorities, such as aboriginals in North America, South America, Australia, and New Zealand, blacks in the United States or "Untouchables" in India are demanding equality of treatment by mainstream peoples and ethnic majorities, condemning the historical and contemporary injustices that have caused their inferior status in political and constitutional arrangements, territorial assignments, social legislation, economic development, and human affairs. Although much more needs to be achieved in this area, as in most other areas of crucial importance to the realization of equality throughout the world, some important gains have been realized in recent years, largely as a result of the efforts of marginalized peoples and ethnic minorities themselves.

Of all the areas where the struggle for equality is manifesting itself throughout the world, none is more conspicuous than the area of gender equality. It has taken women more than one hundred years of cajoling, infighting, lobbying, and protesting to achieve a certain measure of equality with men, and then only in highly selected parts of the world. While specific advances were realized in this domain in the nineteenth century and the early part of the twentieth, largely as a result of the women's suffrage movement, most gains have been realized only in the past thirty or forty years. Much remains to be accomplished in order to secure gender equality in income, employment, education, legal rights, the elimination of physical and sexual abuse, and medical and reproductive rights, but some important gains have been recorded in recent years through the pioneering achievements of women's organizations, and of individual women such as Betty Friedan, Gloria Steinem, Germaine Greer, Michele Landsberg, and Shirin Ebadi.

In much the same way that women have been battling for equality with men, so physically and mentally challenged people, seniors, and children have been battling for equality as well. Here also some important gains have been realized in recent years, despite the fact that much remains to be accomplished. There is an emerging consciousness throughout the world that physically and mentally challenged people should be able to look after their own affairs, and can make valuable contributions to society; that seniors should not be subjected to physical abuse, mental cruelty or income manipulation, and must be accorded the freedom and independence they need to live fulfilling lives; and that children should not be exploited for economic, social, sexual or commercial purposes. As is the case with women and the women's movement, many of the gains that have been recorded in recent years result from persistent efforts on the part of these groups themselves as they struggle to improve their economic, financial, and social circumstances and fight for equal treatment under the law.

It is impossible to discuss the struggle for equality without recognizing the need for a reasonable measure of income, employment and educational equality throughout the world. Income equality will be realized only when people, countries, and governments in every part of the world make a much stronger commitment to eliminating disparities in the production and distribution of income, employment, education, wealth, and resources among the diverse people and countries of the world. This is of crucial importance if humanity is to go fruitfully into the future, since it is in this area, perhaps more than any other, that resentment and hostility are building up.

While equality in all areas of human life is imperative, it is important to point out that some impressive gains have been recorded in the struggle to create equality by governments and international institutions. For example, in 1948, the General Assembly of the United Nations approved the Universal Declaration of Human Rights. Based on the principle that all people are equal regardless of race, colour, age, gender, creed, ethnic origin, education or geographical location, the Declaration focuses on the need for public and private commitment to equality for all citizens. Similar rhetoric has been reproduced in the human rights legislation of many individual countries.

There is an intimate connection between culture and the struggle for equality. It is in the domain of culture that the historical and contemporary struggle for equality is most easily recognized, as well as most readily understood. Many cultural organizations throughout the world are formally committed to racial, income and gender equality, and are working diligently to do something concrete and constructive about it. Many anthropologists, sociologists, and cultural scholars have argued that every country, culture, and group of people in the world possesses a value, dignity and importance in its own right, which cannot be denied and must never be taken for granted. It is this, in their view, that makes all countries, cultures, and groups of people in the world equal. From this perspective, countries, cultures, and groups of people are not to be categorized as either civilized or primitive, sophisticated or backward, but merely as different, because they perceive the world differently, act in the world differently, and value things in the world differently. This outlook helps to counter the idea that some countries, cultures or groups of people are superior to others or more advanced than others.

As a result of such developments the struggle for equality is more conspicuous throughout the world than ever before, though much remains to be accomplished through the formulation, implementation, and enforcement of equity legislation; the elimination of unfair trading practices, and of exploitative commercial and financial policies; the termination of human rights abuses, and of social and economic injustices; and the recognition of the rights of women, children, and minorities. The indications that things are moving in a favourable direction augur well for the future.

The Necessity of Identity

It is impossible to deal with the struggle for equality without also dealing with the necessity of identity. People cannot live without identity, either as individuals or as members of groups, communities, regions, countries, cultures or civilizations. Identity is deeply etched in human consciousness and the collective imagination everywhere in the world.

There can be no identity without sharing certain similarities, since identity is achieved by recognizing the common bonds that connect people together. At the same time, there can be no identity without maintaining specific differences, for too much sameness can obliterate identity by destroying its distinctive character. Identity is thus achieved and sustained by walking a tightrope between similarity and difference. This is a balancing act fraught with difficulties. A slip in the direction of too many similarities can cause people to rebel, if only to protect themselves from the numbing effects of uniformity. A slip in the direction of too many differences can be equally dangerous, since people mistrust and fear what they are unable to understand. This makes finding the right mixture of sameness and distinctiveness, or unity in diversity, one of the greatest challenges of all.

It is within this context that it is possible to understand why people and countries in every part of the world are expressing the need for identity as never before. People know what is in their best interests and what is not, regardless of what powerful institutions say or powerful leaders and countries do. Take globalization, for example. It is by no means coincidental that the trend towards globalization has brought with it a commensurate trend towards the assertion of identities. The more globalization takes place, the more people lose control over their domestic and international affairs, and institute countervailing measures aimed at restoring such control, through the quest for sovereignty or autonomy, or the resurfacing of interest in neighbourhoods, communities or regions.

People know that globalization, like colonialism, can be a thin disguise for the advancing of the interests of some people, institutions, classes, and countries at the expense of others, rather than a device for promoting and protecting their interests, improving their standards of living, and addressing their needs. Adam Smith recognized this more than two hundred years ago when he wrote that "People of the same trade seldom meet together, even for merriment and diversion, but the conversation ends in a conspiracy against the public or some contrivance to raise prices."

Whenever self-interest works against people, groups or countries rather than for them, they tend to try everything in their power to assert and protect their identity. This has been shown in countries and regions as diverse as the former Soviet Union, the former Yugoslavia, Taiwan, Sri Lanka, Spain, Ireland, Peru, Mexico, East Timor, and the Middle East, as well as in reactions among some sections of the public to the liberalization of trade, and to the actions of multinational corporations and international institutions such as the World Bank, the International Monetary Fund or the World Trade Organization.

It would be a mistake to assume that globalization is the only factor causing these reactions, but it has been a major contributory factor to the extent that it has contributed to the erosion of people's identities, customs, and values, as well as a breakdown in their social systems, political processes, geographical boundaries, and often entire cultures.

Developments in communications and politics are also contributory factors, as they tend to undermine people's sense of identity and belonging, which is tied up with the maintenance of the very differences being stamped out by the standardization of media products, the emergence of larger and larger trading blocs such as the European Union, and the concentration of wealth and power in fewer hands. This is causing a loss of identity for an increased proportion of the world's population, as well as a growing sense of frustration, powerlessness, and alienation. Ghettoization, ethnocentrism, xenophobia, nationalism, and racism are the inevitable consequences. The more power is globalized, centralized, standardized, and homogenized, the more people demand control over the political processes and the economic policies affecting their lives. The protests against globalization in Seattle, Washington, Quebec City, Genoa, Cancun, and elsewhere have been seen by many observers as expressions of this demand. The problem, of course, is that the assertion of identity is often manifested in negative rather than positive ways.

Like many other major developments in the world, the necessity of identity is deeply rooted in culture. Identity is concerned with the preservation and sharing of people's most cherished values and customs, which have been built up over generations and have come to seem indispensable.

The Focus on Creativity

Humanity looks to creativity to provide the theoretical ideas, insights, and ideals, as well as the practical methods, tools, and techniques, that are needed to come to grips with the world's most complex and difficult problems. It is to creativity, therefore, that humanity must look for answers to the host of demanding and debilitating problems that have loomed up on the global horizon in recent years.

The focus on creativity is occurring in many different areas. In the first place, it is occurring in the arts, sciences and humanities, with the constant search for new, better and more innovative ways of doing things. In the second place, it is occurring in community, regional, national and international development, where politicians, planners, policy-makers, and governments are searching for "convergent possibilities" and "clustering effects" that will have favourable effects. This search is taking them deep into the realm of the arts, social change, urban development, advertising, the mass media, microenterprises, and the communications industries, where creative developments often have a catalytic effect on all aspects of social life, as Richard Florida points out in his book *The Rise of the Creative Class*. Finally, it is occurring as people attempt to find more fulfilment and happiness in their lives. This is largely because consumerism and materialism are not delivering the satisfaction and meaning in life that many people are hoping to achieve.

There is, of course, an intimate connection between culture and creativity, which has provided the impetus required to fuel the development of cultures and civilizations, and to propel them to higher and higher levels of accomplishment.

The world would not enjoy the incredible diversity of cultures and civilizations it does today without the capacity of creativity to trigger dynamic developments in the arts, sciences, education, economics, politics, education, technology, and all other areas of life.

Culture as a Crucial Force

Many developments indicate that culture is emerging as a crucial force in the world. The most important development by far is the increased attention being accorded to culture by more and more people and countries throughout the world, regardless of whether this results from the growing realization that reality has more to do with culture than anything else, from recognition of the fact that the world is comprised primarily of many different cultures and civilizations, from increasing intercultural interaction, mixing, and borrowing, from globalization, or from increased interest in cultural diversity.

Another major development is the involvement of most of the world's governments in a variety of cultural concerns, ranging from the preservation of cultural heritage to citizens' participation in cultural life. A third was the creation of the World Decade for Culture and Development by UNESCO in 1989, and of the World Commission on Culture and Development by the United Nations in 1993. Both these initiatives were designed to examine the vital role that culture plays in global development and human affairs, and to promote a systematic and sustainable approach to cultural policy.

A related development is the establishment of many courses and institutions in the field of cultural studies. As the world becomes more involved in a variety of cultural issues and people become more culture-conscious, there is a need to broaden, deepen, and intensify knowledge and understanding of culture and cultures in general, and of the reasons for differences between cultures in particular. It is impossible to understand such developments as changes in communications, technology, and society, the rise of Islamic fundamentalism, the terrorist attacks on the United States, conflicts in the Middle East, hostilities between developed and developing countries, or the tensions in the Balkans, Chechnya, India, Pakistan, and Kashmir, China, Tibet, and Taiwan, Afghanistan, Iraq, Spain, Catalonia, Sri Lanka, and elsewhere in the world without understanding a great deal more about cultures and the ways in which they function.

A final development in this area is the realization that, like economics, religion, politics, technology, and other powerful forces, culture plays both positive and negative roles. On the one hand, it can play a unifying role when it unites people through the sharing of values, customs, and identities. On the other hand, it can play a divisive role when people are separated from one another as a result of cultural differences. When this happens there can be deep divisions, which will have to be understood and dealt with effectively if cultural conflicts are to be minimized or avoided in the future.

While these developments confirm that culture is playing a crucial role in the world, they do not explain why more and more people, countries, governments, organizations, and educational institutions are looking to culture to play that role. In the first place, the development dream has turned sour and many feel that culture possesses the capacity to set things right, largely by providing a more effective framework than the economic framework, situating development issues, problems, and possibilities in context, and providing a more effective means of achieving balance and harmony between economics and the environment, consumption and conservation, competition and cooperation, people and technology, scientism and humanism, and materialism and spiritualism. Javier Pérez de Cuéllar, former Secretary General of the United Nations, summed this up best when he said in a speech in 1994:

> Today, rethinking development is necessary on a world scale . . . It was believed, not so long ago, that the economy was the base, the infrastructure. That is wrong: the historians of the "long history" have shown that the decisive element is culture . . . Without a large cultural transformation, development is doomed to the destiny of ghost towns.

In the second place, it is through culture that it may be possible to come to grips with the world's most demanding, debilitating and difficult problems: the environmental crisis, pollution, poverty, homelessness, hunger, unemployment, the gap between rich and poor nations, and between rich and poor people, ethnic tensions, violence and terrorism, the dehumanization of life, and the constant threat of nuclear, biological or chemical warfare. This is because culture possesses the capacity to address these problems in a sustained, systematic, equitable and integrated way, rather than in a piecemeal, partisan, inequitable, and fragmented way.

In the third place, culture has a great deal to contribute to human well-being because it places a much higher priority on the human dimension in development than on products, profits, consumption or the market.

In the fourth place, culture possesses the potential to make a substantial contribution to the realization of peace and harmony. This is particularly important at the contact points between different cultures, although it requires the establishment of numerous safeguards to ensure that cultures are used in constructive rather than destructive ways, as forces for liberation and fulfilment rather than for enslavement and oppression.

In the fifth place, it is through culture that strong connections can be made among the diverse peoples and countries of the world. This will not happen, however, without a great deal more emphasis on cultural education and international cultural relations, which can help people to understand their own culture as well as the cultures of others. With this can come a greater sense of appreciation and sensitivity for the strengths, and the shortcomings, of all the various cultures, as well as increased tolerance and understanding of cultural values and practices that are different from one's own.

In the sixth place, culture is concerned with the ultimate ends and ideals of humanity, as well as the values that may be needed to achieve them. Unlike economics, which focuses on a specific part of the whole, culture focuses on the whole, the complex relationships that exist between the parts and the whole, and particularly the need to realize balanced, egalitarian and harmonious relationships between the parts and the whole. This is why the Canadian cultural scholar Fernand Dumont wrote (in Ostry, p. 160): "I have always considered a collective project as something mainly cultural. The economy is not an end in itself: culture is." The social critic Jane Jacobs reinforced the view when she wrote (Jacobs, p. 147): "Like language, economic life permits us to develop cultures and multitudes of purposes, and in my opinion, that's its function which is most meaningful for us."

Finally, and most importantly, culture is central to human existence because it is concerned with human needs in all their diverse forms. While economic needs form a very important component of this because they are concerned with people's material requirements and the ever-recurrent problem of physical survival, they are part and parcel of a much larger and more comprehensive process. This is why more and more people throughout the world are coming to the conclusion that it is culture that is the real foundation of human existence. Without a much better understanding of this, it will not be possible to deal effectively with humanity's greatest opportunities and fundamental problems. Ultimately it is culture that possesses the potential to unlock the secrets of creativity and sustainability, and to realize a renaissance in global development and human affairs.

6

Foundations for a Cultural Age

Culture constitutes the topmost phenomenal level yet recognized—or for that matter, now
imaginable—in the realm of nature.
—Alfred Kroeber and Clyde Kluckhohn (1963), p. 290

If a cultural age is to function effectively, it will have to be erected on firm foundations. Without this it will be not be possible to realize the full potential of culture or to achieve the aims and objectives established for it. Of the foundations that will have to be created, four stand out from all the rest: achieving general agreement on the nature of culture, broadening and deepening understanding of cultures, interpreting history from a cultural perspective, and capitalizing on culture's great practical and theoretical tradition.

The Nature of Culture

Achieving general agreement on the nature of culture is the most difficult to realize because there are so many different concepts and definitions of culture in use throughout the world. Today, this is causing confusion, misunderstanding, and uncertainty for many people. For some people culture is the arts. For others it is the legacy from the past, or leisure-time activity. For still others it is the "cultural industries" of publishing, radio, television, film, video, and sound recording. For others again, it is a state of mind, a way of life, a set of shared values, symbols and beliefs, a means of interacting with the natural environment, or the organizational forms of different species. This makes it essential to reach general agreement on the nature of culture before anything else is addressed. It would be foolhardy to predicate any age, but particularly a cultural age, on a concept that causes confusion and misunderstanding rather than acceptance and a reasonable measure of certainty.

How are we to proceed when there are so many different concepts and definitions of culture from which to choose? While many approaches to the problem are possible, the most promising one involves examining the way in which culture has evolved as a concept over a history spanning some two thousand years (see Schafer 1998a, pp. 13–65).

The concept of culture can be traced back to the Romans, who associated it with cultivation of the mind, as when Cicero wrote that *cultura animi philosophia est* ("philosophy is the cultivation of the soul"). This view remains influential today since, while most scholars see culture as something substantially broader and deeper than this, many people continue to think of culture in terms of individual self-refinement.

During the Middle Ages, culture was associated more with the arts than with philosophy, another approach that remains influential: most countries and governments use a similar concept of culture as art in their official definitions of the word. There are legitimate reasons for this. The arts have long been recognized for their capacity to provide countries with a distinctive identity through their concern with excellence, creativity, beauty, truth, inspiration, freedom of expression, and a sense of "place." Moreover, the arts are often responsible for propelling societies to higher and higher levels of accomplishment through their capacity to create signs, symbols, stories, myths and legends, metaphors and beliefs that are then diffused through the process of cultural communication and enrichment.

Towards the middle of the nineteenth century, in the hands of Matthew Arnold and other social critics, culture came to be associated with education, in the sense of the pursuit of excellence and perfection, as individuals and societies alike acquired greater knowledge and understanding, and set out, in Arnold's phrase (p. 70), "to make the best that has been thought and known in the world current everywhere." In Arnold's view, it was not sufficient for people to learn and understand without giving anything back in return. It was also essential for people (whom Arnold, being of his time, calls "men") to ensure that "the best" was made accessible to all citizens and to future generations (p. 69):

The great men of culture are those who have had a passion for diffusing, for making prevail, for carrying from one end of society to the other, the best knowledge, the best ideas of their time; who have laboured to divest knowledge of all that was harsh, uncouth, difficult, abstract, professional, exclusive; to humanize it, to make it efficient outside the clique of the cultivated and learned, yet still remaining the *best* knowledge and thought of the time, and a true source, therefore, of sweetness and light.

Even as Arnold was writing, Tylor and other anthropologists were beginning to view culture in substantially broader terms than his, launching the holistic understanding of culture discussed in the previous chapter. They had discovered that, while there were all sorts of words to describe the specific activities in which people engage as they set about meeting their individual and collective needs, and working out their complex relationships with the world, there was no word to describe how all these activities are woven together to form a whole. "Culture" was the word they chose to designate that whole. Accordingly, Franz Boas, Ruth Benedict, Margaret Mead, Ralph Linton, Bronislaw Malinowski, Alfred Kroeber, Edward Hall, and numerous other anthropologists have defined culture as "the sum of all activities in a society," "all manifestations of a community," "the totality of material and non-material traits," "the sum total of ideas, conditioned emotional responses, and patterns of habitual behaviour," or "the total body of belief, behaviour, knowledge, sanctions, values, and goals that mark the way of life of any people" (all quoted by Kroeber and Kluckhohn, pp. 81–84). Their intention is not to downplay or denigrate the parts of the whole, but rather to recognize that those parts are always combined in specific combinations and arrangements to form a whole that is greater than the parts or the sum of the parts.

Interest in this holistic way of looking at and thinking about culture has become prevalent not only among anthropologists but also in cultural institutions such as UNESCO. After many years of defining culture largely as the arts, the finer things in life, heritage, and "the cultural industries" of publishing, radio, television, film, video, and sound recording, UNESCO has started to define culture in far more expansive terms, as the total way of life of a people. This holistic view was confirmed in 1982, when the following definition was adopted at UNESCO's Second World Conference on Cultural Policies in Mexico City (UNESCO 1987, p. 41):

Culture may now be said to be the whole complex of distinctive spiritual, material, intellectual and emotional features that characterize a society or social group. It includes not only the arts and letters, but also modes of life, the fundamental rights of the human being, value systems, traditions, and beliefs.

The arguments for adopting this holistic understanding of culture were set out even more forcefully in the planning documents and working papers for the World Decade of Cultural Development (1988–97) referred to earlier (UNESCO 1987, p. 16):

> Without neglecting the importance of creativity as expressed in intellectual and artistic activity, they [the participants at the Second World Conference on Cultural Policies] considered it important to broaden the notion of culture to include behaviour patterns, the individual's view of him/herself, of society, and of the outside world. In this perspective, the cultural life of a society may be seen to express itself through its way of living and being, through its perceptions and self-perceptions, its behaviour patterns, value systems, and beliefs.

As long as people and countries are in no danger of losing their cultures, it is easy to define culture in partial rather than holistic terms, whether as the arts, the humanities, heritage, or the "cultural industries." However, as soon as culture is threatened or there is a danger of losing it, as is the case for many countries and peoples today, there is a sudden realization of the comprehensive character of culture as a total way of life. Clearly, there is nothing quite like the threat of cultural extinction or foreign domination to bring about a rapid realization of the holistic character of culture.

It is impossible to view culture in holistic terms without extending it to all groups, classes, activities, people, and institutions. Culture in this sense is all-inclusive. It is education and the environment as well as economics, pop music as well as classical music, science as well as art, business as well as recreation, technology as well as sports, industry as well as religion, politics as well as social affairs, popular activities as well as elite activities. This is what more and more people mean when they say that they are products of their culture. This is probably why the Nigerian writer and Nobel laureate Wole Soyinka views culture as "Source," from which all things flow and to which all things return (p. 21):

> We need therefore to constantly reinforce our awareness of the primacy of Source, and that source is the universal spring of Culture. It is nourished by its tributaries, which sink back into the earth, and thereby replenish that common source in an unending, creative cycle. That one tributary proves more aggressive, domineering, more seemingly nourished than others does not transform its egalitarian quotient.

Perceived this way, culture is concerned with the entire set of ways in which people visualize and interpret the world, organize themselves, conduct their affairs, elevate and enrich life, and position themselves in the world. Since each component of this holistic understanding of culture enriches our knowledge and understanding of culture as a concept, it pays to examine each component in turn.

First, people's ideological, mythological, cosmological, aesthetic, scientific, religious and ethical beliefs and convictions constitute the cornerstone of culture, because they provide the axioms, assumptions, and premises on which culture is based. They function very much like the submerged part of a huge iceberg: while they are more implicit than explicit, they are always there, just below the surface. As a result, they are of crucial importance to the overall understanding of culture and cultures because they are intimately connected to the natural environment, the global situation, the world system, the human condition, concepts of space, time, life, death, reality, and the universe, and theories of development and change.

Second, culture includes how people organize themselves with respect to economic systems, social processes, political procedures and government activities, technological and communications policies, and ecological practices, whether in neighbourhoods, communities, towns, cities, regions, countries, cultures, civilizations or the world system overall. These activities are undergoing profound change as a result of shifting trading practices, globalization, computerization, commercialization, demographic developments, pluralism, and new economic, political, social, environmental and technological realities.

Third, culture includes how people make and carry out their decisions about family life, child-rearing, consumer behaviour and expenditure, living arrangements, gender relations, and personal preferences and practices. Just how important these things are is indicated by the enormous importance of family life, child-rearing, and gender relations in the modern world.

Fourth, culture includes how people elevate and enrich their lives through education and training, artistic and scientific preferences, spiritual practices, moral values, and all those things that make life deeper, richer, and more meaningful than it would otherwise be. It is in this domain that many of the signs, stories, and rituals are created that are used to understand culture in the holistic sense, providing the building blocks, tools, and techniques to unlock the secrets of culture.

Finally, culture includes how people position themselves in the world in respect of geographical location, temporal situation, geopolitical processes, and territorial manoeuvring. These factors play a critical role in determining the ways in which distinct groups of people in different parts of the world situate themselves in space, relate to the natural environment and the world around them in a specific, practical sense, interact with each other, and occupy particular pieces of the planet.

When culture is defined in this all-encompassing sense, it can be visualized as a huge tree with roots, trunk, branches, leaves, flowers, and fruit, to adopt the metaphor favoured by Dr. Min Jiayin of the Chinese Academy of Social Sciences. Mythology, religion, ethics, aesthetics, philosophy, cosmology, and the like constitute the roots. Economic systems, technological practices, political and governmental processes, social structures, environmental policies, and the like constitute the trunk and branches. Artistic works, educational endeavours, moral codes, buildings, spiritual activities, and the like constitute the leaves, the flowers, and the fruit. This metaphor contributes a great deal to unlocking the secrets of culture. Just as every tree is a dynamic and organic whole composed of many interconnected parts, so too is culture. Just as all the component parts of the tree play integral and indispensable roles in the effective functioning of the tree, so all the component parts of culture perform a similar function.

Culture, then, when stripped to its essence, is concerned with three matters: worldview, values, and people. It is clear, in the first place, why culture is concerned with worldview: the way in which people visualize and interpret the world has a crucial bearing on how they live, act, and value things in the world, both individually and collectively. Without a vastly improved understanding of worldview in general, and the specific worldviews of people in different parts of the world in particular, humanity could easily experience higher levels of environmental degeneration, a great deal more poverty, pollution, violence, terrorism and suffering, and increased conflict among the diverse cultures and civilizations of the world. It is a frightening prospect in view of the high levels of these atrocities today, but one that is possible if much more attention is not accorded to the impact that worldviews have on every aspect of the human condition.

In the second place, as the US anthropologists Alfred Kroeber and Clyde Kluckhohn pointed out in 1963 (pp. 340–41):

> values provide the only basis for the fully intelligible comprehension of culture, because the actual organization of all cultures is primarily in terms of their values. This becomes apparent as soon as one attempts to present the picture of a culture with reference to its values. The account becomes an unstructured, meaningless assemblage of items having relation to one another only through coexistence in locality and moment, an assemblage that might as profitably be arranged alphabetically as in any other order, a mere laundry list.

Values are important because they assign weights or priorities to the component parts of culture. How much emphasis is placed on the economy compared to the environment? How much emphasis is placed on products, compared to people and matters of human well-being? How much emphasis is placed on the arts compared to the sciences? How do politics, education, business, and technology fit into the equation, and how much emphasis is placed on them? How these values are determined in particular parts of the world varies a great deal from culture to culture and from one part of the world to another, according to people's needs, wants, preferences, policies, practices, and circumstances. Some people may prefer to put a great deal of emphasis on the economy, products, the sciences, politics, and technology, while others may prefer to put a great deal of emphasis on the environment, ethics, people, religion, the arts, education, and the humanities. It all depends on how people decide to order the component parts of their cultural life.

The intimate connections among culture, worldview, and values make it apparent why culture is so concerned with people, for it is people who create worldviews and values as they set about meeting their individual and collective needs. Their needs to breathe, bond, eat, belong, create, procreate, recreate, work, communicate, reflect, love, and so on give rise to the complex set of requirements that constitute culture in general and cultures in particular.

What is steadily unfolding here are some of the main reasons why culture is of such vital importance to the world of the future, as well as why it is essential to achieve a general agreement on the nature of culture if firm foundations are to be established for a cultural age. As a Chinese proverb says, the beginning of wisdom lies in calling things by their right names.

Culture is concerned, as we have seen, with the whole, and not just a part or parts of the whole. The US anthropologist Ruth Benedict illustrates this point by using the metaphor of making gunpowder (1963, p. 33):

> The whole, as modern science is insisting in many fields, is not merely the sum of all its parts, but the result of a unique arrangement and interrelation of the parts that has brought about a new entity. Gunpowder is not merely the sum of sulphur and charcoal and saltpetre, and no amount of knowledge even of all three of its elements in all the forms they take in the natural world will demonstrate the nature of gunpowder. New potentialities have come into being in the resulting compound that were not present in its elements, and its mode of behaviour is indefinitely changed from that of any of its elements in other combinations.

Culture is also concerned with the myriad relationships that exist among the parts of the whole. It was this that the British literary and social critic Raymond Williams had in mind when he wrote about the critical importance of cultural theory (1961, pp. 46–47):

> I would then define the theory of culture as the study of relationships between elements in a whole way of life. The analysis of culture is the attempt to discover the nature of the organization which is the complex of these relationships. Analysis of particular works or institutions is, in this context, analysis of their essential kind of organization, the relationships which works or institutions embody as parts of the organization as a whole.

It is not difficult to identify some of the most important of these relationships as far as the world of the future is concerned: human beings and the natural environment; economics and ethics; technology and people; rich and poor countries; rich and poor people; women and men; and materialism, ethics, and spiritualism. Broadening and deepening understanding of these and other strategic relationships, as well as the priorities that should be placed on them, holds the key to lessening many of the world's tensions, pressures, conflicts, and confrontations.

Finally, as has been emphasized throughout this book, culture is concerned with the need to achieve balanced, harmonious, and equitable relationships between the parts and the whole. This is imperative if excesses, imbalances, and deficiencies in the world system, in people's lives, and in economics, technology, and all the other parts of the whole are to be reduced, or, even better, eliminated.

This completes our examination of the nature of culture. With this cornerstone in place it will be possible to broaden and deepen understanding of the character of cultures. Fortunately, we now have a very specific concept of culture in place to assist with this process.

The Character of Cultures

If culture in the broadest sense is a whole composed of many interdependent parts, so is each specific culture. This makes every culture distinctive and unique, with its own particular set of characteristics, though there are different ways of classifying them depending on which parts of each whole are emphasized, be it activities; geographical areas; groups of people defined by ethnicity, religion, or some other factor; or some other set.

To broaden and deepen understanding of the point that every culture is a whole made up of many interdependent parts, consider Jewish culture, Armenian culture, and the cultures of aboriginal peoples (although any culture could be used to illustrate the same point).

The groups chosen as examples have been able to keep their cultures together as wholes despite formidable challenges and deplorable conditions. Faced with the perpetual threat of extinction, Jewish, Armenian and aboriginal cultures have remained remarkably intact over hundreds, indeed, thousands of years because these peoples have repeatedly created, recreated and reordered the component parts of their cultures in the light of rapidly changing conditions and terrifying historical events. They have done this through a variety of initiatives and devices: the sharing of myths, legends and rituals; the telling of stories; the preservation of customs, traditions, beliefs, and identities; the development of specific signs and symbols; the enjoyment of communal feasts and celebrations; the establishment of vast networks of international contacts and support mechanisms; the evolution of many indigenous art forms and musical works; the use of humour; and engagement in a great deal of social interaction. If this were not the case, Jewish, Armenian and aboriginal cultures would have split apart and died out a long time ago.

Unfortunately, it is not possible to see cultures as wholes or total ways of life, which makes it exceedingly difficult to know them in the comprehensive, holistic sense. There are three aspects to this problem that must be dealt with. First, it is not possible to know all the parts of cultures because there are too many of them. Second, it is not possible to know any part in great detail because every part is a vast and complicated entity in its own right, regardless of whether it is an activity, a geographical region, an ethnic or religious group, or anything else. Finally, and perhaps most importantly, it is not possible to have total knowledge of the ordering process that is used to bind all the component parts together because this is conducted by many different people, institutions, and groups in society. How, then, is it possible to "know" cultures in the holistic sense? According to Giles Gunn, the best place to start is with the parts, and with the dynamic interplay that is constantly going on between the parts and the whole. In his book *The Culture of Criticism and the Criticism of Culture* he states (p. 95):

> We cannot understand the parts of anything without some sense of the whole to which they belong, just as we cannot comprehend the whole to which they belong until we have grasped the parts that make it up. Thus we are constantly obliged to move back and forth in our effort to understand something "between the whole conceived through the parts which actualize it and the parts conceived through the

whole which motivates them" in an effort "to turn them, by a sort of intellectual perpetual motion, into explication of one another."

For people interested in getting to know cultures as wholes, the best place to start is with their own culture and their own specific part of the whole—their job, their family, their community, their life, their geographical location—considered, not in isolation, but rather as a part of their culture as a whole. While this cannot provide a complete solution to the problem, it starts the process moving in the right direction by compelling people to think about the larger context in which their own experiences are situated.

To progress further in this area, it is necessary to turn to people who possess the ability to sense how cultures as wholes are put together, as well as the ability to communicate this to others. Invariably, they are artists, scholars, historians, philosophers, critics, and other types of creative people who possess the necessary intuitive and sensorial skills, as well as expressive and communicative abilities. Robert Redfield, a cultural anthropologist who spent his life studying cultures as wholes, comments on the ability that these types of people possess as follows (pp. 158–59):

> Still farther from where we just now stand are those who study the relations of parts to parts, of elements abstracted out from the whole in strict and limited relationship to each other, generally described . . . They are those who make a science from chosen parts of human wholes, placed in relation to other such parts, but not in relation to all the parts of the original whole. Over there, on that other side, are all those who strive to present the concrete reality of each human whole as each, in itself, is. They are a various group. Included are novelists, philosophers, historians, philosophers of history, literary people, critics of literature and of art, historians of art, and writers of personal reminiscence. These people describe human wholes—personalities, civilizations, epochs, literatures, local cultures—each in its uniqueness.

The old adage that a picture is worth a thousand words is a cliché, but it speaks volumes about the ability of people such as artists to communicate knowledge, information, and insight into cultures as wholes that it is impossible to convey or communicate in any other way.

Redfield calls this "the ability for portraiture," commenting (pp. 161–62):

> The characterizations of the artist . . . are of course not precise at all, but very much of the whole is communicated to us. We might call them all portraits. They communicate the nature of the whole by attending to the uniqueness of each part, by choosing from among the parts certain of them for emphasis, and by modifying

them and rearranging them in ways that satisfy the "feeling" of the portrayer. . . . In
the portraitures accomplished by art, exaggerations, distortions and substitutions
of one sort or another play important parts. Caricature and satire are special forms
of portraiture. Each describes the whole by overemphasizing something felt to be
significantly true of the whole. Metaphor and analogy offer different and parallel
images for understanding the whole, as does the parable: a narrative standing for a
human something other than itself.

Take, for example, the way in which the US television producer Ken Burns
has used baseball and jazz to broaden and deepen understanding of American
culture as a whole.

Baseball and jazz are both highly symbolic of that culture because they are
populist forms of expression, and the United States has a very populist culture.
Baseball is the "national game" and jazz is one of the country's most indigenous
forms of musical expression. As a result, they have something extremely powerful
to say about American culture that could not be communicated otherwise.
Using baseball and jazz also makes it possible to bring to the fore a number
of other strategic aspects of American culture in the holistic sense, particularly
relations between whites and blacks, the competitive urge that is arguably
characteristic of American culture, the creation of new and popular forms of
recreation and cultural expression, and the commercialization of popular forms
of entertainment. This made it possible to shed a great deal of light on the
character and evolution of American culture at very crucial periods in the course
of its development.

Another example of this is the way in which the nineteenth-century Czech
composer Bedřich Smétana used the Vltava (the river also known as the Moldau)
to say something extremely powerful about Czech culture as a whole. There
is something about the way in which Smétana depicts the Vltava majestically
flowing through the Czech countryside, from its inauspicious beginnings
to its meanderings past vast forests, famous castles, and other historic sites,
that communicates a great deal about the character of Czech culture as it was
understood in Smétana's day. Not only did the Vltava dominate Czech culture at
a very crucial stage in its development, by linking villages, regions, and activities
together, it also dominated Czech culture as long as water transport was central
to so many economic activities. What is true of the Vltava and Czech culture is
equally true of many other waterways and other cultures, such as the Yangtze in
China, the Ganges in India, the Po in Italy, the Volga in Russia, the Amazon in
Brazil or the Mississippi in the United States, "Ol' Man River" itself.

While artists *use* parts of the whole such as rivers, baseball, jazz and the like to say extremely powerful and symbolic things about cultures as wholes, they also *create* parts of the whole to achieve similar effects. An excellent illustration of this is Irving Berlin's song "God Bless America":

> God Bless America,
> Land that I love.
> Stand beside her and guide her
> Thru the night with a light from above.
> From the mountains, to the prairies,
> To the oceans white with foam,
> God bless America,
> My home sweet home.

Berlin created a part of the whole that has something extremely powerful and profound to say about American culture as he and many others have known it. Not only has this inspiring song helped to bind Americans and the United States together in the comprehensive and cohesive cultural sense, it also says something very meaningful and patriotic about the expansiveness and beauty of the country, and the faith that many Americans have in their culture and their identity. At no time, perhaps, was this more in evidence than during the period following the 9/11 terrorist attacks on the United States, when "God Bless America" was heard almost as frequently as the national anthem.

A similar function is performed for British culture, or at least some versions of it, by Hubert Parry's setting of William Blake's poem "Jerusalem":

> And did those feet in ancient time
> Walk upon England's mountains green?
> And was the holy Lamb of God
> On England's pleasant pastures seen?
> And did the countenance divine
> Shine forth upon those clouded hills?
> And was Jerusalem builded here
> Among these dark satanic mills?

It is interesting, in this regard, to find "dark satanic mills" so often interpreted as a reference to the industrial revolution, though Blake was in fact expressing his opinion of the Christian churches of his time. This is an example of how a culture can absorb and assimilate a particular part by altering its meaning.

British culture has also been symbolized by Edward Elgar's setting of A. C. Benson's "Land of Hope and Glory", just as Jean Sibelius's "Finlandia" is still seen by many Finns as symbolizing and communicating a great deal about their national culture. There are comparable works in every culture, for every culture has its own inspiring and symbolic "parts of the whole," communicating vital information and feelings to people about the culture as a whole, in the attempt (not always successful) to bind them together in space and time, and give them a sense of unity. They may also be musical compositions, as, for example, in the case of Spanish culture, which is expressed and celebrated in Joaquin Rodrigo's *Concierto de Aranjuez* and *Concierto de Andaluz*, Enrique Granados's *Goyescas* and *Danzas españolas*, Isaac Albéniz's *Iberia*, and Manuel de Falla's *Noches en los jardines de España* and *El amor brujo*. Their evocations of hot days, sultry nights, splendid architecture, and majestic monuments rival, if they do not surpass, Miguel de Cervantes Saavedra's classic *Don Quixote de la Mancha*.

However, painters, novelists, poets, playwrights, film-makers, and other creative people also possess the capacity to produce evocative works of this type: for example, Shakespeare in the context of British and other Anglophone cultures, Omar Khayyam, Rumi, and Sadi in Persian culture, Monet and other Impressionists in French culture, or Tolstoy, Dostoevsky, Pasternak, and Solzhenitsyn in Russian culture.

Indeed, any part of a culture can say something powerful, profound, symbolic, and meaningful about it. Sports may do so, as is the case with baseball in the United States, or soccer in Brazil and Argentina. Individuals, or more usually the legends about them, may do so, as Confucius does for China, Gandhi for India, Nelson Mandela for South Africa or Martin Luther King Jr. for the United States. So too may buildings such as the Taj Mahal or the Great Wall of China.

It is this fact that makes it essential to examine very carefully the different parts of any culture, but particularly those parts that have become symbolic of the culture as a whole. The cultural anthropologist Clifford Geertz called this kind of examination "thick description." While the picture that emerges is always only approximate, because cultures are too vast and complex to be wholly seen or known, it is an exceedingly important function nevertheless. It is through "thick description" that people can piece together an understanding of their own culture, and the cultures of others, as dynamic and organic wholes. Artists can be particularly helpful here. As Edward Hall contends (1966, p. 74, Hall's emphasis):

> It is the artist's task to remove obstacles that stand between his audience and
> the events he describes. In so doing, he abstracts from nature those parts which,

if properly organized, can stand for the whole and constitute a more forceful, uncluttered statement than the layman might make for himself. In other words, *one of the principal functions of the artist is to help the layman order his cultural universe.*

Without sustained and systematic exposure to the works of artists, popular as well as classical, historical as well as contemporary, it is not possible for people to get to know, understand or experience their own culture as a whole, or other cultures as wholes. Nor is it possible for people to "order their cultural universe" effectively.

It should not be assumed, however, that the role of artists is limited to the functions outlined so far. Artists can also *change* cultures. Mark Twain, through *The Adventures of Huckleberry Finn* and other novels, and Alex Haley, through his book *Roots*, each did a great deal to challenge stereotypes of whites and blacks in the United States, and to promote greater equality. *The Adventures of Huckleberry Finn* in particular revolutionized the language of fiction by using vernacular speech. This ability of artists to change cultures should be constantly borne in mind, since it may be required to make fundamental changes in the various cultures of the world in the future.

Further, while artists and the works they make may be the best vehicles for helping people to get to know, understand, and experience their own culture and other cultures, they are not the only vehicles available. Architecture plays a particularly important role in this regard because it makes concrete statements that are often highly symbolic. One need only think of the Forbidden City in Beijing, the Taj Mahal in Agra, the Ring in Vienna, the Empire State Building in New York, the Guggenheim Museum in Bilbao, the Opera House in Sydney or the Eiffel Tower in Paris, and what they each symbolize. Virtually every country in the world uses architecture to make profound and highly visible statements, from cathedrals, presidential palaces, and legislative buildings to public squares and monuments of famous people.

Language and the "cultural industries" of publishing, radio, television, film, video, and sound recording do the same, providing the communication tools and distributive mechanisms that bind people together, and make the works of artists, architects, historians, and others known to the public. So too do athletes, sports teams, and sporting events, because they represent parts of the whole that are often highly symbolic and therefore have something extremely powerful to say about cultures. Think, for example, of what Pele symbolizes in the case of Brazilian culture, Wayne Gretzky in the case of Canadian culture, Joe DiMaggio, Babe Ruth, and the New York Yankees in the United States, traditional acrobats in Chinese culture, or the Olympics and the FIFA World Cup for most contemporary cultures around the world. Anthropological and sociological studies also do this because they tend to deal with cultures in the comprehensive, holistic sense, and therefore with the patterns, themes, worldviews, values, social structures, and interrelationships that comprise cultures.

Personality studies do this as well because, as Ruth Benedict contended, cultures are often "personalities writ large": for example, Theodore Roosevelt or John F. Kennedy in relation to the United States, Nelson Mandela or Desmond Tutu in South Africa, Mao Zedong in China, Margaret Thatcher in Britain or Charles de Gaulle in France. Religious and philosophical treatises do this because they tend to deal with the totality of human experience or fundamental aspects of it, and therefore with the interconnected and interrelated activities of people's lives. Scientific studies do this because they have a profound effect on the worldviews that underlie cultures. Ecological, economic, geographical and historical studies do it because they reveal how cultures have imprinted their holistic character on very specific parts of the natural and human environment.

One of the first people to write about cultures in the broader, deeper and more comprehensive sense was the German poet and philosopher Johann Gottfried von Herder, considered by some to be one of the founders of anthropology (though it should also be pointed out that he has been criticised by others as one of the pioneers of modern racism and ultranationalism). Although Herder was writing at a time when it was not commonplace to write about cultures, at the turn of the eighteenth and nineteenth centuries, he had a remarkable understanding of the holistic character of cultures, as well as the ways in which cultures develop and are manifested in space and time. He likened cultures to organisms in order to emphasize their dynamic, cohesive, evolutionary and comprehensive character, and set out his ideas in his *Outlines of a Philosophy of the History of Man* (1791). In Herder's view, the most important factor in the development of cultures is not the individual, but the group, and many factors contribute to the creation and development of cultures, including history, heredity, tradition, education, interaction with other cultures, and, most importantly for Herder, climate, geography, and nature (quoted by Ergang, p. 90):

> Man is no independent substance, but is connected with all the elements of nature;
> he lives by inspiration of the air, and derives food and drink from the most unlike
> productions of the Earth; he employs fire, absorbs light, and contaminates the air he
> breathes; awake or asleep, at rest or in motion, he contributes to the change of the
> universe; shall not he also be changed by it?

The factors affecting the creation and development of cultures vary a great deal from one part of the world to another, so, according to Herder, every culture exhibits a specific "national character," most plainly visible in its arts, language, literature, and religion. It was but a short step from this for Herder to conclude that the world is very much like a garden, with all sorts of flowers growing in it. Each culture has its own particular fragrance, colour, design, and distinctive features. The challenge, in Herder's view, is to make it possible for every culture to develop its national character, or "circle of happiness," to the fullest extent, thereby realizing its full potential and becoming all that it is capable of being.

In retrospect, it is clear that Herder's views had both positive and negative effects, particularly when they were combined with the views of other writers. On the positive side, Herder and other scholars helped to inspire the creation of many valuable artistic and scholarly works aimed at broadening and deepening understanding of culture, "national character," and the influence of art, landscape, history, geography, climate, and nature on the development of cultures. On the negative side, Herder's views had a profound influence on the growth of extreme nationalism and racism in Europe and elsewhere in the world in the nineteenth and twentieth centuries. In combination with many other developments taking place at the time, this resulted in the fighting of two major world wars, the deaths of millions of people, and a great deal of unrest. This was not part of Herder's intention. He was much more concerned with the contributions that different groups of people can and, in his view, should make to the common cultural heritage of humankind, as Robert Ergang has argued (pp. 263 and 265):

> The nationalism, however, which Herder advocated was not the narrow nationalism of the later nineteenth century. Herder's nationalism was in its essence humanitarian; it was built around the principle of the essential unity of mankind as a whole. Hence his nationalism is free from the reproaches which may be brought against nationalism of the violent and exclusive type. He did not, like later nationalists, endeavour to inculcate in the minds of his countrymen an absolute faith in their superiority over all other nationalities. . . . His conception of nationality pointed toward toleration and mutual enrichment. His message in brief was: each nationality has its peculiar duty to perform for the common good of mankind, and its special contributions to make to the common fund of civilization.

Despite this, there is no doubt that Herder's views had some effect on the growth of nationalism and racism, largely because he tended to view cultures as homogeneous and closed systems rather than as open and heterogeneous systems. He tended to place a great deal of emphasis on cultural similarities and uniformity, the separation of one culture from another, the distinction between one group and another, and, inevitably, the inference that some cultures, races, and groups are superior to others.

This example of the positive and negative impact of Herder's ideas reinforces the point that it is imperative to be ever watchful for, and mindful of, the actual and potential uses and abuses of cultures, particularly when too much power is concentrated in too few hands, and cultures are exploited for political, military or imperialistic purposes. It is imperative to establish the necessary safeguards to ensure that cultures are not abused in this way, safeguards that include democratic and benevolent forms of government; a strong private sector to counterbalance the potentially dangerous power of the public sector; assurances that too much power is not concentrated in too few hands; cultural agencies and institutions at arm's length from government and the political process; numerous and varied cultural relationships between countries and cultures; the democratization and decentralization of institutions, resources, and opportunities; and, above all, freedom of expression, movement, and participation in decision-making.

At the time Herder was writing, and for some time afterwards, most cultures were much more closed, homogeneous, and uniform than they are today. Not only was there much less interaction going on among the various ethnic groups around the world, but most people in each culture shared the same or very similar ethnic, religious and linguistic identities. It is also true that Herder was writing largely about European cultures and had little knowledge of cultures elsewhere in the world, and it has been claimed that European cultures were much more diverse in Herder's day than they later became.

In any case, it is clear that cultures are generally much more open, heterogeneous and diverse today, largely as a result of developments in transportation, communications, technology, globalization and trade. There is much more interaction today, not only within cultures, but also between cultures. There is also a great deal more interethnic and intercultural mixing and borrowing, and a great deal more travel and migration than in any previous period of human history. As a result, a majority of cultures are much more diverse than before, bringing together different ethnic, religious and linguistic groups. These developments pose problems for the character of cultures as wholes composed of many parts and require new understandings of culture, particularly in respect of the ways in which various activities are combined together. After hundreds of years of thinking about cultures largely in terms of religious and ethnic groups, or geographical regions, it is going to take a quantum leap in human consciousness to think about cultures in these more complex terms.

Nevertheless, such a leap is of crucial importance to the world of the future. The ways in which people combine all the various activities in which they are engaged to form total ways of life are bound to have a crucial effect on their well-being, as well as on the vitality and sustainability of cultures in every part of the world. Cultures that fail to achieve balanced and harmonious relationships among the many different activities comprised within them, or fail to situate themselves effectively in the natural and global environment, are bound to find that their days are numbered.

It will also require a quantum leap in human consciousness to think about cultures as open, diverse, heterogeneous, and inclusive, rather than as closed, uniform, homogeneous, and exclusive. Increasing numbers of people have multiple cultural identities and allegiances, which necessitates new understandings of what the various ethnic and religious groups that comprise cultures have to give and to gain. It also necessitates the creation of many more connections among peoples, subcultures, ethnic and religious groups, geographical regions, and environmental, social, economic, educational, political, artistic, scientific, technological, religious and spiritual activities. There are still elements of closedness and exclusiveness in every culture that make it difficult for outsiders to penetrate it or for insiders to change it, but cross-fertilization, communication, exchange, and inclusion must increasingly take the place of separation, non-communication, isolation, and exclusion within and between all cultures.

Clearly, it will take time to make the transition that has just been described. It may be helpful in this regard to look at a couple of cultures that appear to manifest some of the capabilities that will be required to make these quantum leaps in the years ahead. Canadian culture, to take one example, is already relatively diverse, heterogeneous and open, because it is comprised of a broad array of different activities, regions, and ethnic and religious groups all interacting with one another (as discussed in the present author's *Culture and Politics in Canada*). Compared to most other countries in the world, Canada has a much more open immigration policy and has allowed more influences from outside, and particularly from the United States, to penetrate its borders. While this is starting to change as a result of the terrorist attacks on the United States and the need for greater security measures, Canadian culture is still generally seen as a mosaic rather than as a melting pot, being composed of numerous ethnic and religious groups and "subcultures" that, apart from the First Nations and other aboriginal peoples, derive their identity and distinctiveness from other parts of the world, which is why Canada is often described as a land of immigrants. Indeed, it has been argued that Canadian culture is rapidly becoming a microcosm of the global macrocosm, with people from every part of the world contributing to its development and composition. Canada has shown that multiculturalism, the official recognition of pluralism and cultural differences, can work, and that cultures do not have to be uniform, homogeneous or closed in order to function effectively.

What is true of Canadian culture is also true of Swiss culture, though in an entirely different way. Standing at the crossroads of Europe, and including people belonging to German, French, Italian, Romansch, and other linguistic and ethnic groups, Swiss culture is more diverse than most of its European counterparts, though it is less diverse or multicultural than Canadian culture. Swiss culture too functions very effectively as a whole, because all the ethnic, religious and linguistic groups and geographical regions that comprise it have been able to create structures, such as the system of cantons, or the practice of holding referendums on major political issues, that bind the various parts of Swiss culture together.

While such structures vary from culture to culture, every culture in the world uses a variety of devices to bind its component parts together. These devices may be signs and symbols, such as flags, national anthems, official emblems and languages, national holidays, citizenship activities, and various types of civic celebrations. Myths, legends, rituals, and stories also play an important role, as do values, value systems, and value hierarchies. These are all important because they help people to coalesce all the various activities in which they are engaged into organized and meaningful wholes, as Jerzy A. Wojciechowski has pointed out (Wojciechowski, p. 54):

> the hierarchy of values underlying each culture is the principle of internal cohesion of a culture, which bonds the various elements of a culture together and structures them into an organized whole composed of interdependent parts . . . The hierarchy of values underlying a culture integrates elements of knowledge into a world view, determines, to a large extent, attitudes and reactions to life situations, and offers a general framework for man's conscious presence in, and relationship to, the world. Central to each culture are convictions about the universe and about man, about his nature, his relation to the external world, his place in the universe, the meaning of human life, the supreme values, and the distinction between right and wrong, good and evil. The sum of these convictions forms in each case a unique and distinctive system, differing from culture to culture, even though some of its elements are similar in different cultures. It is this system which shapes the beliefs, attitudes, and behaviour of individuals.

Spatial factors are also important in providing cohesiveness to cultures. Every culture in the world occupies a very specific piece of territory, binding people together and giving them a sense of place, and particularly pride in place. On the one hand, people are anxious to receive the benefits that derive from sharing space together. On the other hand, they are anxious to protect their space whenever it is threatened. This explains military build-ups throughout the world, which may well increase in the future as population increases and people's spaces are used up, invaded or threatened.

All these devices bind the component parts of cultures together to form wholes. It is this process that gives cultures their distinctiveness. While the result is generally less particularistic or ethnocentric than earlier forms of "national character" tended to be, and therefore, arguably, less prone to nationalism, chauvinism, racism or political manipulation, the effect is still to bring together bundles of beliefs and assumptions to form cultural wholes.

Since cultures are structured differently and have different qualities and capabilities, some are known for their architectural achievements, others are known for their music or art, still others are known for their cuisine, and others again are known for their customs, traditions, regional variations, community celebrations, historical development, or use of colour and language. This is what makes the exploration and discovery of the architectural, musical, artistic, culinary and historical complexities, intricacies and accomplishments of all the various cultures of the world alluring and attractive. There is a rich mine of materials, artefacts, and activities here to reward determined explorers. Standing behind this, of course, are cultures in the holistic sense, which are increasingly revealed as more knowledge and understanding of their parts, and the ways in which these parts are put together to form wholes, is acquired.

It would be a mistake to conclude that expanding knowledge and understanding of cultures in the holistic sense is essential only for theoretical, intellectual, or educational reasons. It is also essential for practical and political reasons. As the terrorist attacks on the World Trade Center and the Pentagon, the conflicts in the Middle East, the tensions between Islamic and non-Islamic countries, and the pressures between eastern, western, southern, and northern cultures confirm, there are profound differences among the diverse cultures of the world, not only in their details but as total ways of life. Without a much better understanding of the character of cultures in general, and the reasons for such differences, humanity will pay a severe price in the future, particularly given the increased interaction among cultures today. This makes expanding knowledge and understanding of cultures in the holistic sense a categorical imperative.

The Cultural Interpretation of History

Broadening and deepening understanding of the nature of culture and cultures is imperative if firm foundations are to be laid for a cultural age. So too is interpreting history from a cultural perspective. This is yet another pillar that will have to be manoeuvred into place if a cultural age is to function effectively.

Interpreting history from a cultural perspective is essential because humanity needs accurate and authentic interpretations of the past to carry forward into the future. Interpretations of history have powerful effects, as illustrated in the case of the "economic interpretation of history", because they provide answers to some of humanity's most profound and pressing questions. Where did human beings come from? Why have they evolved the way they have? What are the most basic forms of human settlement and activity? What activities have human beings considered to be most important? Where do human beings stand at present? Perhaps most importantly, where should humanity go from here? Without accurate and authentic interpretations of history, it will not be possible to interpret the past correctly, understand the present properly, or confront the future effectively.

From a cultural perspective, what stands out most clearly is the fact that people in every part of the world have struggled to build cultures in the holistic sense, as the first and foremost act of human effort and ingenuity, whenever and wherever people have come together for the express purpose of living together in the world and working out their association with the world. While economic activities have constituted an essential component in each culture, because they have been concerned with people's material needs and physiological requirements, and the ever-recurrent problem of survival, they have been only part of a substantially broader, deeper, and more fundamental process. Cultures in this sense constitute the basic building blocks of human society and the real foundations of human existence. The fact that all the diverse cultures of the world have been wholes composed of an intricate interlacing of numerous interdependent parts is evident from the very beginnings of human life on Earth. Crucially, then, the cultural interpretation of history, in contrast to other interpretations, is consistent with reality, the human condition, and the nature of historical development, because this history is viewed from a comprehensive, egalitarian, and multidimensional perspective, rather than a partial, partisan and one-dimensional perspective.

History viewed in this way is a continuous process involving the ebb and flow of different cultures and civilizations. The German historian Oswald Spengler called this process (p. 18) "a picture of endless formations and transformations, of the marvellous waxing and waning of organic forms." Whether cultures actually rise and fall, or merely pass through periods of greater and lesser dynamism and creativity, history in the all-encompassing, holistic sense involves the building up and fading out of many different cultures: Chinese, Indian, Egyptian, Islamic, Greek, Roman, Mayan, European, African, Asian, Latin American, North American, Caribbean, Middle Eastern, and so forth. While all these cultures have had their positive and negative aspects, their strengths and weaknesses, there is no group of people or society anywhere in the world that has not experienced this miraculous process at one point or another in its history.

This is why the historian Karl Weintraub contended that the most important question in historical interpretation is this (p. 1): "how can a civilization or a culture be understood and presented in all its complexity, and yet as an intelligible and structured whole?" Weintraub's own answer was as follows (pp. 2–3):

> In this delicately fashioned network the arts may have their ties to religion and economic values, morality may affect the constitutional arrangements and in turn be affected by political realities, a mood reflected in literature may also come to the fore in a social custom, and a scientific insight may work back upon a religion belief. . . . This double concern with what has been called by anthropologists the synchronic and the diachronic mode of culture implies, on the one hand, the study of connections between cultural factors in their structural relationship, and, on the other hand, the study of the gradual changes, either by the introduction of new factors or by a shift in emphasis among the existing relations, resulting in a modification of the cultural configuration. In the world of the cultural historian all things touch one another.

One of the first historians to interpret history from this broad cultural perspective was the nineteenth-century Swiss historian Jacob Burckhardt. His own artistic training served a very valuable purpose, since Burckhardt was aware that every artistic work is a whole composed of many interrelated parts, regardless of whether it is a painting, a play, a building or a musical composition. This helped him to understand how any attempt to interpret history from a cultural perspective requires coming to grips with the comprehensive and interdependent nature of cultures, and therefore with the fundamental relationships between the parts and the whole.

Burckhardt applied this principle to the interpretation of the culture of Italy in the fourteenth, fifteenth and sixteenth centuries. The parts of the whole that he used to shed light on the culture of Renaissance Italy were the state as a work of art, the development of the individual, the revival of antiquity, the discovery of the world and of man, society and festivals, and morality and religion. Through the detailed examination of these parts and by paying close attention to the complex interrelationships and interconnections among them, Burckhardt was able to produce a portrait of the culture of Renaissance Italy as a whole. What makes Burckhardt's portrait particularly powerful is the way in which he uses works of art and architecture to depict and confirm his case that a culture can be revealed through a detailed examination of its parts. Perhaps this is why Florentines of the fifteenth and sixteenth centuries saw culture as "the first and greatest of all needs," according to Burckhardt, and therefore of central rather than marginal importance. As Burckhardt put it (Vol. I, p. 229):

> The age in which we live is loud enough in proclaiming the worth of culture, and especially of the culture of antiquity. But the enthusiastic devotion to it, the recognition that the need of it is the first and greatest of all needs, is nowhere to be found but among the Florentines of the fifteenth and early sixteenth century. On this point we have indirect proof which precludes all doubt.

It was this technique of using the arts and architecture to shed light on the holistic character of cultures that Burckhardt used to great advantage in his lectures and writings on ancient Greek culture, which were left incomplete on his death in 1897.

Just as historians and scholars such as Voltaire, Gibbon, Condorcet, Buckle, Goethe, Moeser and Guizot had paved the way for Burckhardt, largely by struggling to overcome specific methodological problems in the development of the cultural interpretation of history, so Burckhardt paved the way for such historians as Huizinga, Spengler, and Toynbee. What all these cultural historians share in common is the quest to understand cultures as wholes that exude very specific ways of life and are composed of many different elements. It is this that makes the cultural interpretation of history more accurate than the economic interpretation of history. It is impossible to point to any culture that has been preoccupied exclusively with economic needs. Regardless of how destitute people have been, they have never neglected the need for social organization, recreation, religious and spiritual understanding, artistic expression, mythology, play, symbolism, governance, training, and just plain idling. These needs have been every bit as important to people's overall survival and well-being as their economic and material requirements. Seen from this perspective, economic needs do not cause other needs, any more than other needs cause economic needs.

This is not to say, however, that cultures cannot be dominated by certain themes, of which economics may be one. Indeed, it is clear that cultures have been dominated by different themes just as ages have been dominated by different ideas. Whereas the dominant theme in one culture may be aesthetic or religious, in another it may be scientific, political, technological or economic. For example, during the Middle Ages the dominant theme in many European cultures was religion. This is apparent as soon as attention is focused on the central role that the church played in shaping most if not all aspects of life. In the early modern era, in contrast, the dominant theme in many European cultures was aesthetic, as is confirmed by the use of the term "Renaissance" to refer to the return to the arts of antiquity. In our own time, the dominant theme in many cultures, particularly Western cultures, is economic. It makes sense, therefore, to talk about "medieval religious culture," "Renaissance aesthetic culture" or "Western economic culture."

The fact that different cultures have been dominated by different themes is brought home with startling clarity in the modern world. Think, for example, of the profound differences between the culture of the United States, on the one hand, and the culture of the Taliban in Afghanistan, on the other hand. Whereas the dominant theme of American culture is economics, as epitomized by the World Trade Center before it was attacked by terrorists, the dominant theme in Taliban culture is religious fundamentalism. This has caused numerous pressures, tensions, and conflicts between the two cultures, and others associated with them, because the differing symbols and themes of the two cultures have aroused fear, misunderstanding, suspicion, and mistrust.

While there is a pressing need for greater understanding between the different cultures of the world, awareness of the fact that cultures can be dominated by different themes serves a very valuable purpose. It confirms the fact that history has been dominated by different themes, thereby challenging the central premise of the economic interpretation of history. The cultural interpretation of history asserts that history can be dominated by different themes at different times and in different places. This makes history the product of a greater degree of free will, and a smaller degree of determinism, than in the economic interpretation of history, and is therefore much more consistent with the actual facts of the matter.

While it is not possible to say in advance what theme or themes will dominate history in the future, because the future is always an open book to be charted in accordance with humanity's needs, ideas, and assets, the cultural interpretation of history brings to an end the belief that history must be dominated by one theme and one theme only, namely economics. In so doing it opens the doors to a more fluid and flexible way of understanding the past, comprehending the present, and confronting the future. This demonstrates how essential it is to interpret history from a holistic, impartial and egalitarian perspective, rather than a specialized, partial and partisan perspective. It has been the development of cultures, not just economics, that has been the central concern of humanity, making the challenge of the future one of broadening and deepening understanding of how cultures can be developed most effectively, and of the lessons to be learned from the cultural interpretation of history.

One lesson is surely the need for environmental sustainability, sensitivity, and awareness. It is impossible to view history from a cultural perspective without recognizing that the development of cultures has been strongly influenced by the natural environment and the intimate associations that people have with it. Just as cultures provide the context within which the various parts of cultures are situated, so the natural environment provides the context within which whole cultures are situated. As the historical development of cultures has shown, time and again, cultures that are insensitive to the natural environment run the risk of overextending themselves and collapsing.

Another lesson is how essential it is to try to interpret history impartially. What a cultural interpretation of history provides here is the realization that people, countries, and cultures in every part of the world have made strong, lasting and valuable contributions to human development, global progress, and the cultural heritage of humankind. This confirms the equality, value, and dignity of all people, countries, and cultures, not just some of them. Fortunately, significant advances have been recorded in this area in recent years, as noted earlier, despite the fact that much remains to be accomplished. Such developments augur well for the future because they signal the need for a more just and equitable world characterized by more equality between men and women, among ethnic groups, among the diverse peoples of the world, and between the developing countries of sub-Saharan Africa, Asia, Latin America, the Caribbean, and the Middle East, on the one hand, and the developed countries of Europe, North American and elsewhere, on the other.

There is also a more sinister side to history that must also be taken into account in all future developments: the countless conflicts and confrontations between the different cultures and peoples of the world, and the record of acts of brutality, barbarism, violence, and oppression. As the history of colonialism, imperialism, Nazism, fascism, and "cultural revolutions" throughout the world confirms only too well, there are always problems when too much power is concentrated in too few hands and there are major inequalities in the world. This makes it imperative, as indicated earlier, to be ever mindful of, and to create safeguards against, the abuses of culture. Without cultural education, aimed at broadening and deepening understanding of cultural differences, and international cultural relations aimed at intensifying cross-cultural communication, it will not be possible for people or countries to experience order, stability, and security, rather than instability, chaos, and violence.

There is one final lesson to be learned from the cultural interpretation of history, and that is the importance of taking non-material factors into account in all future development. One of the biggest problems with the economic interpretation of history is that it reduces everything to materialism and ignores non-material factors. The cultural interpretation of history, in contrast, recognizes the importance of ideas, theories, motives, emotions, images, ideologies, personalities, ethics, and spirituality in history. This is particularly true with respect to ideas, since it has become evident in recent years that ideas, especially creative ideas, play a quintessential role in driving major developments throughout the world.

The Great Cultural Tradition

If a cultural age is to develop properly in the future, it will also be necessary to capitalize on culture's practical and theoretical tradition. Just as the economic age is predicated on a solid tradition of theoretical and practical accomplishments in the field of economics, so a cultural age will be predicated on a solid tradition of theoretical and practical accomplishments in the field of culture.

There is, however, a significant difference between the two traditions. Whereas the economic tradition is reasonably well-known—as a result of the agricultural, industrial, technological, and commercial revolutions, the amount of attention devoted to economic thought and practice in the mass media and educational institutions, the historical and contemporary encounter with economics, and the fact that we are living in an economic age—the cultural tradition is virtually unknown throughout the world. This makes broadening and deepening knowledge and understanding of the great cultural tradition one of the most pressing requirements for a cultural age.

The practical side of the cultural tradition is as old as history. Wherever there have been attempts to improve the human condition, and to elevate and embellish life, there also the practical side of the great cultural tradition is to be found: in the efforts of peasants and labourers in every part of the world, in the works of artists, scientists, scholars, and educators, in the commitment of religious and spiritual leaders, and in the determination of humanists, social activists, business people, and politicians. It is also manifested in all the oldest cultures of the world, as epitomized by Stonehenge and Carnac, the settlements at Ur, Catal Huyuk and Alaca Huyuk, and the pottery and utensils of prehistoric times.

China and Egypt were probably the first areas of the world to recognize that the fruits of culture can be multiplied many times over when the practical development of culture is attended to in earnest. There is ample evidence of this in the various cultures created in China from ancient times, as well as in the numerous publications, exhibitions, and television programmes on Chinese and ancient Egyptian culture, both of which are still making their presence felt in the world today. One can only marvel at the countless treasures being unearthed in recent archeological digs in China, the throne of Sitamon, the funeral mask of Tutankhamen, the pyramids of Giza, the Sphinx, Thebes, Abu Simbel, or the tombs of the pharaohs, and appreciate the lofty heights to which the practical side of the great cultural tradition can be raised when the development of culture is pursued with vigour and imagination.

These accomplishments were perpetuated in brilliant style by the ancient Greeks and Persians. In Greece, such accomplishments reached their zenith in Athens, Mycenae, Delphi, Sparta, Corinth, and elsewhere, thanks to the efforts of such visionary rulers as Pericles and the triumph of the *polis*, the ancient Greek city state. As in China and Egypt, a kind of renaissance flourished there in ancient times, a renaissance known for its outstanding aesthetic, intellectual, political, economic and social accomplishments. In Persia, where it also culminated in a brilliant civilization, it is epitomized in many elegant and decorative buildings, such as those at the imperial cities of Susa, Persepolis, and Pasargadae.

There is hardly a place on Earth or an epoch in history that has not benefited from the practical side of the cultural tradition. Alongside the cultures already mentioned can be placed the Inca, Maya and Aztec civilizations of the Americas, the Ashanti and Benin cultures of Africa, the Heian and Ashikaga eras in Japan, the Gupa and Moghul cultures of India, the Medician and Elizabethan periods in Europe, and countless others. It would be a mistake, too, to conclude that the practical side of the great cultural tradition is limited to large-scale cultures. Cities such as Beijing, Kyoto, Bangkok, Venice, Vienna, Buenos Aires, Quito, Isfahan, Marrakesh, Jerusalem, Istanbul, Samarkand, San Francisco, Cairo, Sydney, Quebec City or Mexico City are inconceivable without practical contributions from a host of individuals and institutions. In each of these cases conscientious efforts on the part of people and organizations of all kinds have been needed to turn these places into cultural treasures in their own right. Stretching back to the very beginnings of history and reaching right up to the present, the practical side of the great cultural tradition has been steadily developing and gathering momentum for thousands of years, giving rise to the wealth of cultural achievements and masterpieces we know and appreciate today.

There is an equally valuable constellation of accomplishments on the theoretical side of the great cultural tradition, created by generations of scholars working in such disciplines as anthropology, sociology, the arts, philosophy, history, geography, ecology and biology. What makes their accomplishments important is the fact that what they have had to say is relevant to the human condition in general, as well as to developments at local, regional, national and international levels, whether they have been addressing the formation of human personalities, the development of towns, cities, regions or countries, the character and classification of cultures, the natural environment, the importance of creativity, diversity, equality, and identity, the role of the state in cultural life, the diffusion of culture throughout the world, or the meaning of progress.

As far as the formation of personalities is concerned, the most prominent contributors are Matthew Arnold, Thomas Carlyle, Georg Simmel, John Cowper Powys, Johann Wolfgang von Goethe, Ruth Benedict, Margaret Mead, Gordon Allport, Anthony Wallace, Edward Sapir, John Harding, Irving Hallowell, John Honigmann, Abram Kardiner, Géza Róheim, and Ralph Linton. They have made their contributions by focusing on the role that cultures play in shaping personalities. Arnold, for example, emphasized how important it is for people to attend to the harmonious development of all the powers that comprise human nature. Carlyle formulated a "law of culture" predicated on the belief that people should "cast off all foreign and especially all noxious adhesions," and "stand in their full stature." Goethe urged people to "live in the whole, in the good, and in the beautiful." Benedict, Mead, Sapir, and Kardiner focused attention on the formation of "national character" and "national identity." Powys, perhaps the most persuasive commentator on the role of culture in the development of personalities, made his view clear in his book *The Meaning of Culture* (p. 8):

> The art of self-culture begins with a deeper awareness, borne in upon us either by some sharp emotional shock or little by little like an insidious rarefied air, of the marvel of our being alive at all; alive in a world as startling and mysterious, as lovely and horrible, as the one we live in. Self-culture without some kind of integrated habitual manner of thinking is apt to fail us just when it is wanted the most. To be a cultural person is to be a person with some kind of original philosophy.

What is significant about all these contributions is the way in which they attempt to broaden and deepen understanding of what it means to be "a whole person" and to "live a full life." Such writers and thinkers have been at the cutting edge of attempts to develop a perception of personality formation based on the integration of all the mental, physical, emotional, aesthetic and spiritual factors that comprise human existence. This may prove to be one of the greatest challenges of all in the years ahead.

In relation to the role of culture in the development of towns, cities, and, regions, Lewis Mumford, Friedrich Ratzel, Leo Frobenius, Fritz Graebner, Franz Boas, Clare Wissler, Amos Rapoport, John Agnew, John Mercer, David Sopher, Richard Sennett, and others have focused attention on "culture centres," culture areas," "cultural circles," or "cultural complexes." For example, Ratzel, Frobenius, Graebner, Boas, and Wissler shed a great deal of light on how such complexes are created and coalesce, how they develop in space and time through the sharing of values, traditions, and ways of life, and how these are transmitted and diffused to other parts of the world. Mumford shed a great deal of light on how culture acts as an integrating and powerful force in urban development, largely by providing cohesion, balance, order, belonging, and pride of place. He also enhanced understanding of the ways in which human settlements have developed historically, as well as how essential it is to incorporate culture fully into community planning and development.

These contributions have a great deal of relevance to the world of the present and the future, especially now that more than half of the world's population is living in urban settlements. Perhaps this is why more and more attention is being focused on the role that culture can play in community and urban development. It was the former Minister of Culture of Greece, Melina Mercouri, who first proposed the idea of "cities of culture" at the inaugural meeting of the Ministers of Culture of the European Union in Athens in 1985. The idea has since caught on elsewhere, as more and more communities seek to focus on what makes them dynamic, creative, inspiring, and unique (see Landry). This helps to explain the burgeoning interest in liveable and sustainable cities, as well as the importance of cultural districts and corridors, and the key role played by creative individuals and activities in urban development and municipal affairs.

Another seminal contribution to the theoretical side of the great cultural tradition was made when Edward Burnett Tylor formulated his anthropological definition of culture in 1871. This has had a profound effect on cultural thought because it focused attention on culture as a whole, and not just some limited part of it. A related contribution came from Alfred Kroeber and Clyde Kluckhohn in their book *Culture: A Critical Review of Concepts and Definitions* (1963). This comprehensive compendium is essential reading for anyone interested in plumbing the depths of culture. Not only does it expand knowledge and understanding of the many different concepts and definitions of the term, it also expands awareness of those qualities that are most relevant to culture, including worldviews, values, value systems, patterns, and beliefs. In so doing, it focuses attention on those ideals that have been accorded the highest priority by human beings down through the ages.

Yet another valuable contribution came when anthropologists such as Lewis Henry Morgan, Franz Boas, Bronislaw Malinowski, Alfred Reginald Radcliffe-Brown, William Halsey Rivers, A. H.Lane-Fox Pitt-Rivers, Edward Evans-Pritchard, Raymond Firth, Leo Frobenius, Lucien Lévy-Bruhl, Margaret Mead, Ruth Bunzel, Ruth Benedict, and others began studying cultures in depth and on the ground by travelling to the South Pacific, the Northwest coast of North America, the interior of sub-Saharan Africa, and many other parts of the world in the late nineteenth and early twentieth centuries. Working under conditions of extreme hardship, these pioneering scholars and others like them contributed greatly to broadening and deepening understanding of cultures in every part of the world. Their work was not always free of errors, which is understandable in view of the fact that they had little initial knowledge of the cultures they were studying and field work was still in its infancy (see Peacock on the problems involved). Yet there is no doubt that their achievements did much to enhance the knowledge and understanding of culture that are needed more than ever if conflicts and confrontations between the diverse cultures of the world are to be avoided, or at least minimized.

The work of such cultural scholars as Pitirim Sorokin and F. S. C. Northrop has also done a great deal to enhance knowledge and understanding of different types of cultures, as well as the ways in which cultures can be classified and analyzed. For example, in his pioneering work, *Social and Cultural Dynamics: A Study of Change in Major Systems of Art, Truth, Ethics, Law and Social Relationships* (1957) Sorokin identified four principal types of cultures—sensate, ideational, idealistic, and mixed—each of which has a distinct set of characteristics. In setting out his views on this subject, Sorokin created a typology of different types of cultures and signalled the need to shift from sensate cultures to ideational, idealistic and mixed cultures if environmental sustainability and human fulfilment are to be achieved. While Northrop's views on culture were different than Sorokin's, he was equally interested in different types of cultures. In his seminal book *The Meeting of East and West* (1946) Northrop drew on concerns at the time about the relationship between the United States and Japan to focus on the need to develop effective methods for ensuring that occidental and oriental cultures complement rather than conflict with one another. His research remains relevant today because it enhances understanding of the development of both East and West, and the interactions and tensions between them.

Related contributions have been made by such historians as Oswald Spengler, Arnold Toynbee, Johan Huizinga, Jacob Burckhardt, Fernand Braudel, W. M. F. Petrie, Joseph Ki-Zerbo, Peter Burke, and Karl Weintraub, who have each shed a great deal of light on how cultures develop over long periods, and on the reasons for the growth and decline of different cultures. Why, for example, does the light go out in some cultures? Spengler contended that all cultures pass through four distinct stages analogous to the four seasons, moving from creation through flourishing to decline and death. Toynbee saw the reasons for cultural decline in the inability of cultures to respond to challenges, particularly as these challenges grow stronger while the capacity to respond gets weaker.

Yet another contribution has come from the US anthropologist Edward Hall, whose work explores how different cultures interact, and how values and worldviews are transmitted between cultures, groups, and individuals. As cultures interact more frequently, and as people move more freely from one culture to another or from one part of the world to another, the need for intercultural understanding, communication, and exchange increases proportionately. Hall and others have helped to provide the context for this development by focusing on the various ways, both verbal and non-verbal, in which cultural communication takes place and conflicts can be avoided.

Economists have also made significant contributions to the cultural tradition. John Maynard Keynes, William Baumol, John Kenneth Galbraith and others have been strong advocates of cultural development as it relates to the arts, social affairs, education, and the humanities. Keynes, for example, was a champion of the arts both in private, as a leading light of the Bloomsbury Group, and in public, as Chairman of the wartime body that, after his death, became the Arts Council of Great Britain. Baumol turned his attention late in life to the complex connection between economics and the arts, and discovered that the main reason why artists encounter financial difficulties is not that they mismanage their funds or are frivolous with their money, but that, in many cases, they create handcrafted products and are involved in labour-intensive activities. They are forced to compete in a mechanized age but cannot take advantage of technological gains as corporations can. This led Baumol to develop his theory of the income gap, which has had a profound effect on arts management because it explains why artists need public assistance to cover the shortfall between earned income and total expenditure, just as educational institutions, hospitals, and other institutions do. Galbraith too made a strong case for the development of the arts and humanities, both in his writings as an economist, and in his activities as an adviser to US Presidents Kennedy and Johnson.

A final noteworthy set of contributions has come from poets, philosophers, educators, and diplomats, including Rabindranath Tagore, Mahatma Gandhi, Octavio Paz, Carlos Fuentes, Elise Boulding, Wole Soyinka, Léopold Senghor, Takdir Alisjahbana, Soedjatmoko, and many others. Each in his or her own way has helped to broaden and deepen understanding of the role that culture plays in society and in the development of cultures. For example, Tagore and Gandhi saw the world largely in terms of the interaction between different cultures, religions, and peoples. Soyinka, as we have seen, views culture as the "Source" from which all things flow and to which all things return, and Alisjahbana views culture as the very foundation of human existence. These and other writers have shown that it is impossible to understand many of the developments taking place today without understanding the powerful role that cultures play in human affairs.

It is on the foundation of such thoughts, ideas, and findings that the theoretical foundations for a cultural age should be established. Just as the economic age is predicated on the theoretical contributions of the economists discussed in Part I of this book, so a cultural age should be predicated on the contributions of the scholars mentioned here, as well as of their colleagues and successors. Their legacy has been largely ignored over the past two hundred years or so because the world has been preoccupied with economics, but it will need to be known and used throughout the world on an unprecedented scale from now on, since it provides the theoretical underpinnings for a more authentic way of looking at the human condition. As the Russian film-maker Sergei Eisenstein put it, "we need thought as a film needs light, for clarity and definition." If, as Ralph Waldo Emerson wrote, thoughts are the antecedents and ancestors of action, then it is through the thoughts of generations of cultural scholars that the actions will be forthcoming that are most essential for the world of the future.

7
Functioning of a Cultural Age

The systematic interpretation of culture brings us close to the thesis that global development is in reality the development of cultures and civilizations.—Nada Svob-Dokic (1991), p. 299

Now that firm foundations have been laid for a cultural age, it is possible to turn our attention to how a cultural age would function in fact. What worldview would underlie it, what model of development would drive it, and what concerns would dominate it?

A Cultural Worldview

One of the biggest challenges for a cultural age will be piecing together, making known and using a cultural worldview to replace the economic worldview, which has the advantage of being reasonably well-known and accepted throughout the world. Since there are obviously many different concepts and definitions of culture in use throughout the world today, the most promising approach in piecing together a cultural worldview may be to examine what individuals and institutions working in the cultural field have been most concerned about. While construction of this worldview from ideas and practices across such a wide range of disciplines is fraught with difficulties, and is subject to numerous qualifications and generalizations, it simply must be done if we are to ascertain the way in which the world would be viewed from a cultural perspective.

From anthropology, sociology, history, and philosophy there is the concern with the whole, discussed in an earlier chapter. From the arts there is the concern with excellence, creativity, beauty, diversity, and the search for the sublime, as well as the ways in which knowledge and understanding of cultures are enhanced through signs, symbols, and stories that stand for the whole. From the humanities there is the concern with people, cooperation, equality, and the connection between spiritualism and materialism. From ecology, biology, and other disciplines that have a close historical and contemporary affinity with culture there is the concern with the natural environment, other species, and the relationships, including the similarities and differences, between these and human beings. While none of these concerns is exclusive to any of the disciplines cited, it is these disciplines that tend to place a relatively high priority on them.

When these concerns are looked at in totality, they provide the basis for the construction of a cultural worldview. In contrast to the economic worldview, a cultural worldview would be predicated on the conviction that the best way to view the world and everything in it is through the prism of culture. The priority would be placed on the whole, not just on economics or any other part of the whole, and on the need to achieve balanced, harmonious and equitable relationships between the parts and the whole. This would then be used to address the complex challenges and opportunities involved in making improvements in society, the human condition, and the world system. What would be of the greatest concern for a cultural worldview is the way in which people tie together all the various activities in which they are engaged to form a whole or total way of life.

Concern with space and time would be another crucial aspect of a cultural worldview. In spatial terms, this would mean placing the emphasis on the relationship between human beings and their institutions, on the one hand, and the natural environment, or "the land," as well as specific places, on the other. In temporal terms, it would mean placing the emphasis on the ways in which human institutions have developed over time, as well as where they stand at present and where they are headed in the future. For culture, this would mean focusing attention on the theoretical and practical heritages that the diverse peoples and countries of the world have built up, as well as the entire cultural heritage of humankind. For specific cultures, it would mean focusing on the relationships between people and traditions, customs, and identities.

It should be pointed out here that a cultural worldview would not reject the economic worldview. Rather, it would subsume the economic worldview, and a great deal else, in a broader, deeper, and more fundamental way of looking at the world. Further, just as the economic worldview is a collective worldview, so too would a cultural worldview be. It may differ substantially from the individual worldviews of people and institutions working in the cultural field, just as the economic worldview may differ substantially from the individual worldviews of people and institutions working in the field of economics. However, this does not alter the fact that it is possible to talk about a cultural worldview in the collective sense.

The development and use of a cultural worldview in this collective sense could prove valuable and timely at the present juncture in history. In the first place, it would place humanity in a much stronger position to make sensible and sustainable decisions about future courses and directions in planetary civilization. In the second place, it would provide an opportunity to make a breakthrough in environmental matters because a high priority would be placed on the relationship between people and the natural environment. In the third place, it would render a better perspective on the numerous conflicts between groups of people, countries, and cultures. The large majority of these conflicts are far more than economic conflicts, even though many economic factors may be involved, such as control and ownership of land, or access to natural resources and wealth. Rather, they are cultural conflicts to the extent that they also involve such factors as differences in worldviews, values or traditions, as, for example, in the Middle East, Afghanistan, Iraq, and elsewhere in the world. A cultural worldview would place the priority on unity, synthesis, inclusion, and holism, rather than division, separation, exclusion, and polarization.

Development of Culture and Cultures

Since the development of culture and cultures would be the major consequence of adopting a cultural worldview, it is necessary to examine what this means in practice.

Developing culture in depth means placing the priority on the quest for knowledge, wisdom, beauty, and truth; the importance of creativity, excellence, compassion, caring, and sharing; the need for equality, diversity, identity, and unity; respect for the needs and rights of others; appreciation of the cultural heritage of humankind; and the search for the sublime. These are ideals that people and countries in every part of the world have valued highly, despite significant differences in their worldviews. It also means placing a great deal of emphasis on the arts, humanities, education, learning, spirituality, philosophy, ethics, anthropology, sociology, ecology, and biology, since these activities and disciplines have very close connections with culture. This would help to ensure that culture's highest, wisest and most enduring ideals would be located at the core of the development process.

Developing culture in breadth means ensuring that people have access to as many cultural options and opportunities as possible, and are able to participate as actively and fully as possible in all aspects and dimensions of cultural life. Every individual and every ethnic group has a great deal to give to the development of culture, as well as a great deal to receive in return. Governments, corporations, foundations, and local, regional, national and international organizations would have to play forceful and proactive roles in cultural development and policy here, and remove as many barriers to access and participation as possible.

Specific cultures would also have to be developed in depth and breadth. Such development would be comprehensive, involving the development of all activities in society, and not just certain activities. The Dutch historian Johan Huizinga had this in mind when he wrote (quoted by Karl Weintraub, p. 216) that "the realities of economic life, of power, of technology, of everything conducive to man's material well-being, must be balanced by strongly developed spiritual, intellectual, moral, and aesthetic values."

Development would also be coherent, so that all the component parts of cultures are properly situated. Given the innumerable difficulties involved, this may well turn out to be one of the greatest challenges in the development of cultures. Situating the component parts of cultures properly is most essential in the case of economics, if it is to serve human, social and environmental interests, and not merely commercial, industrial, financial and corporate interests. The specific goals of economics, such as production, consumption, investment, growth, and so on, would have to be brought into line with, and constrained by, the broader and deeper cultural goals of access, creativity, equality, compassion, cooperation, and safeguarding the natural environment and cultural heritage of humankind.

Positioning economies properly within cultures would reduce the strain on scarce resources, because much more emphasis would be placed on activities that make fewer demands on them. It would also humanize economies by placing a higher priority on income and resource sharing, job creation, training and retraining, diversity, distribution, cooperation, and inclusion than on consumption, exploitation, uniformity, profits, competition, exclusion, and the market. Clearly, strong economies are needed to deliver the improvements and investments in technology, capital accumulation, and material living that are required to eliminate poverty and hunger, but strong economies must be positioned properly within cultures if economic excesses and imbalances are to be prevented. Technology, communications, the arts, education, health, the sciences, religion, politics, and all the other component parts of cultures must also be properly positioned. There are always problems when priority is given to any part over the whole, regardless of what part it may be.

Developing cultures that are cohesive is equally important. This would necessitate creating strong connections between activities, ethnic groups, geographical regions, and so on. Where such connections exist, cultures are likely to remain intact, and soar to higher and higher levels of accomplishment. Where they do not exist, cultures can become unglued and split apart. Cultures can easily fall prey to complex communications problems, particularly where geographical size or formidable terrain makes staying in touch difficult or impossible. They can also succumb to tribal divisions or ethnic unrest when ethnic or linguistic groups visualize their futures in terms of isolation, exclusion, and separation, rather than integration, togetherness, and inclusion. It is here that artists, arts organizations, and the creative industries have a key role to play through their ability to create parts of the whole that stand for the whole.

Another key requirement would be the development of cultures that are civilized, meaning that resources are shared equally, there are no major disparities in income or wealth, and discrimination and violence are eliminated, or at least reduced. The objective here would be to create a level playing field on which all citizens and groups can find a place. This should go a long way towards ensuring that cultures have a human face, and that people's needs, rights, and responsibilities can be dealt with in a fair, equitable, open and compassionate manner.

Finally, having adequate control over decision-making processes, and development policies and practices, is essential. Regardless of whether cultures are local, regional, national or international, possessing adequate control over internal affairs and external relations is mandatory if cultures are not to become the victims of standardization, imperialism, globalization or commercialization. Governments, citizens, and community groups will have to work to ensure that decision-making processes and development practices are in domestic rather than foreign hands, and that a reasonable amount of cultural programming is indigenous, rather than imported or imposed. What is at stake here is the survival of cultures into the future.

A Cultural Model of Development

There are many different ways to perceive and define development, but most would agree that development is concerned with the fulfilment of human needs. If human needs are to be dealt with effectively in the future, it will be necessary to evolve models of development that are equal to the task. They must be capable of doing justice to all human needs, and not just certain human needs. They must also be capable of coming to grips with the many different problems associated with people's needs, as previously discussed. A cultural model of development would be capable of dealing effectively with the shortcomings of the economic model of development, as well as with the needs of people and countries in every part of the world.

While the diagram of the cultural model of development (below) has been greatly simplified, it displays the main features of the model and illustrates why it is essential to take a cultural rather than economic approach to development. It is clear from the diagram that, when development is viewed from a cultural perspective, its scope and subject matter are enormous, comprising six fundamental matters:

(1) culture as a whole and cultures as wholes;

(2) the component parts of culture and of cultures;

Figure 2. A Cultural Model of Development

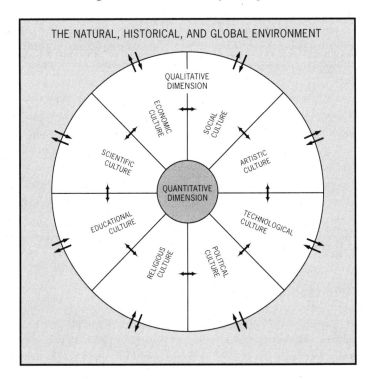

(3) the relationships between the component parts of culture and of cultures;

(4) the interactions between the component parts and the whole of culture or of cultures;

(5) the relationship between the quantitative and qualitative dimensions of culture and of cultures; and

(6) the relationship between culture and cultures, on the one hand, and the natural, historical and global environment, on the other.

The most important priority is to develop culture as a whole and cultures as wholes (the complete circle), but a very important aspect of this is developing the component parts of culture and of cultures in their own right. These component parts are depicted in the diagram as the "economic culture," the "social culture," the "political culture," and so on, since they all share culture in common. Each can be developed most effectively when it is developed in terms of the uniqueness, creativity, excellence, integrity, and diversity inherent within it. Given the highly specialized nature of the modern world, a great deal is known about each of these component parts and how to develop them most effectively, even if the resources are not always available to achieve this.

Far less is known about how to deal with the complex relationships between and among the component parts. What, for example, is the relationship between the economic culture and the social culture, and how can this relationship be dealt with most effectively? Or to cite another example, what is the relationship between the technological culture and the religious culture? Understanding these relationships and coming to grips with them looms ever larger in the overall matrix of concerns that must be addressed.

It is also imperative to examine very carefully the dynamic interplay between the component parts of culture and of cultures, on the one hand, and culture and cultures as wholes, on the other. A larger and larger price will be paid if these relationships are not understood and dealt with effectively.

Turning now to the relationship between the quantitative and qualitative dimensions of culture and cultures, it is the qualitative dimension that is more difficult to deal with, because it is so difficult to measure and define. Nevertheless, breaking culture and cultures down into quantitative and qualitative elements serves the very useful purpose of focusing attention on the material and non-material dimensions. This in turn helps to draw attention to the natural environment, consumption of renewable and non-renewable resources, the rapid rate of population growth, and the finite carrying capacity of the Earth. It is obvious from the model that the larger the quantitative dimension of culture and cultures, the more pressure is exerted outwards on the qualitative dimension. In effect, the more time, money, and energy are spent on the production, distribution, and consumption of material goods and services, the more pressure is exerted on the natural environment, resources, and other species, and the less time, money and energy are available for social interaction, spiritual renewal, friendship, human love, family, recreation, the arts, and other things that make life richer, fuller and more meaningful.

This leads us to the most important relationship in the cultural model of development, namely the relationship between culture and cultures and the natural, historical, and global environment. History confirms time and again that when culture and cultures are not positioned properly in their environment, the consequences are devastating in terms of environmental exhaustion, cultural conflict and confrontation, and repetition of the mistakes of the past. There may be nothing more important to the world of the future than situating culture in general and specific cultures in particular effectively in their environment. On the one hand, this means ensuring that all the diverse cultures of the world are predicated on values, policies, and practices that ensure environmental sustainability, human well-being, and harmony between all people and countries of the world. On the other hand, it means ensuring that all the diverse cultures of the world are based on understandings of the past that are as accurate as possible.

It is imperative to examine very carefully the impact that culture and cultures have on the natural environment. Rather than taking the natural environment as a given or taking it for granted, as the economic model of development tends to do, the cultural model opens up a commanding place for the natural environment at the very core of the development process and in every aspect of development activity. Since all human activities are composed of material and non-material elements, it is essential to examine in great detail the material draws and ecological impacts that different types of human activities have. For example, manufacturing, commercial, transportation, and technological activities draw and impact heavily on the natural environment, because the material component of these activities is high and the potential for damage is great. Conversely, many artistic, educational, social, and spiritual activities draw and impact lightly on the natural environment, because their material component is low and the potential for damage is significantly reduced.

The implications of this for local, regional, national and international development are clear and unequivocal. As world population increases and more pressure is exerted on the natural environment, a great deal more emphasis will have to be placed on activities that draw less on the natural and global environment, and do as little environmental and global damage as possible. In the economic model, human needs with a high degree of material input and output are given a high priority because they produce higher levels of material living and more rapid rates of economic growth. This puts a great deal of strain on the environment. In the cultural model, in contrast, the satisfaction of human needs is much less dangerous and demanding, since the emphasis is placed on achieving a judicious balance between the quantitative and qualitative dimensions of development, and between people's material needs and their non-material needs.

Attention also needs to be focused on the dynamic and reciprocal interplay between the natural environment and culture. Just as culture, and specific cultures, affect the natural environment by constantly pressing outwards, so the natural environment affects culture and cultures by constantly pressing inwards. There are many examples of this. Scientists, for example, are concerned with expanding knowledge and understanding of everything that exists from the outer reaches of the cosmos to the smallest forms of plant and animal life. Artists have been concerned with expanding human awareness of the natural environment for centuries, primarily by enhancing our appreciation of its beauty and grandeur. The natural environment also has an uncanny way of striking back when it is exploited and abused, by way of hurricanes, floods, tornadoes, earthquakes, droughts, global warming, and the collapse of cultures that have failed to take the natural environment fully into account.

Culture and cultures must also be properly positioned in the global environment. As recent developments indicate, every culture is situated in the world and interacts with other cultures in very specific ways. As globalization increases and cultures interact more frequently and extensively with one another, a great deal of thought and attention will have to be given to how cultures are positioned in the world, and what threats and dangers they may pose to other cultures. Without the creation of many more connections between the diverse cultures of the world, conflict and confrontation will be inevitable, and harmony and peace will not be achieved. This requires a dramatic increase in international cultural relations, as well as many more opportunities for intercultural communications and exchange. These are the real keys to solidarity, friendship, and understanding.

Culture and cultures must also be situated properly in the historical environment. This means protecting the legacy of artefacts, ideas, ideals, values, traditions, monuments, and beliefs that has been built up over the course of history. This legacy provides people and countries with connections that create a continuous bond between past, present, and future generations, as well as the means of differentiating between right and wrong, good and evil, valuable and valueless, meaningful and meaningless. Without protection of the cultural legacy of humankind from the ravages of time, people and countries will be unable to learn from the past, maintain their distinctive identities and diversities, and preserve their cherished ways of life. However, this also means coming to grips with the cultural baggage that people and countries inherit from the past, particularly where this baggage is negative, since it creates hostilities and resentments that stand in the way of achieving peace and harmony. The "truth and reconciliation" initiatives instituted in South Africa and other countries offer a ray of hope in this regard, indicating a willingness on the part of specific groups to admit the wrongs of the past, and to seek reconciliation and forgiveness. Another set of examples concerns the attempts now being made to right the wrongs that have been done to aboriginal peoples, in New Zealand, Australia, Canada, the United States, Mexico and other countries, through the resolution of land claims, the provision of greater control over the development of indigenous activities, the preservation of distinctive cultural traditions, and the installation of self-government for aboriginal peoples.

This completes our analysis of the cultural model of development, which provides the contextual, conceptual and practical framework required to make sensible and sustainable decisions about a variety of community, regional, national, international, and planetary matters. It does so by incorporating the natural, historical, and global environment fully into the development equation, as well as by recognizing that development is an interactive, egalitarian, inclusive and holistic activity. It also addresses two of the greatest shortcomings of the economic model of development: failure to take the natural environment into account in planning and decision-making; and the tendency to treat development as an economic activity rather than a multi-dimensional and comprehensive cultural activity.

Key Cultural Concerns

Just as the economic age is driven by a number of powerful forces, so a cultural age would be dominated by a number of fundamental concerns. It is important to identify and examine these concerns, since they flow inevitably from the conviction that culture and cultures should be made the centrepiece of society, and the principal preoccupation of municipal, regional, national and international development.

It is essential to emphasize, once again, that the dominant forces of the economic age would not disappear in a cultural age. Rather, they would be incorporated into it, along with much else. It simply is not possible to create material resources without these forces, as they provide the wherewithal required to fuel economic growth, drive economic development, and propel countries to higher and higher levels of commercial attainment. Moreover, they are so deeply ingrained in the world system, people's lives, and development that it seems unlikely that they could ever disappear. They would, however, be constrained by the key concerns of a cultural age.

To illustrate this point, take the questions of specialization and holism. What specialization is to the economic age, *holism* is to a cultural age. However, specialization would not disappear, because it will always be required to increase knowledge and understanding of the component parts of culture and cultures, as well as to increase production, productivity, and efficiency in all areas of life. Nevertheless, holism would be to a cultural age what specialization is to the economic age. Holism does not reject the need for knowledge and understanding of specific parts of the whole, but incorporates this into the quest to broaden and deepen knowledge and understanding of what is more fundamental: the total way of life of people, and the need to achieve harmonious relationships between material and non-material requirements.

This would not be the only benefit to be derived from making holism a key concern. Many individuals, institutions, groups, and countries have become so caught up with, and dependent on, specialization that their futures are in jeopardy. As long as the demand for their particular specialization is strong there is no real problem, but as soon as the demand diminishes there are serious problems indeed. While this has been going on steadily since the industrial revolution, and has been a basic concern for a long time, it is assuming alarming proportions today as a result of globalization, the liberalization of trade, rapid changes in technology, and new environmental and ecological realities. More and more individuals, institutions, groups, and countries are discovering that excessive dependence on a highly specialized skill, profession, production function or handful of products can lead to unemployment, underemployment, and obsolescence. Holism could prove valuable here as it puts the emphasis on the cultivation of many diverse skills and the ability to function in a variety of contexts, rather than the cultivation of a single skill within a single context.

What makes *human well-being* a key concern of a cultural age is the fact that it has been pushed into the background over the past two hundred years or so, while concern for products, profits, and the market has been pushed into the foreground. Do people have enough food, clothing, shelter, security, education, recreation, and social, artistic, health and spiritual amenities? Are they able to participate actively, freely and fully in the life of the community, region, country, and culture in which they live? Are social, religious, linguistic, economic and financial barriers to access and participation breaking down or building up? Are these and other obstacles preventing people from improving their lot, and expanding their range of opportunities and choices? These are the questions that must be asked and answered if human well-being is to be a key concern, making it possible to address people's needs and requirements in a sustained, systematic, proactive and egalitarian manner.

This fact has been brought home with striking clarity in recent years as a result of the violent reactions of some groups of people to free trade and globalization. They claim that these arrangements do not place the priority on human well-being, but rather on corporate profits, excessive rates of economic growth, exploitation of the natural environment and labour, and promotion of the interests of powerful institutions such as the World Trade Organization, the World Bank or the International Monetary Fund. To this must be added the fact that some free trade agreements have been negotiated in secret, with little or no input from the public, civil society, or social and environmental organizations.

Distribution would also be a key concern in a cultural age. Despite the advances in production, productivity, and productive capacity over the past fifty years, the distribution problem has yet to be solved and, if anything, it is worse than ever. Not only are there substantial disparities in income, wealth, power, and resources, but these disparities are getting more conspicuous. If this problem is to be dealt with successfully in the future, distribution will have to become a mainstream concern rather than a marginal one. If as much progress can be made in the area of distribution over the next one hundred years as has been made in the area of production over the past one hundred years, the greatest single obstacle to global harmony, peace, and stability will have been overcome.

Sharing and *compassion* are also essential to ensure human survival and well-being, and to make it possible for all people and countries to live with dignity and respect. This would go a long way towards addressing some of the most obvious causes of hostility and resentment in the world. If the focus is on giving rather than taking, dispersion rather than accumulation, it will become possible to shift from looking after oneself to concern for others, from survival of the fittest to concern for the plight and well-being of the majority of people and countries in the world.

A great deal of emphasis will have to be placed on *altruism* if this is to be achieved. Not only is the world in need of individuals who can make commitments to causes that are greater than themselves, altruism is also needed to address the world's most difficult, demanding and debilitating problems.

Regrettably, the world seems to be moving farther away from altruism rather than closer to it. The erosion of religious beliefs and practices in many parts of the world has brought with it a significant loss of interest in things that are greater than the self. Then there is the increase in affluence and materialism throughout the world, and the effect this is having in freeing people from dependence on others while at the same time fostering a preoccupation with the self and self-sufficiency. To these trends against altruism should also be added the tendency to develop concern for rights without a commensurate concern for responsibilities, and the need to give something back to community and society in return for the safeguarding and promotion of human rights.

It would, then, be beneficial if more people took President John F. Kennedy's advice: "Ask not what your country can do for you, but what you can do for your country." But this advice does not apply simply within any one country. Without a revival and diffusion of altruism, it is difficult to see how or why rich countries would increase their aid and assistance to poor countries, reduce or eliminate their oppressive debt loads, or help them to deal effectively with poverty and address the needs of the disadvantaged.

The arts have long had concerns that are fundamentally linked to culture, and would therefore be key concerns of a cultural age. Foremost among these concerns are *excellence, creativity, beauty*, and *the search for the sublime*. The challenge is to aspire to the best that can be achieved, regardless of the audience for which it is intended or the field in which it is created, and to emphasize the role of creativity in all areas of life, so that discovering new and better ways of doing things with fewer resources, and more effective and efficient results, becomes standard practice in science, business, industry, government, medicine, welfare, and education as much as in the arts.

There would also be much to be gained from making the creation, conveyance, and cultivation of beauty a key concern in a cultural age. Everybody appreciates beauty and derives a great deal of satisfaction and inspiration from it, whether in songs, paintings, poems, landscapes or thoughts, and every culture, country, and civilization in the world possesses a profuse legacy of beautiful works. These legacies need to be much better known and used throughout the world, for beauty knows no bounds and requires little or no knowledge, commentary or interpretation. People everywhere in the world need beauty in their lives on a daily and full-time basis if they are to achieve meaning, fulfilment, and happiness.

Finally, there is the contribution that the arts can make to the search for the sublime, as they inspire people to reach above and beyond themselves in the quest for the unattainable. Scientists also display this ability when they make major breakthroughs in research and exploration, but it is an ability that artists possess in abundance. Through their expression of profound thoughts and feelings in simple, straightforward and compelling ways, artists are responsible for much of the inspiration that is needed to propel people, communities, countries, and cultures to higher and higher levels of accomplishment.

What makes *democratization* and *decentralization* key concerns of a cultural age is the fact that they expand the range of options and opportunities available to people by making it possible for them to engage in all aspects and dimensions of cultural life. This is why it is imperative to break down the barriers to participation. Aggressive action will be required on the part of governments against those barriers that prevent the realization of human rights or contravene the need to treat all people equally, as well as those that impede particular groups from playing an active role in society and gaining access to the resources they need. This is the message underlying UNESCO's "Recommendation on Participation by the People at Large in Cultural Life and Their Contribution to It," adopted in Nairobi in 1976. Without democratization and decentralization, cultural development becomes static, pedantic, sterile, and elitist rather than dynamic, fluid, flexible, and egalitarian. In the words of Augustin Girard, a French authority on cultural development and policy (p. 137):

> decentralization of activities . . . is at once the first step in the direction of cultural democracy and, at the same time, essential to cultural creativity, vitality and freedom. Thus decentralization is necessarily the guiding principle of cultural democracy.

Democratization is needed to provide full access to existing institutions and resources, as well as to provide opportunities to create new institutions and resources. However, any institutions and resources are controlled by powerful elites, who have a vested interest in maintaining the status quo, in which they exercise control. Democratization can only be achieved through a great deal of struggle, and may well result in harassment, intimidation, and even imprisonment. Further, creating new institutions and resources often involves very great risks. Even so, experience shows that when artists, craftspeople, scientists, and scholars have been provided with funds to create new institutions and resources, those funds are seldom wasted or squandered and the returns are usually far greater than the funds expended. It does not take a great leap of imagination to visualize the numerous benefits that could accrue from a comprehensive programme of assistance to talented individuals to create alternative institutions and resources. Ultimately, this may be the litmus test for democratization.

Like democratization, decentralization is necessary if people's needs, rights, and responsibilities are to be attended to properly. Unlike economic development, which tends to be centralized in nature, and national and international in character, cultural development tends to be decentralized in nature, and local, regional or "grassroots" in nature. Biserka Cvjeticanin, Director of Culturelink and a former Deputy Minister of Culture in Croatia, put her finger on the crux of the problem when she pointed out that (p.1):

> The trend towards globalization has favoured the establishment of planetary networks, but at the same time it has triggered an opposite process, that of "localization," with different cultures asserting cultural pluralism and diversity rooted in local cultural traditions. In contradistinction to cultural universalism, we now witness a return to individual cultures, traditions, and values. There is a constant tension between these two phenomena, universal and particular.

More and more people throughout the world are recognizing that it is "localization" in general, and the quality of life in neighbourhoods, communities, cities, and regions in particular, that is the decisive factor in life. If these fundamental human collectivities lack a diversified array of cultural institutions and amenities, and reasonable access to them, and if people lack control over the decision-making processes and planning structures governing their lives, no amount of national or international development will make up the difference. It is through localized activities and institutions that people learn to cope with the centralizing, standardizing and homogenizing effects of economic, political, commercial, and technological development. It is little wonder that in recent years there has been a rapid proliferation of "grassroots" organizations aimed at restoring people's sense of identity, solidarity, belonging, and control over the decision-making processes affecting their lives. Their appearance is part and parcel of the reaction to globalization, the creation of larger and larger trading blocs, the growth of multinational corporations, and the concentration of financial and commercial power in fewer hands.

If problems as fundamental as these are to be dealt with successfully, a great deal of emphasis will have to be placed on cultural development at the local, municipal and regional level. This will require, among other things, a dramatic increase in the funds available for cultural development at this level; the creation of plans and policies capable of expanding localized resources and institutions; the broadening of participation in planning and decision-making; the commissioning of creative people to enhance the aesthetic state of neighbourhoods, communities, cities, and regions; and the employment of "cultural animators" to act as catalysts for change by helping to take culture out of the hands of narrow elites and special interest groups, and to place it under the control of society as a whole. Without this, it is difficult to see how municipal and regional authorities will be able to respond to the needs and demands of their citizens, especially now that, as we have seen, more than half of the world's population lives in urban environments.

Alongside democratization and decentralization there is a dire need for *cooperation*. Indeed, cooperation should become so contagious in a cultural age that it spreads to all people, institutions, governments, countries, and cultures in the world. At present, however, competition is valued far more highly than cooperation is. People have been competing for such basic necessities as food, clothing, shelter, income, and employment for so long that competition has come to seem normal or even "natural," as the widespread belief in slogans such as "the survival of the fittest" confirms. Moreover, competition is deemed by the proponents of the prevailing ideology to be the key to a healthy and vigorous economy, because it is deemed to yield the best possible situation for producers, consumers, and society as a whole. Competition also plays a major role in motivating people to higher levels of accomplishment. Yet cooperation will be needed far more than competition in the future. It will simply not be possible to come to grips with the complex problems confronting humanity through competition, which would aggravate these problems more than it alleviated them.

It is obvious why *conservation* should also be a key concern in a cultural age, given the size and growth of the world's population, and the limited carrying capacity of the Earth. There are many ways in which conservation can be achieved: by eliminating duplication and waste whenever and wherever they are encountered; by placing much more emphasis on permanence, recycling, and repair, rather than on obsolescence, acquisition, and new purchases; and by trying to realize E. F. Schumacher's dictum that "small is beautiful." The arts can be used to good advantage here, for what lies at the root of many artistic activities is the desire to achieve a great deal with the utmost simplicity.

This brings us to what would be the final major concern of a cultural age: *spirituality*. Spirituality is not an alternative to materialism, just as holism is not an alternative to specialization. Spirituality recognizes that material needs exist and constitute a very essential part of life, but goes beyond materialism by placing the emphasis on the need to achieve harmony and balance between the material and non-material dimensions of life. It is through culture that this harmony and balance is achieved most effectively. This means deriving maximum fulfilment from all the physical, emotional and intellectual experiences that constitute life, as well as combining all these experiences to form an integral consciousness. In the words of Duane Elgin and Colleen LeDrew (p. 19):

An integral culture and consciousness involves a new way of looking at the world. It seeks to integrate all the parts of our lives: inner and outer, masculine and feminine, personal and global, intuitive and rational, and many more. The hallmark of the integral culture is an intention to integrate, to consciously bridge differences, connect people, celebrate diversity, harmonize efforts, and discover higher common ground. With its inclusive and reconciling nature, an integral culture takes a whole-systems approach, and offers hope in a world facing deep ecological, social and spiritual crises.

A Cultural World System

The present world system undoubtedly yields numerous benefits for people and countries in every part of the world, and for the world as a whole, but it is not without its problems. In the first place, it is divided into two unequal parts, developing and developed, and income, resources, wealth, and power are not shared equally. The destructive and dangerous effects of this division have already been discussed.

In the second place, the system is unbalanced in the sense that priority is given to the development of all the municipal, regional and national economies of the world, as well as the global economy. This gives rise to the vast panorama of bilateral and multilateral relationships among the diverse economies, countries, governments, and international institutions of the world, relationships that are intended to facilitate the movement of goods, services, resources, capital, information, technology, and people at speeds and in volumes hitherto unknown. Since the central purpose is to build up the commercial, industrial, financial, agricultural and technological capabilities of countries, priority is given to these relationships in international development and global affairs. Since bilateral and multilateral relationships are much more difficult between countries than within them, because of differences in worldviews, values, customs, languages and so on, ways have to be found to overcome these difficulties, and these are provided by international artistic, educational, social, athletic and spiritual relationships. The result is that these latter types of relationships are seen as marginal and supportive, rather than valued in their own right, and little time, energy, attention or funding is devoted to them.

In the third place, as we have seen, the human element is missing from most international relationships, since much more emphasis is placed on products, profits, finance and so on. This above all makes it imperative to develop a world system that is capable of coming to grips with all the problems facing humankind, not just the economic ones. In order to develop this new system, a great deal more attention will have to be given to how culture in general, and all the various cultures of the world in particular, can be developed most effectively and interact most efficiently.

By far the most important priority in this regard is building up artistic, social, athletic, educational, humanistic and spiritual relationships between countries to the point where a reasonable measure of equality and parity is achieved between them and commercial, industrial, financial, agricultural and technological relationships. This would make it possible to put the emphasis on human well-being rather than on products, profits, and the marketplace, and also to enhance communication across ethnic, linguistic, geographical and political boundaries.

Despite the vast importance of commercial, industrial, agricultural, financial and technological relationships, they tend to be cold and impersonal, largely because they deal with profits and products rather than people. Thus the potential for war, aggression, conflict, violence, and terrorism is always present. This is precisely where the arts, humanities, education, social affairs, and spirituality come in. Human feelings and expression are their very essence. Equally important is the fact that relationships in these areas could provide a strong stabilizing force when commercial, military, political, financial, industrial and technological relations are in flux. They could help to cushion the shocks that result from erratic swings in the pendulums of political, economic and military power. Comprehensive programmes of exchanges involving musicians, composers, writers, painters, theatre and dance companies, symphony orchestras, scholars, athletes, social, spiritual and religious leaders, and development workers could provide the cement that would keep people, countries, and cultures together when other forces are operating to split them apart. In this way peace, stability, security, and friendship would be more readily achieved and maintained in the world.

To this should be added the fact that relationships in the arts, social affairs, sports, education, the humanities, and spiritual affairs can do more than anything else to eradicate the fear, suspicion, misunderstanding, and mistrust that result from inability to understand the signs, worldviews or values of others. The communications revolution and the steady emergence of an interdependent world make it possible to reduce these negative factors in human affairs through a massive build-up of such positive and humane relationships, predicated on in-depth encounters with the creative accomplishments of all cultures, peoples, and countries. Thus the whole world could be brought into intimate, personal contact. This is an opportunity that is far too important to the future of the world to be passed up.

Achieving a reasonable measure of parity among all the diverse economic and non-economic relationships between people, countries, and cultures is also the key to evolving a world system that is unified, balanced, equitable and integrated. In such a system, decisions would be made on the basis of what is in a country's or a culture's best cultural interests, not merely its best economic interests. The relevant question should always be whether a relationship with other countries and other cultures contributes to a country's or a culture's cultural interests as a dynamic and organic whole, regardless of the economic, commercial, financial or technological implications. In the words of Verner Bickley and John Philip Puthenparampil (p. 9 of their collection):

> If all national cultures, quintessentially, are considered as representing, as they do, "ways of life", values and "symbolic systems" which are significant and meaningful in the lives of particular peoples, it should be possible to conceive of ways in which intercultural relations could be perceived and evaluated. Firstly, it will be agreed that transactions which have an adverse impact on the dignity and wholeness of cultures cannot, for that reason, be defended. Secondly, in any organization of purposes intended to be served by intercultural transactions a high place has to be given for purposes which serve to enhance the dignity and vitality of cultures. Thirdly, good cultural relations are those which have a positive impact on cultures and contribute to their "autonomous development." Fourthly, a fundamental aim of intercultural relations/transactions will be the development of a scheme of shared values and "mutual consequentiality" among cultures.

Placing the emphasis on what is in the best cultural interests of countries and cultures would change the ways in which countries and cultures interact with and relate to one another, causing new patterns to form and new possibilities to emerge. This is particularly important in a world where cultures and countries are becoming increasingly multicultural and multiethnic in nature, with a great deal more intercultural mixing, and a greater emphasis on cultural identities, diversities, and differences. Mahatma Gandhi put the case well (in a passage quoted by the World Commission on Culture and Development, p. 73):

> I do not want my house to be walled in on all sides and my windows to be stuffed. I want the culture of all lands to be blown about my house as freely as possible. But I refuse to be blown off my feet by any.

What makes Gandhi's counsel particularly wise is the fact that he warns against being blown off one's feet by any culture, thereby signalling the dangers that result when countries and cultures become closed, homogeneous, and chauvinistic, rather than open, diverse, and responsive to outside influences. As the Romanian scholar Mircea Malitza has pointed out (p. 102):

> Cultures in watertight compartments are doomed to oblivion. Dialogue is essential. The choice between the development of a national culture and an increase in exchanges with the outside world is a false one. Interdependence cannot be denied. The cultures which have blossomed are those which have had the advantage of innumerable influences, received and transmitted in accordance with a process of unceasing enrichment.

The poet T. S. Eliot expressed similar sentiments when he wrote in his *Notes Towards the Definition of Culture* (1948) that the development of culture depends on two interrelated factors: the ability to go back and learn from domestic sources and the past; and the ability to receive and assimilate influences from abroad. Both capacities are imperative if cultures are to develop properly and interact effectively across the total spectrum of cultural achievements. Interaction with other countries and cultures, and international scrutiny and evaluation, are the best defences against ossification, parochialism, and chauvinism.

One of the biggest problems in the development of the world system of the future is the need for cultures to retain their distinctive identity and traditions while simultaneously being able to absorb and integrate influences from other parts of the world. In the past, cultures have been able to cut themselves off from other parts of the world, but as a result of the phenomenal changes in communications, technology, and trade this is now exceedingly difficult, if not impossible. Virtually all cultures in the world are now compelled to deal with all the dynamic developments going on in the world, and to open up to external influences while struggling to retain their identities. The solution to this problem lies in creating a global federation of world cultures, in which all cultures would benefit from, and contribute to, developments taking place in other parts of the world, while maintaining their distinctiveness.

Just as culture in general and specific cultures in particular are wholes composed of many interconnected parts, so too is the world system. As a result, there is much to be learned from the functioning and development of cultures as dynamic and organic wholes that is relevant to the development and functioning of the world system. In the first place, attention should be focused on the development of worldviews and values that are consistent with the world system as a whole, not just particular parts of this system. Otherwise excesses, imbalances, and deficiencies are experienced that are not in the best interests either of particular cultures or of the world as a whole. The best example of this is the environmental crisis, as we have seen throughout this book so far.

Putting the emphasis on the world system as a whole also shines the spotlight on the need to achieve unity and harmony in the world system as a holistic entity, not just selective parts of it. This is imperative if people, countries, and cultures in every part of the world are to live in peace and harmony rather than conflict and confrontation. What is desperately needed here is a global system that breaks down the barriers separating the developed and the developing parts of the world.

Finally, emphasis should be placed on the need to achieve synthesis rather than polarization and separation in the world system. As free trade protests, anti-globalization movements, and terrorist attacks suggest, it is easy for the world system to become subdivided into opposing camps when commitment to finding an effective synthesis is absent or deficient. If polarization and separation are to be eliminated from the world system, and a real synthesis is to be achieved, governments, countries, and cultures will have to give much more consideration to practices and policies that unite rather than divide, and promote consolidation rather than divergence.

It is equally important to focus attention on the realization of harmonious relationships between the component parts of the world system. Where it is not possible to do this it may be necessary to cut back on certain activities. The Dutch historian Johan Huizinga wrote the following with reference to particular cultures, but it is equally applicable to the world system as a whole (quoted by Karl Weintraub, pp. 219–20):

> A culture which no longer can integrate . . . diverse pursuits . . . into a whole . . . has lost its centre and has lost its style. It is threatened by the exuberant overgrowth of its separate components. It then needs a pruning knife, a human decision to focus once again on the essentials of culture and cut back the luxuriant but dispensable.

As far as the cultural world system of the future is concerned, the "essentials" would be conservation, cooperation, education, the arts, learning, friendship, human love, spirituality, the quest for excellence, beauty, creativity and equality, and the need for free expression. The "luxuriant but dispensable" elements would be *excessive* consumption, production, profits, competition, obsolescence, pollution, consumerism, materialism, and waste.

What is required is what Pitirim Sorokin advocated, a shift from "sensate cultures" to "idealistic, ideational and mixed cultures." Sorokin believed that what is needed more than anything else is a commitment to playing down activities that consume excessive amounts of natural resources, and to playing up activities that conserve resources, and achieve harmony and synergy in the world. The key to this shift lies in creating many more connections between the component parts of the world system, and therefore between countries and cultures. The British theatre and film director Peter Brook had this foremost in mind when he wrote (in his article "The Three Cultures of Modern Man," p. 144) that "the culture of the individual" and "the culture of the state" would be followed by "the culture of links":

> It is the force that can counterbalance the fragmentation of our world. It is to do with the discovery of relationships where such relationships have become submerged and lost—between man and society, between one race and another, between the microcosm and the macrocosm, between humanity and machinery, between the visible and the invisible, between categories, languages, genres. What are these relationships? Only cultural acts can explore and reveal these vital truths.

In a world characterized by a great deal of multicultural and multiethnic mixing, the assertion of ethnic and cultural identities, and increased violence and terrorism, many more connections will be needed between the diverse countries and cultures of the world if the world system is to function effectively in the years ahead. While there are no easy answers to these problems, since they are buried deep in history and the human condition, it is difficult to see how they can be overcome without many more such connections. Paul J. Braisted had this in mind when he wrote more than sixty years ago (1944, p. 25):

> Cultural cooperation is so directly a national interest that it should furnish the fundamental motivating principle in governmental foreign service, replacing or reordering all lesser motives. It should become the controlling principle in personnel selection and training, in establishment of new standards of service, and fresh criteria of effectiveness.

Indeed, all relationships are cultural relationships when the world system is viewed from a cultural perspective. Economic, political, military, technological and commercial relationships are included in culture when culture is visualized and defined in holistic terms. They make profound cultural statements in their own right, are integral parts of cultures as dynamic and organic wholes, and have powerful cultural implications and consequences. One need look no further than the impact that the economic, political, military, technological and commercial relationships of the United States have on all the various cultures and countries of the world to confirm this.

If all international relations are cultural relations when the world system is viewed from a cultural perspective, all countries and cultures are developing countries and cultures. They are struggling to make improvements in the various social, political, economic, artistic, scientific, educational, and spiritual components that comprise them, as well as striving to achieve harmonious, synergistic and equitable relationships between these components. No country or culture in the world can consider itself to be developed in the cultural sense, as there is always room for improvement.

This represents a significant departure from the present practice, since it breaks with the well-established tradition of making a distinction between developed and developing countries on the basis of a few highly selective economic criteria. It also has major implications for the world system of the future, because it means that no distinction would be made among the different countries and cultures of the world. This, in itself, could remove one of the biggest obstacles to world peace, security, and stability. A much more unified and integrated approach could be taken to the world system, based on the conviction that all the diverse countries and cultures of the world have different assets and abilities to contribute to global development and progress.

8

Priorities for a Cultural Age

Will humans make the choices that need to be made to bring about a future world at peace?
—Elise Boulding (2000), p. 256

While many priorities may be identified for a cultural age, among the most essential are a new environmental reality; an all-out assault on the barriers to the fulfilment of human needs; new meanings of wealth, a new corporate ideology; a new political system; a cultural approach to citizenship; a breakthrough in education; the creation of liveable and sustainable cities; and a united world. Coming to grips with these priorities is imperative if peace, harmony, and progress are to be achieved.

A New Environmental Reality

Given the size and growth of the world's population, and the finite carrying capacity of the Earth, a new environmental reality is mandatory if human survival and global well-being are to be assured. As Greenpeace, the Sierra Club, Friends of the Earth, and many other organizations have advocated for years, a new environmental reality must be based on three fundamental prerequisites: cleaning up the natural environment whenever and wherever necessary; conserving resources, arresting climate change, stopping the loss of other species, and preventing the spread of greenhouse gases, pollution, and toxic substances; and increasing awareness of the fragility of the natural environment. The first prerequisite requires environmental action after the fact; the second requires environmental safeguards and precautions before the fact; and the third requires an entirely new association between people, the natural environment, and other species.

A great deal of progress has been achieved in recent years by taking environmental action after the fact. While these measures do not provide a total solution to the environmental crisis, cleaning up oil spills after they happen, burying nuclear materials and toxic substances, and dealing with colossal accumulations of waste have accomplished a great deal in terms of sound environmental management and effective ecological practices. Much of the progress that is needed in this area will have to come from North America and Europe, as well as Japan and other developed countries, since they are among the world's most significant polluters.

While environmental action after the fact has been and remains essential, it pales by comparison to the need for environmental safeguards and precautions before the fact. A battery of initiatives is required, both preventative and precautionary.

On the preventative side, the most urgent initiatives are reducing the use of fossil fuels (oil, gas, and coal); developing new technologies and alternative sources of energy such as wind, geothermal, solar, hydrogen and tidal power; instituting and enforcing rigorous standards with respect to emissions from trucks, vans, and cars; preventing the use of toxic substances such as chlorofluorocarbons and pesticides; purifying water and air; and protecting endangered species. Since these preventative measures are unlikely to occur on their own, governments will have to play a proactive role if real progress is to be achieved. This is a cause for concern because most governments have not demonstrated a capacity to deal with these problems effectively. This is particularly important with respect to establishing and enforcing rigorous standards for emissions, and preventing the spread of toxic substances, since these practices represent the greatest of all threats to environmental well-being.

On the precautionary side, the most important initiatives include increasing the time scale of products so that they last longer, do not wear out so easily, and are recycled at every opportunity; reducing the spatial scale of products so that they take up less room and do not use up as many resources to begin with; recycling and repairing products rather than throwing them out; and shifting from products and activities that are high in material input and output to products and activities that are low in material input and output. Such initiatives would go a long way towards conserving resources and reducing the demands that human beings are making on the global ecosystem. Much could be accomplished in this area if, as discussed in an earlier chapter, more emphasis was placed on products and activities that are labour-intensive rather than capital- or material-intensive.

While action is urgently required on all these fronts, what is required more than anything else is an entirely new association between people, the natural environment, and other species. Unfortunately, the prevailing attitude in many parts of the world is that the natural environment owes people a living, and that humanity will eventually tame the natural environment and bring it under its control. These convictions are deeply rooted in technological beliefs and religious practices, particularly in the western world. Unfortunately, they also underlie the world system. It is believed that humanity will ultimately be able to change weather patterns, control or prevent natural disasters, and regulate the ebb and flow of nature through advances in science and technology. The progressive deterioration of the natural environment and the destruction of the ecosystem are the best indicators of the fallacy of this line of thinking. The forces of nature are too powerful and pervasive to be controlled. Instead, the focus should be on the need to see the natural world in a totally new way, as well as on renewing, revitalizing and respecting it at every opportunity.

The arts have a crucial role to play in this regard, since they have the capacity to broaden and deepen people's awareness with respect to nature and other species, make fewer demands on resources, and help to protect the natural environment from excessive consumption and production. As the late Jane Jacobs argued (p. 127):

> Evidence of aesthetic appreciation accompanies early evidences of Homo sapiens. Nobody who has seen reproductions of the most ancient cave paintings can doubt the aesthetic sensibility infusing them, no matter what other purposes they may or may not have served. Foragers have decorated themselves and their possessions, danced, and made music, all of which must have kept them from doing excessive foraging. Practicing and appreciating art is seldom environmentally harmful. It's especially significant, I think, that aesthetic appreciation includes admiration for the rest of nature: flowers, ocean waves, rocks, seashells, vines, human faces and figures, birds and other animals, the sun, the moon, stars, grasses, butterflies—recurring motifs in art, sometimes rendered literally, sometimes abstractly or formalized—and, in due course, art that shows appreciation of cultivated farmland, wild landscapes, seascapes, streetscapes, monuments, and domestic scenes.

Artistic, environmental and spiritual works are far more than interesting forms of aesthetic, ecological and spiritual expression, or devices for popular entertainment. They are forays into what ecologists and environmentalists call "deep ecology," ways of getting to know the natural world as an aesthetic and spiritual entity. Recognition of this fact is essential if humanity is to be successful in evolving the values, lifestyles, and worldviews that are necessary to realize a new environmental reality. It is a reality that hinges on never taking more from the natural environment than is necessary, renewing the environment at every opportunity, and respecting other species, natural resources, and fragile local, regional, national and international ecosystems.

This is why crossing over the threshold from the present economic age to a future cultural age is essential. There has been an intimate connection between culture and nature stretching back thousands of years — the very word "culture" derives from the Latin verb *colere* meaning "to till" or "to cultivate" — meaning cultural scholars have been concerned about the relationship between human beings and the natural environment for almost as long a period. It is through culture that the development policies and practices can be created to counteract adverse contemporary developments, confirm the Kyoto Protocol and other international instruments, increase human knowledge and understanding of the fragility of the natural environment, and reduce unreasonable environmental demands and expectations.

Fulfilling Human Needs

While a new environmental reality is necessary to ensure the survival of human beings as a species, an all-out assault on the barriers to the fulfilment of human needs is needed to improve the well-being of the majority of people in the world. When a substantial percentage of the world's population is living on less than two US dollars a day, it is not possible to claim that their welfare is being properly attended to.

Accordingly, it is necessary to institute powerful measures to improve the quality of life for all people, but particularly for those living in sub-Saharan Africa, Asia, Latin America, the Caribbean, and the Middle East. At the most fundamental physiological level, this means ensuring that they have sufficient food, clothing, and shelter to ensure survival. There is a great deal that developed countries can do towards this goal, through increasing foreign aid and assistance, both in absolute terms and as a proportion of their gross domestic product; opening up markets for, and reducing or eliminating tariffs on, agricultural and industrial products from these regions; training many more development workers and expanding development opportunities; reducing the debt loads of the poorest countries; promoting gender equality and helping to reduce mortality rates; and supporting the elimination of hunger and homelessness.

The changes that are needed to achieve the fulfilment of human needs also include improving governance, ending corruption, enforcing the rule of law, expanding educational opportunities, and promoting participation in planning and decision-making, not only in the developing countries but in the developed countries as well. This too would make a major contribution to ensuring that people have sufficient amenities in all areas, from fresh water and clean air, to education and health care, as well as social, recreational, artistic and spiritual amenities, to be able to live decent and dignified lives. Clearly, humanity now possesses enough productive capacity to satisfy the elementary needs of citizens in all areas of life and in every part of the world, provided only that it is properly directed. What is lacking is, primarily, the public and private will, and, secondarily, the necessary distributive mechanisms and procedures, to make this dream a reality. When large quantities of foodstuffs, clothing, and other basic necessities are destroyed every year to keep prices high, and when production systems are operating at far less than full capacity, it is difficult to contend that humanity lacks the ability to solve this most endemic of all human problems.

Shifting attention away from products and profits, and towards people and their well-being, is imperative for this purpose. If the United Nations, the World Bank, the International Monetary Fund, the G8, and other international organizations stepped up their financial commitments in this area, and pressured other organizations and institutions to do likewise, the results could be substantial. These efforts could and should be supplemented by other measures to address people's elementary needs, such as more effective distribution of surplus food, clothing, books, computers, and medicine; increased commitments from governments, corporations and foundations to distribute income and wealth more equitably; transfers of appropriate technology to enhance sustainable development; fundamental changes in education and training; and, especially, increasing the capacity of poor people and poor countries to gain access to the credit, capital, real estate, and entrepreneurial skills they need to take control of their own lives.

When human needs are visualized from a cultural rather than an economic perspective, they extend far beyond such economic issues to encompass social, aesthetic, recreational, scientific, health, and spiritual needs as well. A group of scholars and statesmen assembled by the Kapur Surya Foundation in India in 1995 examined crucial issues in global development and human affairs, and concluded (p. 1):

> Development must assure the satisfaction of the minimum basic needs for food, habitat, health, education, and employment, and the quest for inner peace and self-realization. This can only be achieved if we can cultivate need-based, as against

desire-based, lifestyles, which are not superficial or self-indulgent, and are non-destructive of the environment and other cultures. These must be frugal in means and rich in ends, and not beyond the reach of increasing numbers of citizens. While being equitable, development must not sacrifice initiative and excellence, but be ecologically responsible, economically viable, cumulative, life-enhancing, culture-specific, and culturally sensitive.

Such a transformation in understanding with respect to the nature of people's basic material and non-material needs has fundamental implications for public and private policy- and decision-making processes, as well as for the way in which human needs and their fulfilment are visualized and dealt with. It means, for example, that human needs are no longer seen as a hierarchy or ladder, with economic, material and quantitative needs spread out across the lowest rung. Rather, they are seen as a holistic constellation, with economic and non-economic, material and non-material, and quantitative and qualitative needs constantly impinging on one another and interacting with one another. This could bring an end to the assumption that, once people's economic, material and quantitative needs have been met, everything else will fall naturally and inevitably into place. It could also give rise to the realization that a broad spectrum of resources must be put in place if people's choices and opportunities are to be enlarged, and development with a human face is to be achieved. This will require development policies and practices that are capable of addressing people's needs simultaneously rather than sequentially.

It will not be sufficient to address people's needs in all areas of life. It will also be necessary to change attitudes with respect to the contributions that people make to production and productivity, since this affects income distribution, access to resources, people's value to society, and people's sense of identity and self-worth. In the economic age, all these things are viewed largely in material and financial terms, which explains the high priority awarded to economic, industrial, commercial, business and technological production and productivity in the overall scheme of things, since the material, quantitative and monetary component of these activities is very high. This is what most governments, corporations, international organizations, and labour organizations have in mind when they talk about the importance of production and productivity, as well as the need to increase production and productivity if living standards are to be improved. It is a way of thinking about and dealing with production and productivity that can be traced back to the classical economists, and the distinction they made between "productive" and "unproductive" labour. It is this attitude that must be changed if people's needs are to be addressed satisfactorily. It is necessary to recognize that all labour is productive and makes a significant contribution to the fulfilment of human needs, regardless of whether it takes the form of mental, emotional, spiritual, aesthetic or physical activity. The "output" of artists, scientists, scholars, philosophers, social workers, homemakers, teachers, health care workers, and spiritual leaders is every bit as essential, and makes as significant a contribution to development, as material output.

In much the same way as a new understanding of production is needed, so too is there a need for a new understanding of what development is. When development is viewed from a holistic and comprehensive cultural perspective it becomes necessary to include all the factors that contribute to development, the artistic, scientific, social, educational, political, environmental and spiritual alongside, and interacting with, the economic, industrial, commercial and technological. Culture constitutes the essence of development because it is concerned with the totality of human needs, and the ways in which human needs may be addressed most effectively in different countries and cultures.

New Meanings of Wealth

It is commonplace to view wealth today in material, monetary and financial terms. This has a long history. As we have seen in Part I of this book, the mercantilists of the seventeenth and eighteenth centuries viewed wealth as gold, silver, and other precious metals; the classical economists viewed wealth largely in terms of "material products," or, as Adam Smith called them, "the necessaries and conveniences of life"; and the neoclassical, Keynesian and post-Keynesian economists viewed wealth primarily in terms of "goods and services," which is how most countries, economists and people view wealth today. To be wealthy is to be a person who either possesses numerous goods and services, or the income and financial resources to acquire them. This has given wealth a highly material, monetary and financial orientation in the modern era. However, what the world needs now, more than ever, are new meanings of wealth. This is necessary in order to reduce the demands that people make on the natural environment, as well as to describe more accurately what wealth is really all about. More and more people are discovering that possessing, or being able to possess, numerous goods and services is not necessarily a guarantee of satisfaction, happiness or fulfilment in life, or an assurance that one has "wealth" in a broader, deeper and more fundamental human sense.

Culture has a crucial contribution to make to realizing new meanings of wealth. When culture is perceived and defined in holistic terms, wealth comes to be seen as qualitative as well as quantitative, non-material as well as material. What is needed to achieve wealth in this sense is the ability to achieve a harmonious balance among all the forces and factors that constitute life. To be wealthy in this sense is to be a person who derives a great deal of fulfilment from many sources, both simple and profound.

If new meanings of wealth are necessary, so too are new measures of wealth. This is especially important in the collective, public sense, since most countries are engaged in efforts to define and measure their wealth, and compare their wealth with that of others. The key to developing these new measures of wealth lies in developing a set of comprehensive cultural indicators capable of measuring wealth in qualitative and quantitative terms. In the development of these indicators three points are essential. First, indicators from a variety of fields and disciplines—including the arts, the sciences, the humanities, the environment, religion, politics, and health, alongside economics, technology, and business—will have to be brought together and compared. Second, the best indicators from each field and discipline will have to be selected for inclusion in the final set of indicators. Finally, the resulting indicators will have to be refined in order to improve their effectiveness.

While it will take time to develop this set of comprehensive cultural indicators, the most essential of them will probably be environmental indicators, such as the quality of water and air, and levels of toxicity and waste; health indicators, such as longevity, health care, disease control and prevention, and substance abuse; social indicators, such as welfare assistance, participation rates in community, regional and national development, and levels of violence and crime; educational indicators, such as student-to-teacher ratios, access to elementary, secondary and post-secondary education, and student drop-out rates and debt loads; recreational indicators, such as the availability of parks, conservation areas, and leisure-time activities; economic indicators, such as employment possibilities and income opportunities; and aesthetic, political and spiritual indicators, such as the quantity and quality of artistic offerings, the stability of political systems, the provision of safety and security measures, and the diversity of religious and spiritual possibilities. While some of these indicators will be difficult to formulate, because they are much more qualitative than quantitative, and therefore less susceptible to concrete forms of measurement, they must be included in the final set of indicators if wealth in the cultural sense is to be understood and measured effectively (see, for example, Bennett, Mercer, and Toffler 1967).

The development of this set of comprehensive cultural indicators will require a great deal of collaboration among policy-makers, planners, statisticians, and scholars from a variety of fields. It will also require a great deal of cooperation on the part of the United Nations, the World Bank, the International Monetary Fund, the World Trade Organization, the Organization for Economic

Cooperation and Development, the World Economic Forum, UNESCO and other such institutions, since they play the pivotal role in the creation and use of indicators throughout the world. Indeed, the role of UNESCO could be paramount in this, given that it is the principal cultural organization in the world. Not only is it involved in monitoring cultural trends and developments on a regular basis, but it is also in an ideal position to bring together the multidisciplinary teams that are required to ensure that the proposed set of indicators is developed effectively.

The development of these indicators could prove timely in creating new understandings and measures of wealth, intimately connected to securing quality of life for people and countries in every part of the world. (There are precedents in, for instance, the efforts by the Canadian Policy Research Networks to develop a "quality of life index," as described by Goar.) This is imperative if people are to experience happiness, fulfilment and security in their lives, and if humanity is to be successful in reducing the demands it makes on scarce resources. Otherwise, the environmental crisis will broaden, deepen, and intensify, the division of the world into two unequal parts will become more pronounced, and disharmony rather than harmony will characterize people's lives and the world system. This will exacerbate even further the gap between rich and poor countries, and between rich and poor people, aggravating a situation that is already too close to the breaking point.

A New Corporate Ideology

In view of the fact that corporations wield an enormous amount of power and influence in the world, a new corporate ideology is imperative.

In the economic age, corporations are expected to maximize their profits and compete as vigorously as possible, because doing so satisfies the dictates of the economic ideology and economic age most effectively. The justification that is usually given is that this yields the best possible situation for producers, consumers, the economy, and society as a whole. Not coincidentally, it also yields the best possible situation for corporations, corporate executives, and shareholders, since it makes it possible for them to earn high rates of return on their efforts and investments, and look forward to even higher rates of return in the future. These convictions contribute substantially to the prevailing corporate ideology or "corporate culture," as it is often called today.

In recent years, however, vigorous attacks have been launched against this prevailing ideology, as well as against corporations more generally. These attacks have been accompanied by vigorous critiques of "corporate capitalism" on the grounds that it often results in monopoly rather than competition, as well as sweatshops, branding, outsourcing, labour exploitation, and exorbitant incomes for executives. While these developments have created major problems for corporations, what sustains the corporate ideology and makes it so powerful is the fact that it is substantiated by more than two hundred years' worth of economic theory and practice, the support of the world's most powerful national and international institutions, and the full force of the world system. It is this situation, far more than the greed of individuals, that explains why the existing corporate ideology is perpetuated. This situation will not change until a new corporate ideology is created.

The key to creating this new corporate ideology lies in crossing the threshold from the economic age to a cultural age. In a cultural age, corporations would serve human, social and environmental functions, as well as economic ones. Clearly, corporations will always be needed to produce the goods and services that are required to satisfy people's needs, fuel economic growth, stimulate consumption and investment activity, and power industrial and technological development. However, in a cultural age they would also be expected to play a major cultural role, through a careful balancing of commercial and cultural objectives, especially in the communities, cities, regions, and countries in which they function. Some will argue that it is impossible to develop this new corporate ideology because corporations are too deeply immersed in the present world system to alter their behaviour to any great extent. Despite this, it is clear that profound changes are required if corporations want to function effectively in the world of the future. They could well profit from Machiavelli's sage advice to rulers, nearly five hundred years ago: that it is in their best interests to attend to people's needs because this will redound to their advantage in the long run. Corporations and corporate executives have a great deal to gain from improving the quality of life in communities, cities, regions, countries, and the world as a whole.

A great deal of emphasis will have to be placed on corporate cultural responsibility if this is to be achieved. This will require three basic commitments on the part of corporations: taking realistic rather than excessive profits; increasing corporate giving well beyond its present level; and cooperating more effectively in commercial and industrial affairs.

Earning realistic rather than excessive profits is necessary to reduce the hostility aroused by profit maximization, corporate power, and unreasonable financial benefits for corporate executives. It is also necessary to focus attention on the need to invest in worthwhile causes and undertakings, such as reducing the debt loads of countries in sub-Saharan Africa, Asia, Latin America, the Caribbean, and the Middle East; conducting an all-out campaign to stamp out poverty, unemployment, hunger, and human suffering; redistributing surplus food, clothing, building supplies, and text books to needy families and countries; eliminating the exploitation of labour, especially child labour; curtailing human rights abuses, including all forms of gender exploitation; and promoting health care, medical research, and human longevity. Corporate commitment to these and other goals would ensure that corporations are fully engaged in the design, development and functioning of the world system of the future, rather than remaining aloof from it.

Corporations will also have to increase their giving quite substantially if they want to improve the communities, cities, regions, and countries in which they do business. As matters stand now most corporations devote only small proportions of their profits to these requirements. Despite this, there are examples of corporations that have recognized the short-term and long-term benefits that can be derived from making improvements in this area. In Britain, for example, from the late nineteenth century onwards the Cadbury company of Bournville went to great lengths to ensure that those who worked in its chocolate and cocoa factories experienced improvements in their working conditions and quality of life. In the United States similar efforts to improve people's lives and advance community interests have come from offshoots of many large corporations, including the Ford Foundation, the Rockefeller Foundation, the Eastman School of Music, and the Hershey High School for underprivileged children.

It would be a mistake to conclude that such corporate cultural responsibility is a thing of the past. During the past twenty years the Turner Broadcasting Corporation, for example, has contributed large amounts of money to the United Nations to improve conditions for the poorest people and countries of the world, as well as to prevent the spread of HIV/AIDS and other debilitating diseases. The Bill and Melinda Gates Foundation and the Microsoft Corporation have contributed millions of dollars to improving literacy rates, immunizing populations against diseases, and transferring computer and library skills to countries in the "developing world." These examples serve as a clarion call to corporations in every part of the world to increase their financial commitments to levels that are consistent with human, environmental and cultural needs, and not merely their own commercial and financial interests.

The final requirement for the creation of a new corporate ideology is the promotion of cooperation rather than competition. This does not mean that corporate competition would cease in a cultural age. There will always be a need for corporations to compete in order to drive commercial and industrial development, create new inventions, innovations, and technologies, fuel capital accumulation, and increase sales, income, and market share. Yet this would not be the only mode of corporate behaviour in a cultural age, especially as competition itself often leads to monopoly rather than sustained competition. Cooperation would play a much more important role in corporate behaviour. Corporations would spend a great deal more time working with employees, customers, consumers, and other corporations to evolve the decision-making processes and planning structures needed to create a more equitable, viable and secure world.

Without a new corporate ideology, corporations may well be in for a very rough ride in the future. While their prospects are reasonable at present, their long-term prospects are far less favourable. Rapid rates of technological change, escalating terrorist attacks, anti-globalization protests, outrage over fraudulent corporate accounting procedures and investment practices, and growing scepticism over corporate motives and objectives will probably cause many more bankruptcies, mergers, downsizing exercises, and assaults on corporations, producing a great deal more instability as well as more unemployment. This could reduce consumers' incomes and thus the funds necessary to purchase corporate products. This situation could be aggravated by adverse reactions from civil society and consumers' associations. In contrast, a new corporate ideology would make it possible to improve the outlook for corporations.

A New Political System

It is impossible to deal with the most pressing priorities for a cultural age without dealing with the need for profound political changes. During the past sixty years governments have become so immersed in economic affairs that their principal role is now economic rather than political. Consistent with the prevailing economic ideology and the basic tenets of the economic age, governments believe that immersion in economic affairs is the key to everything: increases in wealth, income and standards of living; the generation of consumption, investment and employment activity; improvements in education and health care; breakthroughs in transportation and technology; advances in the arts and sciences; and the enhancement of human welfare and environmental well-being.

This conviction has its origins in the "political economy" of the classical and neoclassical economists, although it was not until after the Keynesian "revolution" that it became commonplace throughout the world. Since the 1940s, governments have been expected to play a forceful economic role in society by controlling monetary and fiscal policy, stimulating business and industry, promoting economic growth, regulating business cycles, managing debts, deficits, and surpluses, administering complex tax systems, and expending public funds to boost the level of aggregate demand. While this has done a great deal to increase economic growth, it is not without its problems.

In the first place, it has made it impossible for governments to deal effectively with the two most pressing problems of modern times: the environmental crisis; and the need to achieve an effective balance between the material and non-material dimensions of development. Indeed, these problems are generally deemed to stand outside the realm of economics altogether.

In the second place, it has made it difficult for governments to act objectively, impartially, and in the public interest. It is impossible for governments to get deeply immersed in one sector of society, in this case the economy, without impairing their capacity to deal equitably with all sectors of society and society as a whole. The effect is that the tail is forever wagging the dog. The most obvious example of this is the way in which corporations have become so powerful and pervasive that they are often able to dictate to governments what is in the best interests of citizens and society. This makes it possible for corporations to subordinate political interests to their will, often through the creation of large industrial zones and free trade areas that are exempt from governmental regulation and the rule of law. This has caused an erosion of political power, and consequently also a loss of interest in politics and the political process on the part of citizens and community groups.

Governments will have to extricate themselves from this situation if they are to act in the public interest, and deal with pressing local, regional, national and international problems and issues. First and foremost, they will need to re-establish their ability to play a political role in society. In order to do this they will have to assert control over corporations and put themselves in a much stronger financial position than they are today. This will be exceedingly difficult to achieve, because many governments have mishandled the policies prescribed by economists, particularly Keynesian economists. Keynes himself advocated creating surpluses in times of prosperity, in order to have funds available to be spent on public works and other activities in times of recession, but instead many governments have increased their deficits in good times in their efforts to accelerate economic growth and satisfy the desires of consumers. Not coincidentally, increasing debt loads have increased the dependence of governments on corporations, as significant proportions of government income in many countries are siphoned off to service debts.

This is not to say that governments should abandon their commitments to developing strong economies and dealing with fundamental economic problems, but governments will have to deal with these problems in a totally new way, redistributing income and wealth more fairly, holding corporations accountable for their financial actions and environmental shortcomings, and situating economics properly within the broader cultural context.

Governments will have to use all the policy tools and techniques at their disposal if they are to achieve this. Legislation and regulation will be necessary to impose full control on corporations and to return the political process to citizens, community groups, and other actors in the public realm. Taxation will be necessary to restore the financial health of governments and strengthen their capacity to address key public issues. While care must be taken not to dampen economic growth or stifle consumption, investment or entrepreneurial activity, a great deal can be achieved through progressive taxation. A new political system would make it possible for governments to achieve balance and harmony between all sectors and segments of society, and to deal equitably and impartially with all citizens and community groups.

Taking a cultural approach to the political process is the key to this new system. When culture is visualized and dealt with in holistic terms, the principal responsibility of governments is to develop culture in general, and cultures in particular, in the all-encompassing sense. There is an intimate connection between culture and politics here, since both are concerned with "the whole," and the need to achieve balanced, harmonious, synergistic and sustainable relationships between the parts and the whole. Governments, above all, possess the authority and the responsibility to deal with all sectors of society on a sustained and systematic basis. All other institutions and groups deal only with specific parts of the whole.

A new political reality is unfolding in the world and it would be foolhardy not to admit it. Vast and complex cultural systems are emerging in every part of the world that are constantly changing and evolving as changes take place in their various parts. While some of these changes can be foreseen, many occur with little or no warning and have devastating effects on cultural systems as wholes through interactions between the parts. Examples include: sudden and unexpected catastrophes such as floods, hurricanes and forest fires; the changes now taking place in many countries in relations between and within the genders, which were not predicted in the days when marriage was generally assumed to be between a man and a woman, and for life; the spread of HIV/AIDS, SARS, mad cow disease, and other infections; and the recent eruption of terrorist attacks in the United States, Britain, Spain, and elsewhere. Governments are thus compelled to deal with abrupt, erratic and often unpredictable changes in cultural systems.

It is no longer a case of developing local, regional and national economies, and then assuming that everything will work out for the best. Rather, it is a case of continuously monitoring and guiding complex cultural systems, and ensuring that they are managed effectively. In order to do this, governments will have to know much more about how complex cultural systems actually function, as well as how changes in their parts interact and affect the systems as wholes. This is why it is necessary to take a cultural rather than economic approach to the political process. Parliaments, cabinets, and caucuses will have to devote much more time to discussing and analyzing the development of culture and cultures in breadth and depth. Ministries of cultural development will have to replace ministries of economic development as the key ministries in government. Cultural models will have to replace economic models as the main devices for government planning and decision-making, and cultural development and policy will have to be accorded the highest priority in the political process. The aim should always be to evolve political policies and practices that include all individuals, institutions, and sectors of society in decision-making, improve the lot of all citizens and community groups, and make it possible for people to live in harmony with the natural environment, each other, other countries, other cultures, other species, and past, present and future generations.

Ministries of cultural development, as well as specially designed cultural agencies at arm's length from government and the political process, will have particularly important roles to play. They will have to be extremely active inside and outside government. Inside government, they will have to act as integrating mechanisms and coordinating vehicles for all departments and agencies, winning respect for culture's most elevated principles, values, and ideals. They will also have to be involved in promoting understanding of the way in which culture can act as a coalescing force, and as a conceptual framework for public policy- and decision-making. Outside government, they will have to become extremely active in sowing the seeds of cultural development in communities, cities, regions, and society as a whole, broadening and deepening participation in the political process, expanding understanding of the vital role that culture can play, and creating a climate conducive to a healthy and vigorous cultural life. Such ministries and agencies will have to possess the powers, and the funding, to execute these responsibilities efficiently, effectively, and in a trustworthy manner. History has shown that such responsibilities are best carried out when they are consistent with the principles of access, participation, equality, democratization, and decentralization.

However, as critics have repeatedly warned, permanent solutions will not be forthcoming without a strong commitment to freedom, independence, and democracy. In particular, when it comes to the political process and its impact on the development of culture, this commitment will require the creation and maintenance of a large and viable private sector, capable of formulating and implementing programmes, initiating activities, providing funds, acting as an effective counterpoise to government, and taking risks.

A Cultural Approach to Citizenship

The signing of the Universal Declaration of Human Rights in 1948 signalled the start of an era in which human rights have become a major political issue. However, it is sometimes forgotten that the Declaration goes beyond the traditional list of civil and political rights, to encompass social and cultural rights as well. Thus, Article 22 of the Declaration asserts that:

> Everyone, as a member of society, has the right to social security and is entitled
> to realization, through national effort and international cooperation, and in
> accordance with the organization and resources of each state, of the economic, social,
> and cultural rights indispensable for his dignity and the free development of his
> personality.

Article 27 asserts that:

> Everyone has the right freely to participate in the cultural life of the community, to
> enjoy the arts, and to share in scientific advancement and its benefits.

While focusing time and attention on human rights has accomplished a great deal over the past sixty years, there is an urgent need to devote time and attention to people's responsibilities, since failure to do so creates a one-sided and distorted view of citizenship. On the one hand, there is what people have a reasonable right to receive from society. On the other hand, there is what people must give in order to receive something in return. It is only when these two requirements are in balance that it is possible to claim that all the requirements of citizenship have been addressed.

Clearly, every person has numerous responsibilities to execute if they want to enjoy certain rights in return. Included among these responsibilities are acquisition of the skills, tools, and techniques that are needed to function effectively in society; participation in the cultural development of the community, the region, and the nation; concern for the plight of people who are less fortunate than oneself; sharing income, wealth, and resources realistically and fairly; recognition of the needs, rights, freedoms, values, and worldviews of others; abstinence from violence and terrorism; and concern for the natural environment, other species, other ethnic groups, and past, present and future generations. It is thus essential to develop a Universal Declaration of Human Rights and Responsibilities.

This has become steadily more apparent as increasing numbers of citizens have become involved in protest movements aimed at addressing responsibilities as well as rights. Although citizens' involvement in these movements can be disruptive and does not always produce concrete results, it makes a significant contribution to social progress nevertheless. There are numerous examples where citizens' coalitions have altered age-old political and bureaucratic practices, confronted corporate and wealthy elites, and challenged international institutions. It is amazing what can be accomplished when citizens work together for the common good of their fellow citizens, as well as the needs and concerns of society as a whole. Augustin Girard recognized how essential this is when he wrote (p. 143) that "cultural development is both the ultimate aim of political action and also the means of giving every individual a sense of his responsibility in the common work of mankind."

It is interesting to note in this regard that concerted attempts have been made in recent years to develop "character education" and "character communities," predicated on the collective as well as the personal, the altruistic as well as the egoistic, the other as well as the self, and responsibilities as well as rights. Concerned about the perceived rise in violence, vandalism, and destructiveness in communities and schools, proponents of character education and character communities put a great deal of emphasis on caring, sharing, self-discipline, fairness, honesty, integrity, equality, justice, respect, commitment, and empathy.

They are helping to pave the way for the development of a secular ethics that will be capable of complementing and enriching religious ethics.

Such a secular ethics would answer the call by the World Commission on Culture and Development (pp. 33–51) for "a global ethics," focused on human rights and responsibilities; democracy and the elements of civil society; the protection of minorities; commitment to peaceful conflict-resolution and fair negotiation; and equity within and between generations. While the Commission recognized that this global ethics would constitute the minimum requirements of citizenship and government, it felt that ample room should be left for political creativity, social imagination, and cultural pluralism. This is imperative if a global ethics is not to become oppressive, overbearing or coercive.

A Breakthrough in Education

At present, very few educational institutions, particularly at the elementary and secondary levels, provide opportunities for people to learn about culture in general and their own cultures in particular. This means that people have to turn instead to personal study, exploration, discovery, general observation, and a variety of learning materials and possibilities. Yet the lack of formal education in the basic rudiments of culture is a cause for concern. If people are to function effectively in the specific cultures in which they live, and if many of the tensions and conflicts that exist throughout the world are to be reduced or overcome, much more will need to be known about the diverse cultures of humankind. The problem is compounded by the fact that it is difficult to learn about culture in the holistic sense when education is broken down into specialized disciplines. In addition, there are barriers to transcending one's cultural conditioning in order to understand other cultures. As the Mexican futurologist Antonio Alonso Concheiro has written (in Masini 1991, Vol. 2, p. 65):

> we generally assume that cultures are simply different modes of adaptation to nature, different codes for the same fundamental purposes . . . We seldom recognize that in this manner we are only studying and classifying cultures which we invent through our own cultural framework, and not the cultures themselves. In other words, we generally reach for and obtain only ethnocentric visions of other cultures.

Despite the difficulties involved in teaching and learning about culture and cultures in the holistic sense, no greater mistake could be made than to abandon the attempt. Although people may never get to know and understand their own culture, or the cultures of others, in some ultimate, metaphysical sense, the very fact that they make the effort enhances the prospects for peace, harmony, tolerance, appreciation and respect throughout the world.

An ideal cultural education would contain four key ingredients: learning about culture in general; learning about one's own culture in particular; learning about the cultures of others; and learning to live a creative, constructive and fulfilling cultural life.

Fortunately, there are now many educational materials available to assist in learning about culture in general, as well as a rapidly expanding array of articles, reports, and other publications dealing with every specific culture in the world. The emphasis should be on broadening and deepening understanding of the various parts of one's own culture, as well as on how these parts are organized and orchestrated to form a whole. This would require a great deal more emphasis than at present on integrated, holistic and horizontal approaches to education.

Yet, clearly, everybody is involved in many different cultures simultaneously, since they are involved in local, regional and national cultures, and may also possess a variety of ethnic origins and cultural backgrounds.

Learning about the cultures of others would be equally important, but, unfortunately, this is the most neglected area of education in every part of the world. Not only is the education of most people limited to their own culture, there are very few opportunities to learn about the cultures of others. The upshot of this is the rise in violence, terrorism, racism, and xenophobia throughout the world, as fear, misunderstanding, and mistrust increase, and the potential for cultural conflict and confrontation is heightened. It is therefore essential to ensure that people's education in this vital domain of human life is broadened and deepened as much as possible. There are many organizations that provide valuable services and learning opportunities in this regard, including UNESCO and its regional centres, as well as the Council of Europe, the Maison des Cultures du Monde, Culturelink, the Transnational Network for Appropriate/Alternative Technologies (Tranet), the Intercultural Institute of Montreal, the Zentrum für Kulturforschung, the Cultural Information and Research Centres Liaison in Europe (Circle), CultureGrams, the Austrian Cultural Documentation Centre and International Archives for Cultural Analysis, and Greenwood Publishing.

The world of the future will be characterized by a great deal more interaction and mixing among its diverse peoples and cultures. Not only will this help people to become aware of the strengths and the shortcomings of their own cultures, it will also increase respect for the cultures of others and the reality of cultural differences. This development is already being foreshadowed, as, for example, in the discussions, exhibitions, and arts events at the First Universal Forum of Cultures in Barcelona in 2004.

The ideal cultural education concerns, above all, learning to live a creative, constructive and fulfilling cultural life. That will require skills and understanding that extend well beyond what is needed to function effectively in the economy, to include the capacity to develop one's own identity, and to make a contribution to those aspects of cultural life that require improvement; respect for other people, countries, ethnic groups, cultures, and species, and the natural environment; and development of the sensitivities that are required for responsible citizenship. There is much to be learned from the way in which cultures have developed that is relevant to this goal. Just as the challenge in developing cultures is to develop all their parts, and achieve balance among them, so the challenge in personal development is to develop all the human faculties and achieve harmony among them. If, as Ruth Benedict contended, cultures are "personalities writ large," then people are "cultures writ small." Here lies the secret of leading a creative, constructive and fulfilling cultural life. It is culture, not economics, that provides the wherewithal to knit all the diverse parts of people's lives together to form a coherent whole. It does so by placing the priority on the whole, as well as the need to achieve synergistic and sustainable relationships between the parts and the whole. This is why people in the cultural field are so concerned with the education of "the whole person," in order to help people to live integrated lives and realize their full potential.

It is difficult to see how education of "the whole person" can be attended to effectively without a comprehensive and integrated education in the arts. As Walter Pitman argues in his book *Learning the Arts in an Age of Uncertainty* (1998), arts education provides the key to developing all the various facets of the human personality in concert by focusing attention on the development of the cognitive and affective abilities of the individual. Through comprehensive and integrated education in the arts, people learn to develop the creative capabilities that are needed to function effectively in society, as well as to apply their creative capabilities to problem-solving and all the various challenges they encounter in life. This in turn is not possible without life-long learning, or education for life, beginning in the earliest years of childhood, strongly influenced by the family, and deeply rooted in the educational system. It is education filled with the joys and rewards of creativity and discovery, and fuelled by the desire to make improvements in all domains of life.

It is culture that best facilitates this process, because culture provides the breadth of vision and the depth of understanding needed to illuminate a clear and viable path to the future. In the final analysis, it is through culture in general and cultural education in particular that vast new vistas and fertile avenues are opened up for exploration and discovery, bringing people into contact with the finest accomplishments of all the different cultures of the world and the very best that humanity has to offer. Cultural education is far more than a vocation, it is a way of life.

Liveable and Sustainable Cities

Of all the changes taking place in the world today, none is more evident than the growth of cities, in size, scope, density, and complexity, in every part of the planet. More and more people are looking to cities to solve their problems, and to provide higher standards of living, greater safety and security, economic and ecological sustainability, and improvements in the quality of life. If cities lack the prerequisites that are needed for happy, healthy and secure living, no amount of development at the regional, national or international level will make up the difference.

With the growth of cities have come attempts to determine what makes cities "liveable," and prevents them from becoming degrading and depressing. One factor is the provision of stimulating work and strong social programmes. Another is the maintenance and enhancement of urban infrastructure, from educational institutions and libraries to health services, effective transit systems, a variety of housing styles and types, and ample and attractive public spaces. To this list should be added the diversity of artistic, athletic, culinary, commercial and shopping opportunities that cities offer at their best, as well as the features that vary from city to city, such as historical sites, open-air markets, and captivating ways to idle away leisure time.

The arts have a crucial role to play in enhancing the urban environment. They provide fulfilment and happiness to millions of city dwellers, through art galleries and museums, theatre and dance companies, orchestras and art centres, concerts and poetry readings. They contribute to the attractiveness of cities, not only through the activities of professional organizations but also through community arts centres and festivals, murals, buskers, landscaping, and the artistic expressions of young people and children. They contribute to social cohesion by engaging large numbers of people in the artistic process, both as participants and as members of audiences. They contribute to the economies of cities by generating investment and expenditure on facilities, hotels, restaurants, tickets, clothing, transport, and tourism, as well as by attracting businesses and skilled workers. They also make an important contribution to cross-cultural communication by bringing people together in peaceful rather than violent ways, making it possible for them to communicate effectively across ethnic and linguistic divides. This will be increasingly important in cities where populations are becoming more diverse and multiethnic.

The arts also contribute to the liveability of cities through the creative energy and synergy that they inject into all aspects and dimensions of city life. By creating many of the concepts, styles, and techniques that are needed to institute change, artists and arts organizations help to pave the way for many other types of development. It is not surprising that many planners, policy-makers, and researchers are focusing on the role that "the creative industries" play in urban development by producing "clustering effects" and "convergent capabilities" that link different sectors of cities together. Equally important is the contribution that the arts can make to the revitalization of cities. In recent years dynamic creative activities have injected new life into cities, after years of neglect, often by stimulating concentrations of artistic resources in downtown cores or other key locations. Inspired by corporate executives, arts administrators, planners, educators, and other citizens, such districts do a great deal to rejuvenate cities that are dying from the inside out.

Given all these contributions, the role of the arts must be seen in a new light. Rather than being the icing on the cake of urban living, the arts should be seen as the centrepieces that are needed to create liveable cities. Governments and corporations need to recognize this and do something concrete about it. Too often, they are anxious to squeeze all the economic and tourist potential out of the arts without providing a great deal in return.

Creating liveable cities should go a long way towards creating sustainable cities, but much more will be required. Water supplies will have to be more dependable and reliable, as well as free from contaminants and imperfections. Air quality will have to be substantially improved. Gridlock will have to be overcome, and transit systems will have to be upgraded and enhanced. Waste disposal and urban sprawl will have to be curtailed. Streets and neighbourhoods will have to be safe to walk in, day and night, and free from sexual predators. Programmes will have to be created to help immigrants and other newcomers to become fully integrated into urban life. Much more attention will have to be given to emergency preparedness, affordable housing, safety and security, crumbling infrastructure, ecological management, crime prevention, and programmes for young people. Policies will have to be predicated on taking a holistic and egalitarian approach to municipal planning and decision-making, in order to build cities that are comprehensive and creative rather than segmented and imitative. The focus should be on providing stores, workplaces, and schools that are close at hand rather than miles away, so that people can walk to them rather than drive, and enjoy the urban experience rather than merely tolerate it. In her many writings on the "death and life" of cities, the late Jane Jacobs emphasized the need to provide a balanced and diversified array of amenities at the neighbourhood or local level, so that cities can become liveable and sustainable.

Unfortunately, the approach that has often been taken to municipal planning and decision-making in the past has been piecemeal and exclusive, rather than systematic or inclusive. Yet, like cultures, cities are cultural wholes composed of many diverse and interdependent parts. Not only do these parts vary greatly from one another, but they also vary greatly in the way they are combined to form wholes. These parts must be successfully integrated into the whole, and harmonious relationships must be established between and among them, if cities are to function effectively. Here culture enters into urban development in a very different way than other factors do. Culture is the cement that binds the parts together to form the whole. This is what makes it possible to talk about the "culture of cities" and mean something profound and fundamental by the phrase. It is also what makes culture *the* most important factor in urban development. Without culture in general and cultural cohesiveness in particular, cities are merely smorgasbords of disconnected and unrelated parts, rather than integrated, coherent, dynamic and organic wholes.

Radical change will also be needed in the ways in which cities are financed. Without the ability to raise revenues, address pressing problems, and negotiate effectively with other levels of government, municipal governments will not be able to deal effectively with environmental degeneration, gridlock, declining medical facilities, deteriorating infrastructure, out-of-date social programmes, inadequate transit systems, insufficient housing, or the effects of homelessness, unemployment, and poverty. The short-term solution requires making it possible for municipal governments to increase their revenues, for example through increased property taxes, gasoline taxes, user fees on publicly owned and operated facilities, lotteries, licensing charges for garbage collection and other services, cost-sharing arrangements with other levels of government, and taxes on hotels, restaurants, and other commercial establishments that profit greatly from municipal development but pay little of the cost of providing services. The experience with these types of taxes in the United States and many European countries suggests that when municipal governments possess the authority to impose taxes of this type everyone benefits. In the long term, however, what will be required is a change in constitutional arrangements, and a redistribution of powers among national, regional, and municipal governments. The beneficiaries of these changes will be people, who, as Charles Landry has pointed out, are the most valuable and precious resources of any city. Seen from this perspective, every individual and every institution has a crucial contribution to make to the development and enrichment of cities.

A United World

The world is deeply divided today along economic, political, military, religious, technological, and cultural lines, but the cultural divisions are the most crucial. At least this is the opinion of the US political scientist Samuel P. Huntington (1993, p. 23):

> World politics is entering a new phase, and intellectuals have not hesitated to proliferate visions of what it will be—the end of history, the return of traditional rivalries between nation states, and the decline of the nation state from the conflicting pulls of tribalism and globalism, among others. Each of these visions catches aspects of the emerging reality. Yet they all miss a crucial, indeed a central, aspect of what global politics is likely to be in the coming years. It is my hypothesis that the fundamental source of conflict in this new world will not be primarily

ideological or primarily economic. The great divisions among humankind and the dominating source of conflict will be cultural. Nation states will remain the most powerful actors in world affairs, but the principal conflicts of global politics will occur between nations and groups of different civilizations. The clash of civilizations will dominate global politics. The fault lines between civilizations will be the battle lines of the future.

Huntington subscribes here to the understanding of cultures and civilizations as "total ways of life." It is his view that it is impossible to understand many of the most difficult problems confronting the world today, such as in Afghanistan, Iraq, Israel and Palestine, or the Islamic world in general, without having recourse to broader and deeper notions of culture. While countless economic, political, and military factors are involved, particularly ownership of land and other resources, the assertion of military might, access to production, distribution, and consumption opportunities, and control of technology, resources, and technological capabilities, these factors do not begin to account for the numerous tensions and conflicts in the world.

Cultures can affect people, countries, and the world in positive and negative ways as indicated earlier. On the one hand, they can be sources of fulfilment and happiness, highlighting all that is most desirable and worthwhile in the world. On the other hand, they can be sources of brutality and oppression, bringing to the fore all that is most troublesome and despicable. This makes it imperative, as noted previously, to be ever watchful and mindful of the various uses and abuses of culture, as well as develop safeguards to ensure that these human collectivities are used in constructive rather than destructive ways. In order to do this, it is essential to build strong bonds among the diverse cultures and peoples of the world. In the words of Verner Bickley and John Philip Puthenparampil (p. 8):

> If culture, fundamentally, is the "depth dimension" of a people or nation, then the ideal of intercultural transactions is seen as the effectuation of an "interior bond" between peoples, which has a greater value and significance than other kinds of relationships, of a political or economic nature only. Because culture, basically, is value- and worldview-oriented, intercultural transactions are capable of performing a critical and educative function. . . . Cultural interchanges bring the insights and perspectives of the participating cultures to one another, and thus help to modify narrow monocultural views to produce alternative and more flexible approaches and responses to human problems.

The arts and education have a vital role to play here. Music, drama, painting, literature, dance, philosophy, ethics, and learning expose the real heart, soul, and spirit of countries and cultures. Performances by African dance troupes, Asian acrobatic groups, Latin American pop stars, and European musical ensembles have captivated large audiences across the world. Think, for example, of how the song "Amazing Grace" has touched imaginations beyond the confines of religious services, because its message that spirituality can "save a poor wretch like me" has touched a nerve.

It is not difficult to visualize the kind of world that could result from building strong bonds between countries, cultures, and peoples, particularly those that have little or no contact with each other at present. Humanity should not rest until people in North America, Europe, Australia, New Zealand, and Japan have much more knowledge and understanding of the worldviews, values, and traditions of people in Asia, Latin America, sub-Saharan Africa, and the Middle East, and vice versa. Intimate connections at "cultural contact points" are imperative if the many tensions throughout the world are to be lessened or overcome.

It is also essential to get at the root causes of tensions, most of which have to do with the fact that the world is divided into two unequal parts, and income, wealth, resources, and power are not shared equally. If problems as complex and debilitating as this are to be overcome in the future, it will be necessary to create a world characterized by justice, equality, and opportunity for all people and all countries. When culture is perceived and defined in holistic terms, the emphasis is on unity and synthesis rather than division and separation, so the potential exists within culture to create the conditions for a united world. What is needed, now more than ever, is the public and professional will to create a united world in which economic criteria such as gross domestic product would no longer be used to separate countries, and less and less attention is paid to the stereotyping that results from labelling certain countries and cultures as backward or underdeveloped.

There are numerous examples in business, industry, medicine, the arts, the sciences, education, politics, and the mass media where cooperation among individuals, institutions, countries, cultures, and civilizations has produced results that could not have been realized in any other way. Such results thrive on the creative energy and synergy that derives from bringing people together, even where they have vastly different worldviews and ideas. Paul J. Braisted summed it all up as long ago as 1944 (p. 28):

> Cultural cooperation is described as the way in which the world's peoples can work together, voluntarily, constructively and to mutual advantage, in building a progressive, orderly and more kindly society.

As we have seen in this chapter, many new commitments will be needed if cultural cooperation is to be achieved. Most of these commitments will require dramatic changes in attitudes and behaviour on the part of the richer, more powerful and more privileged nations of the world. Until those who possess and control income, investment, employment, capital, technology, and resources commit themselves to cultural cooperation and sharing, not as a vague moral duty but as a fundamental necessity, humanity will be saddled with a world system that is unjust, unfair, and inimical to global harmony and world peace. As Braisted and his co-authors later emphasized (1972, p. 14):

> Mankind is faced with problems which, if not dealt with, could in a very few years develop into crises worldwide in scope. Interdependence is the reality; worldwide problems the prospect; and worldwide cooperation the only solution.

With this plea for worldwide cooperation and sharing, our discussion of the priorities that would be essential for a cultural age is complete.

9
Flourishing of a Cultural Age

Culture is like a tree, a fabulous tree, in which each branch is formed differently from its neighbour, each flower has its own colour and fragrance, each fruit its special sweetness. This wealth and abundance has developed naturally. Each culture and each people bears its individual stamp, but the branches are all shoots of the same trunk and are fed by the same sap. If the branches are cut and detached from the trunk, the flowers wither. We are all members of the great society of mankind; our national cultures are part of the culture of the whole world, which we must continue building up.—Kaj Birket-Smith (1965), p. v

If a cultural age is to flourish in the future, a new vision will be essential. This vision must be capable of producing a transformation in the world system, the human condition, and the ways in which people interact with each other, as well as with the natural environment and other species.

The key to realizing this vision lies in a renaissance, not revolution or general evolution. General evolution is not possible because the current economic age is based on foundations that are not compatible with environmental, human and global well-being, or with coming to grips with the world's most difficult, demanding and debilitating problems. Revolution is not possible because it is too frightening to contemplate, particularly in view of the fact that more and more nations possess biological, chemical and nuclear capabilities that are capable of causing mass destruction. This leaves a renaissance as the only viable alternative. This renaissance should be so bold in design and daring in execution that it makes it possible for people, cities, and countries in every part of the world to look to the future with hope and enthusiasm, rather than pessimism and anxiety.

A Cultural Renaissance

In thinking about the type of renaissance that is most needed for the future, it is helpful to look back at the past. The cultural renaissance that occurred in Italy in the fourteenth and fifteenth centuries, and fanned out to encompass much of the rest of Europe, and other parts of the world, in the sixteenth, seventeenth, and eighteenth centuries was a renaissance in perception. It changed the way people looked at the world, and therefore how they interpreted the world, acted in the world, and valued things in the world. Viewing the world, not from a two-dimensional and religious perspective, but from a three-dimensional and aesthetic, humanistic perspective, opened the doors to a broader, deeper and more fundamental way of looking at life, society, and the human condition. Something very similar is needed today. Rather than viewing the world from the specialized, partial and partisan perspective of the present economic age, a holistic, comprehensive and egalitarian perspective will be appropriate to a cultural age. It will allow people to focus attention on the whole, on wholes within the whole, and on the need to achieve balanced and equitable relationships between the parts and the whole.

Eventually everything was affected by the cultural renaissance that began in Italy: economic and social life, religion, the arts, the sciences, the humanities, education, community development, rural affairs, and government (see, for example, Burke 1999). There was a blossoming of creativity in all these and other fields, as well as in the interconnections and interrelationships between them, and this has had profound effects on humanity ever since. Many of the most dynamic and strategic developments took place in cities—Florence, Milan, Venice, Pisa, Antwerp, Bruges, Ghent—a fact that should be borne in mind when considering the cultural renaissance needed for the future.

The arts played a crucial role too, by lifting people out of the medieval doldrums, establishing loftier goals and ideals, and providing the new ways of seeing required to produce developments in other areas of life, particularly the sciences. According to W. R. Clement (p. 105):

> one of the key triggers of the Renaissance was the discovery of perspective, or
> paintings and drawings representing three static dimensions. By the early seventeenth
> century the idea of perspective had become the metaphor for that period we call the
> Renaissance. . . . [T]he accessibility of perspective to an ever increasing part of the

population resulted in an intellectual ferment and commitment to exploration of the physical and natural world never before equalled. This metaphorical value served not only the painters of northern Italy, but it travelled well. The metaphor worked for the German artist Dürer, as well as the English poet Henry Vaughn, and supported accessibility to philosophers like Niccolo Machiavelli, Dante Alighieri, Erasmus, and Bruno. The *idea of perspective* was driving the age. In 1610 Galileo called his new invention for viewing the heavens a *perspicillium*. The founder of the academy with which Galileo was affiliated, Prince Cesi, was a more practical Renaissance man—he called it a *telescopium* (distance viewer).

In the early years, seminal contributions to this earlier cultural renaissance were made by painters, sculptors, writers, architects, and composers. Their work in turn spawned a constellation of contributions from later generations of artists who followed in their footsteps. Perhaps artists might make similar contributions to the cultural renaissance that is needed today. It is not coincidental that artists are regarded by some as the antennae of humanity, for they create many of the contexts, styles, and techniques that are needed to make improvements in other areas of life by providing the inspiration and insights to propel people and countries to higher and higher levels of accomplishment. According to Robert Pilon (p. A-24):

> The social purpose of every creative work is to move us, to touch us, to teach us, to make us think, laugh and cry; to lead us to expand our horizons, to question established truths; to open our minds, introduce us to new values, teach us new realities; to challenge the established order while helping society find a new consensus. No society has been able to survive and flourish in the past without recognizing the fundamental social role played by artistic creation, and without integrating into and supporting within it the development of culture. This will be ever more true of the future. A society without culture, without creation, without artists, is a society condemned to stagnation, to withdrawal; a society without soul, without dynamism, in a word, without the vitality that is the very essence of life.

Technology also played a crucial role in the cultural renaissance that began in Italy. Major innovations were needed to communicate the new ideas and methods, above all the invention of printing by Johannes Gutenberg and others in the fifteenth century (or rather, its reinvention, since block printing had been known in East Asia since the third century CE and in Egypt since the seventh century, while movable type had been developed in China more than three hundred years before Gutenberg). The introduction of movable-type printing in Europe made it possible to record, reproduce and diffuse information over long distances in relatively short periods. Printing helped to diffuse the ideas and works of the cultural renaissance from Italy to other parts of the world. A comparable innovation is revolutionizing the ways in which people today record, reproduce, and transmit information and ideas. The internet has the potential to link all members of the human family in ways that were barely even dreamed of in earlier periods. In particular, the internet dramatically reduces the amount of time and resources used in communication, which could have a significant impact on the environment in the long term. While books will always play an important role in communication, because they are durable, transportable, and adaptable to a variety of formats, the internet possesses even greater potential to revolutionize communication, despite the many problems associated with it.

Further, the internet has the potential to enable people in every part of the world to share information more fully, freely, equitably and broadly. Such sharing is imperative if humanity is to go fruitfully into the future. This hits home with striking clarity when consideration is given to the final reason why the earlier renaissance is relevant to the renaissance needed for the future: the need, in both cases, to unleash creativity in all fields of endeavour, as well as to learn from the past—by, as Marshall McLuhan put it, "looking in the rear-view mirror"—in order to unlock the secrets of the future. This makes it possible for people to see the shortcomings of their own period and their own culture, as well as the achievements and accomplishments of earlier periods of history. By reaching deep into the past, the earlier renaissance exposed a vast constellation of historical achievements in philosophy, mathematics, science, the arts, and social, economic and political affairs that were capable of providing springboards for future action. That is why, in 1855, the French historian Jules Michelet initiated the use of the word "renaissance" to describe what had happened: a rebirth of Greece and Rome, with valuable assistance from Muslims, in the Italy of the fifteenth century.

It is not necessary to go back to classical antiquity to uncover the insights and ideas that are most pertinent to the world of the future. However, it is necessary to see that a cornucopia of cultural achievements has been created in the past that is capable of providing an effective base for the cultural renaissance required for the future. We are referring, of course, to the cultural heritage of humankind, and the need to share it more liberally, fully, and equitably if a cultural age is to flourish.

The Cultural Heritage of Humankind

What stands out most clearly when the cultural heritage of humankind is considered in totality is its colossal size and universal character. The world's museums, art galleries, archives, and libraries, as well as people's homes, attics, and basements are filled with vivid reminders that there is hardly a country, group of people, community, region or culture, in any part of the world, that has not made a strong, lasting, and valuable contribution to it.

Take folk music, for example. Every country in the world possesses a vast reservoir of indigenous songs, dances, and musical compositions, commemorating births, deaths, weddings, and other special events, the joys and sorrows of life, and the mystery and vastness of the universe. This fact was brought to light in the early twentieth century when a number of European composers, such as Zoltán Kodály and Bela Bartók in Hungary, or Georges Enesco in Romania, undertook intensive studies of folk music in order to preserve it for posterity and use it in their own compositions. Since that time, interest in the world's wealth of folk music has grown rapidly, especially after UNESCO made a commitment to systematically collecting, preserving, protecting and recording it through its Collection of Traditional Music of the World. As a result of this initiative and others, it is now possible to listen to folk music from every country in the world. Thanks to the foresight of UNESCO and especially of Alain Daniélou, who initiated the Collection along with the International Music Council, authentic music from every region is being preserved for present and future generations.

To take another example, there is a rich array of diverse cuisines throughout the world (see Barer-Stein). Food plays an inextricable role in our daily lives, since, obviously, we cannot survive without it, but food is much more than a tool for survival. It is also a source of pleasure, comfort, and security, a symbol of hospitality and social status, and in most cultures it has ritual significance. What we select to eat, how we prepare it and serve it, and even how we eat it are all factors that have been deeply affected by specific cultures. The world's gastronomic legacy, which is local and regional as well as national and international in character, enriches the lives of billions of people throughout the world, and culinary masters such as Georges-Auguste Escoffier, Julia Childs, Emeril Lagassi or Wolfgang Puck have done much to bring its delights to the attention of the world.

While these two examples provide only infinitesimal glimpses of the colossal size of the cultural heritage of humankind, they underline its pervasiveness and its value as humankind's most precious resource. It includes, in addition to many other things, all the world's finest music, paintings, and literature; all of its most beloved architecture, cities, and historic sites; all the greatest achievements of the civilizations of the past, whether ancient, medieval or modern, and whether in Europe, Asia, Africa, the Americas or Oceania; all of the world's most significant advances in technology, economics, education, social affairs, politics, psychology, and science; and all of its greatest religious and spiritual teachings, its sacred texts, and its most profound philosophical ideas. It is little wonder that Jacob Burckhardt (as quoted by Karl J. Weintraub, pp. 117–18) called this unique resource "the thread in the labyrinth" or "the silent promise" that possesses the potential "to bring an objective interest to everything, to transform the entire past and present world into a spiritual possession." It is a spiritual possession that more and more people, countries, and cultures throughout the world must become familiar with if they want to find fulfilment and happiness in life.

However, the cultural heritage of humankind should not be seen as completed, or static: it is constantly growing and developing. Every day it receives countless contributions from every part of the world, and it is continuously being renewed and revitalized as new sources of knowledge are uncovered, and new materials and artefacts are brought to light. This makes it a living heritage, constantly in need of conservation and renewal if it is to serve humankind to best advantage. In recent years, the maintenance of this unique "heritage of hope" has become highly systematic and sophisticated, involving the work of a battery of skilled and talented curators, technicians, conservation specialists, and the like, as well as the efforts of UNESCO and numerous specialized international organizations. They have been instrumental in raising global awareness of the vital importance of the cultural heritage of humankind, and of the need to protect it whenever and wherever it is threatened. They have also saved Pagan, Angkor Wat and Angkor Thom, Abu Simbel, and many others among the world's most distinguished historic sites and monuments from destruction.

There are many reasons why the cultural heritage of humankind needs to be maintained, but also used more fully. In the first place, it is needed to help people, countries, and cultures in every part of the world to confront and come to grips with the transnational problems of modern times. None of these will be solved without the full use and sharing of the universal fund of knowledge, information, and wisdom that humankind has built up over the ages. It will not be possible, for example, for people to come to grips with the spread of greenhouse gases and toxic substances, or with floods, tornadoes, hurricanes or earthquakes, without sharing all that is known, and all that is still being discovered, about geography, geology and meteorology. Organizations in every part of the world will have to pool their resources, knowledge, and expertise to the utmost if they want to help to prevent such problems from spiralling out of control. Similarly, the world has a profuse legacy of medical and pharmaceutical acumen, including healing practices and procedures, methods of disease control and prevention, and effective approaches to health care and personal fitness. All of it needs to be much better known and used by the diverse peoples, countries, and cultures of the world. This is equally true of agricultural, industrial and commercial knowledge and technology, which could be used to much greater advantage than at present, especially in sub-Saharan Africa, Asia, Latin America, the Middle East and the Caribbean. While there are limits to the extent to which technology and expertise can be transferred from one part of the world to another, there is no doubt that there would be much to be gained, not only for these regions, but for the world as a whole.

The cultural heritage of humankind is a precious gift that past generations have bestowed on present and future generations to assist them in differentiating between right and wrong, good and bad, relevant and irrelevant, timely and timeless. Access to this gift is an inalienable right of every person in the world, and no community, region, country or group of people has a monopoly on it. While people in the more economically developed parts of the world may not be willing to recognize it or admit it, people in the less economically developed countries have a great deal to contribute with respect to what is most valuable and important in life, including how life should be lived and what life is really all about. Many people in small communities and marginalized groups also possess profound insights into relations with the land, spirituality, recreation, education, ecological management, and human fulfilment that have a great deal of relevance at this stage in history.

To this must be added the fact that there is an enormous amount of satisfaction to be derived from the cultural heritage of humankind. Whether they are aware of it or not, every person draws on the cultural heritage of humankind every minute of every day. It is impossible to listen to music, read a book, sit on a sofa, talk on a telephone, use a computer or go to school without having recourse to it.

Since more is always being added to the cultural heritage of humankind than is being subtracted from it, it is essential to create new methods to prevent the erosion of this munificent legacy in the future, which is why the invention and diffusion of computers, the internet, satellites, and the like has been so valuable and so timely. There are numerous problems to be sorted out in connection with the use, ownership, control, and content of these inventions and devices, but they provide a ray of hope in what would otherwise be a depressing situation. Through their capacity to move information from one part of the world to another in incredibly short periods of time they make it possible—in principle, if not always in practice—for people in every part of the world to profit from the very best that humankind has to offer.

World Culture and World Cultures

When considering the cultural heritage of humankind, the question naturally arises whether we should be striving to create a single world culture, shared by all citizens and all countries, or many world cultures, each with its own distinctive identity and capacity to function effectively in an increasingly globalized world.

The arguments in favour of a single world culture are enticing. According to those who advocate it, there has been a relentless trend throughout history towards the creation of larger and larger cultural units, as humankind has moved on from living as nomadic tribes to living, thinking and feeling in terms of settled communities, then cities, countries, continents, and the world as a whole. When this trend is pushed to its logical conclusion, it ends up in the creation of a single world culture shared by all people and all countries. Proponents of such a trend point to the creation of regional trade zones such as the European Union, and the establishment of multinational corporations and international institutions on a scale and in numbers unprecedented in history, as well as to globalization and (though this is more controversial) the establishment of English as a lingua franca, to make their case. Further, many argue that contemporary developments in the mass media, communications, technology, marketing, and international trade make a single world culture inevitable. They point to the popularity of US films, television programmes, and consumer goods, the international diffusion of popular music, advances in satellite communications and technology, the creation of the internet and the appearance of a "global village," and the concentration of media ownership in fewer and fewer hands to confirm this.

For some (not all) who argue along these lines, a single world culture is not only inevitable, it is also desirable, since, in their view, it would open up countless opportunities for cooperation, communication, and collaboration. Once differences in religion, culture, politics, and education have ceased to matter so much, or, perhaps, have even disappeared, the world would be a better, safer and more secure place in their view. Their contention is that since every human being shares the same needs, concerns, and aspirations for food, clothing, shelter, identity, and a decent life, it is high time we emphasized our similarities and downplayed our differences.

Those who oppose a single world culture are quick to counter these arguments. They contend that such a world culture is anything but inevitable, or desirable, and that many factors stand in the way of its ever being realized. Their opposition is based on an equal number of compelling arguments. In the first place, they contend that every movement towards the creation of larger and larger cultural units has spawned, dialectically, reactions towards the creation of smaller and smaller cultural units. In the modern world these reactions are apparent in the reaffirmation of tribes and tribal groups, on the one hand, and, on the other, the creation of all kinds of citizens' coalitions, local associations, and civil society movements, particularly at local and regional levels, as countervailing forces against trade zones, globalization, and the concentration of power and resources in fewer and fewer hands. Most people still derive their identities, their sense of belonging, from small, "human-sized" cultural units, such as the family, the tribe, the ethnic group to which they belong, the neighbourhood in which they reside, or the town, city or region in which they live, because these are more tangible and less abstract than the international or transnational bodies now being created. Also, the world is already divided into so many separate and distinct cultural units that it is highly unlikely they could all disappear. They are too deeply engrained in the human condition.

While opponents of a single world culture generally concede that many contemporary developments have universal implications and consequences, they contend that claims about the emergence of a single culture from such a variety of different trends and events are greatly exaggerated and not really consistent with the facts. Individuals and institutions in positions of power and authority often have a vested interest in promoting the belief that a single world culture is rapidly taking shape, because it helps them to sell goods and services, as well as ideologies, and to promote a particular kind of lifestyle. Yet the world situation is actually very different. People all over the world may watch Hollywood films and listen to western popular music, but they still live in very different cultural contexts, and continue to engage in other activities in their own localities which bear little resemblance to a single world culture.

Most importantly, opponents of a single world culture contend that it would be much more of a curse than a blessing if it ever did come into being. They point to the dangers of imposing uniformity through centralization and homogenization, as well as of control of the world system by powerful elites and countries, colossal corporations and governments, and a small coterie of wealthy individuals. Not only could creativity and diversity be stamped out, but lethargy, apathy, and alienation would become the established pattern. Some opponents even contend that "cultures of resistance" are needed to fight the standardizing, centralizing and homogenizing developments taking place in the world, especially where countries or cultures are in danger of losing their identity, values or ways of life. Denis Goulet, for instance, has written (in Masini 1994, p. 30):

> All cultures and cultural values are assaulted by powerful forces of standardization. These forces homogenize, dilute and relegate diverse cultures to purely ornamental, vestigial or marginal positions in society. The first standardizing force is technology, especially media technology. Television, film, radio, electronic musical devices, computers, and telephones operate, together and cumulatively, as potent vectors of such values as individualism, hedonistic self-gratification, consumerism, and shallow thinking. The second standardizing force is the modern state, a political institution which is bureaucratic, centralizing, legalistic, and inclined to assert control over ideas, resources, and the "rules of the game" in all spheres of human activity. The third standardizing force is the spread of managerial organization as the best way of making decisions and coordinating actions in all institutions. . . The result of these standardizing influences is massive cultural destruction, dilution, and assimilation. The very pervasiveness of these damaging forces, however, gives rise to growing manifestations of cultural affirmation and resistance.

There is a great deal of validity to these arguments. Already the standardizing, homogenizing and centralizing effects of contemporary developments have permeated the world to the point where they threaten local, regional and national cultures, established cultural identities, and marginalized cultures. This is a disturbing development in view of the fact that they also, arguably, threaten originality, creativity, and diversity, the very things that are imperative for environmental sustainability, human progress, and global survival and well-being.

The obvious question, then, is whether there is a way out of the dilemma: Is it possible to have the benefits that might accrue from a single world culture while simultaneously making it possible for people, cultures, and countries to preserve their differences? While it is comparatively easy to visualize what the world would look like and how it would function if a single world culture were to become a reality, it is far more difficult to visualize such a complex balance of world cultures. Yet, clearly, all cultures are becoming "world cultures," in the sense that they are becoming parts of the "global village," and participating in the revolution that is going on in communications technology and international affairs. They are less and less able to tune out developments taking place in other parts of the world, or to insulate themselves from these developments, regardless of how small, remote or insignificant they might be.

The crucial point here is that world cultures have never existed before in human history. Even cultures that have played extremely powerful roles in the world, from ancient China or Rome to Britain, have been national cultures, albeit with powerful international overtones and consequences, rather than world cultures. There were significant parts of the world that were not known to them and were untouched by their influence, and many developments occurring in the world had no effect on them. What is emerging throughout the world today, however, are the first real signs of world cultures in the truly global sense. When they have become fully developed these cultures will be substantially different from local, regional or national cultures. Not only will they be integrated into the world system, they will also be dependent on it, and affected by global developments. The culture of the United States is rapidly becoming the first real world culture in this sense, but a number of other cultures appear to be moving in the same direction, particularly in western Europe and East Asia. Even smaller, less powerful and more remote cultures, in Africa, Asia and Latin America, are steadily moving in this direction. The world knows a great deal more about them than ever before, they know a great deal more about the world as well, and they are being fundamentally and inescapably influenced by developments taking place in other parts of the world.

If all the various cultures of the world will be compelled to function more like world cultures, they will have to develop their global capabilities to the utmost, while simultaneously maintaining their distinctiveness. This is looming larger and larger as one of the greatest challenges facing every culture in the world, as well as the world as a whole, and it has momentous implications. It is a challenge not unlike the challenge confronting local, regional and national cultures in earlier times, although it is infinitely more complex and difficult to manage. People in every part of the world will have to exercise a great deal of control over the public and private decision-making processes affecting their lives, and cope with an array of international developments on a daily basis, if they want their cultures to function effectively as world cultures. In order to do this, five things will have to be done and done well.

First, strong connections will have to be maintained with the past. Not only does every culture in the world possess a rich legacy of historical accomplishments and artefacts, which must be protected from the ravages of time and the incursions of other cultures, but the maintenance of traditions is of crucial importance in developing cultures that are capable of retaining their identity and independence while functioning effectively in the world. Many measures are needed here. One is learning about the historical development of their culture, particularly in the educational system. Another is expanding awareness of traditions in the mass media. Still another is cultural tourism, which has the potential to damage or even destroy traditions, but does provide a way of expanding awareness of their value.

While most countries are becoming adept at cultural tourism, no country in the world is better at it than France. Not only is France divided into a number of distinctive regions, each with its own unique character, but also it is possible to acquire an enormous amount of information on every one of these regions. French planners and administrators are so adept at preserving and promoting their historical traditions that they have developed detailed atlases and dossiers that provide information on the location, condition, and characteristics of virtually every landmark of any significance. Much of the credit for this must go to the French government, which has funded cultural tourism, and culture generally, at a much higher level per capita than any other country in the world. It has also gone much further in developing cultural policies, plans and programmes. It is clear that other governments will have to spend a great deal more on cultural tourism if they too want to maintain connections with their peoples' traditions while simultaneously developing world cultures. It is amazing what can be accomplished through cultural tourism that cannot be accomplished in other ways. Not only does cultural tourism prompt people to get out and explore their own cultural roots and traditions, it also provides a great boost for local, regional and national economies.

Second, control and ownership of strategic industries will have to be in domestic rather than foreign hands. Every country in the world today, with the possible exception of the United States, is experiencing considerable difficulty exercising control and ownership over such strategic industries as the arts, education, the mass media, and communications. This is because of the growing concentration of ownership of these industries in fewer, often foreign hands, as well as the popularity of US films, television programmes, tapes, videos, CDs, and books. Clearly, countries will have to exercise a great deal more control and ownership of these industries if they want to maintain their identity and their autonomy. Despite the protection afforded by linguistic differences, many cultures, especially those in the "developing world," are extremely vulnerable to external influences because they lack strategic industries and infrastructure of their own. This makes building up domestic capacities in the arts, education, media, communications, and technology a categorical imperative for the future. This will require a great deal of action on the part of governments, even in economically developed countries such as Canada, Belgium or Austria, which are located close to major powers or superpowers and have to deal with this problem too, because of the economies of large-scale production, contemporary developments in the mass media and international trade, and the popularity of products emanating from neighbouring countries (respectively, in the examples given, the United States, France, and Germany).

Third, domestic cultural content will have to be increased quite considerably. This is much more than a problem of creating "cultural hardware." It is equally a problem of creating "cultural software." Since artists, scientists, scholars, arts organizations, educational institutions, scientific associations, and the like create much of the content that is required to broaden and deepen understanding of cultures as organic wholes and total ways of life, these individuals and institutions have pivotal roles to play in the creation of domestic cultural content, and therefore in the development of world cultures. What the world needs is cultural content that speaks persuasively to people about the substance and character of their own cultures, and not just the cultures of others. Cultural content that imitates the content of the dominant cultures of the world may be helpful in strengthening the pressures towards a single world culture, but it is not helpful in creating many diverse world cultures, each with its own distinctive identity and capacity to function effectively in a globalized world.

Fourth, indigenous rather than imposed or imported development will have to be pursued. As the world takes on more and more of the characteristics of a "global village," two options present themselves to the large majority of countries and cultures. The first is to imitate the development patterns of other countries and cultures. The resulting "imposed" or "imported" pattern of development usually involves acquiescing to the worldviews and values of other countries or cultures, particularly those that believe they have achieved "development" and are anxious to share it or impose it on others. The second option involves undertaking development that arises organically from a culture's or country's own traditions, while taking care to incorporate relevant developments taking place in other parts of the world. Indigenous development, in this sense, ensures that only those developments and changes that are consistent with a culture's own traditions, circumstances, and needs are adopted. India provides an excellent example of indigenous development in this sense, and has done so ever since Gandhi emphasized the importance of traditional activities, most famously by making and wearing "homespun" clothing. Also, during the sixty years since it achieved independence, India has developed a powerful film industry of its own that rivals Hollywood, addressing themes and ideas that are relevant to the people of India.

Finally, people will have to learn to function effectively in the world on a sustained and systematic basis. In the past, many cultures developed while ignoring changes taking place in other parts of the world. Often this resulted in their becoming so caught up in their own internal affairs that they became self-absorbed and chauvinistic, believing that their culture was superior to others. This was especially true in the nineteenth century and the first half of the twentieth century, but it is still a problem today. In many parts of the world military, religious and political leaders remain anxious to keep their citizens cut off from the outside world because they want to retain undue control over them. In a world characterized by world cultures this would not happen. All cultures would be compelled to deal with global developments and international affairs on a continuous and ever-expanding basis. Moreover, they would be forced to adopt many practices and ideas from the outside, though not at the expense of their own development, or their own domestic and international interests. The focus would always be on building up a culture's or a country's domestic and international capabilities, as well as incorporating ideas and practices that are pertinent. Indigenous development means striking a judicious balance between the internal and the external requirements of development.

While transfers of ideas, technologies, and lifestyles are bound to play a much more powerful role in the future than they have in the past, they are not without their problems. While cultures and countries may seem similar when viewed from afar, they are usually diverse and different when viewed up close. It is not simply a case of taking business and commercial practices, educational endeavours, political procedures or technological activities from one culture, transferring them to another and expecting that they will fit. The field of development is strewn with examples where enormous sums of money have been spent on transfer projects that did not fit well or at all. A great deal more attention needs to be paid to the cultural context in which such transfers take place. This in turn will form part of the process through which all cultures in the world develop their domestic and international capabilities to the utmost. It will not be possible for any culture to become a world culture without substantial improvements in its technological, social, commercial, scientific, economic, political, artistic, educational, and marketing capacities. Functioning in the world on a daily and full-time basis will mean interacting with other cultures and countries on the basis of true equality and continuous communication.

We can now return to the question of whether humankind should be striving to create a single world culture or many world cultures. Can these two ideas be reconciled? Surely they can, and the reconciliation lies in creating a global federation of world cultures. This would make it possible to reap the benefits of a single world culture while simultaneously preserving the diversity, identity, creativity, and equality of many world cultures.

A Global Federation of World Cultures

The belief that all people, countries, and cultures must follow the same path of development has already caused a great deal of stress, anxiety, resentment, and hostility, in response to the conviction that consumerism, commercialism, capitalism, democracy, secularism, economic growth, materialism, and the market are necessary for all. A global federation of world cultures would stand in direct contrast to this conviction, as it would be based on the view that there are many different paths to development, and therefore many different ways of addressing and satisfying people's and countries' needs. Some may well share the priorities of the economic development model, and welcome consumerism, commercialism, and the rest. Others may prefer to emphasize conservation, socialism, spiritualism or environmentalism. It depends on how people and countries decide to address their own specific requirements and order the component parts of their cultures.

In a global federation of world cultures, such notions as "development," "progress," and "the world system" would take on different meanings than they possess today. Development and progress would mean feeling comfortable with the specific directions that people, countries, and cultures follow, rather than acquiescing to the worldviews, values or beliefs of others. The world system would be one that made it possible for many different ways of life to flourish throughout the world, each with its own distinct identity, values, and legitimacy. In this type of world, people, countries, and cultures would exercise the freedom, flexibility, independence, and equality they need to pursue their own particular paths to development, while at the same time participating in the common work of humankind, and engaging in international causes and concerns.

In one form or another, these causes and concerns all relate to making improvements in the quality of life and the human condition. This would not be possible without a vigorous campaign to address people's needs, especially their elementary needs, in a systematic and sustained manner. Nor would it be possible without making fundamental changes in attitudes to the natural environment, and alleviating the enormous pressure being exerted on resources. Gao Xian, senior editor of the Social Sciences Academic Press in China and former Secretary-General of the Chinese Centre for Third World Studies, recognized the quintessential importance of these changes when he wrote (in the two articles cited in the Bibliography) about the "macrocultural approach to development," "the sustainability of sustainable development," and the crucial importance of understanding the complex connections between human beings and nature, human beings in nature, ethical values and the laws of nature, and the intimate connection between human beings and other species. Without such an understanding, there is bound to be more violence, terrorism, conflict, and confrontation in the world as natural resources are used up, and more environmental damage and degeneration take place.

Collective action in addressing these issues would go a long way towards making it possible to attend to other worthwhile international causes and concerns. Especially important in this regard, as we have already seen, would be closing the gap between rich and poor, reducing poverty, homelessness, hunger, and unemployment, terminating human rights abuses and achieving gender equality, and creating a more compassionate, caring and humane world. Yet even these measures would not necessarily ensure a safer world. For this more forceful action will be required, including strengthening international organizations, particularly to ensure that the United Nations becomes the most important political institution in the world, with the power to put the interests of the world as a whole ahead of the interests of particular countries; strengthening international legal systems, to the point where the rule of law applies to all citizens, institutions, and countries regardless of location, influence, wealth or power; and winning the battle against violence and terrorism.

People in different parts of the world will go on choosing to live their lives differently, and holding different opinions with respect to how life is to be lived and the human condition is to be improved, not only for themselves and their families, but also for future generations, people in other parts of the world, and the world as a whole. However, in a global federation of world cultures, they would also be increasingly anxious to participate in international and intercultural communications and activities, in the best interests of all people, countries, and cultures. This would provide a common bond capable of uniting all members of the human family. The Indian poet and thinker Rabindranath Tagore had something like this in mind when he wrote (as quoted by Braisted 1944, p. 5): "We must prepare the field for the cooperation of all the cultures of the world where all will give and take from others. This is the keynote of the coming age."

It is the potential to give and take from each other that makes the creation of a global federation of world cultures so essential. All people, countries, and cultures have something precious to contribute to such a federation, as well as something valuable to receive in return.

In order to create a truly effective global federation of world cultures, it will be necessary to fashion many more opportunities for collaboration among the diverse people, countries, and cultures of the world. Artists would collaborate much more actively with scientists, for example, and people in business, politics, and government would work hand in hand with people in religious

REVOLUTION OR RENAISSANCE

and spiritual institutions. It is through this process that it would be possible to create "unity in diversity," which is, without doubt, what the world needs most in the twenty-first century. There can be no unity without sharing certain similarities, since unity is achieved by recognizing the common connections that bind people, countries, and cultures together. Likewise, there can be no diversity without respecting fundamental differences, for too much sameness kills the creative spark that makes people, countries, and cultures unique. Thus, unity in diversity, like identity, is achieved and maintained by walking the fine line between similarities and differences.

This is what would make the creation of a global federation of world cultures an exciting and compelling prospect. It would make it possible to create many world cultures, each with its own distinctive identity and ability to function effectively in a global world, while simultaneously creating countless connections between diverse peoples, countries, and cultures. This would provide a clear alternative to the relentless march along a uniform path of development towards a single world culture where everybody thinks the same, and sees the world, values things, and acts in the same way. That is what is in store for humanity if it allows the value systems of a few people, countries or institutions to be imposed everywhere. This need not happen. With the development of a global federation of world cultures, people, countries and institutions in every part of the world would retain dignity, value and legitimacy in their own right, while simultaneously participating in the quest to make the world a better place. It was this type of world that Denis Goulet had in mind when he wrote (in Masini 1994, pp. 30–31):

> In an optimistic scenario, humanity advances in global solidarity, and practices ecological and economic concentration as a responsible steward of the cosmos. Numerous vital and authentic cultures flourish, each proud of its identity while actively rejoicing in differences exhibited by other cultures. Human beings everywhere nurture the conscious possession of several partial and overlapping identities, while relativizing each of these identities in recognition of their primary allegiance to the human species.

In such a dynamic and diverse world, ideas, artefacts, and resources would flow much more freely than they do today because people, countries, and cultures would no longer feel threatened by cultural differences. There would be many more opportunities to learn about values and ways of life that are different from one's own and yet provide valuable insights into the human condition. Possibilities for expanding human consciousness and extending human horizons would be greatly enhanced, because there would be many more opportunities for intellectual stimulation, scientific discovery, artistic expression, mutual understanding, cultural enrichment, and personal and collective fulfilment. Many new organizations would be brought into existence in order to advance the interests of people and countries in every part of the world by broadening and deepening understanding of the ways in which culture can improve the human condition and the quality of life of all people and countries.

All these opportunities, and many others, would be made possible through a renaissance in global development and human affairs that would call forth creative capabilities in the arts, the sciences, education, space exploration, the environment, politics, economics, education, technology, spirituality, and social affairs. This is why a renaissance is so badly needed in the world. It would transform the human condition and the world system in peaceful rather than violent ways, largely by transporting humanity out of an age preoccupied with materialism and the market, and into an age preoccupied with human welfare and environmental well-being. Without such a renaissance it is difficult to see how the quality of life and the state of the environment will be improved throughout the world.

Epilogue

When we think of the world's future, we always mean the destination it will reach if it keeps going in the direction we can see it going in now; it does not occur to us that its path is not a straight line but a curve, constantly changing direction.—Ludwig Wittgenstein (1980), p. 3e.

D ue to developments over the last few centuries, and particularly over the last fifty years, the entire world is now living in an economic age. It is an age that has achieved many remarkable things and produced countless benefits, especially for people and countries fortunate enough to enjoy them. Foremost among the benefits are substantial improvements in living standards and the quality of life for more and more people throughout the world, phenomenal increases in the production of goods and services and the realm of consumer choice, and major advances in science, technology, industry, agriculture, education, and health care.

Despite this, it is becoming increasingly apparent that the economic age is the cause of some of the world's most difficult and demanding problems. This is particularly true with respect to the environmental crisis, climate change, depletion of the world's natural resources at a disturbing rate, the persistent gap between rich and poor countries and rich and poor people, and tensions between the "developed" and "developing" parts of the world. These problems are bound to become more severe and life-threatening as population increases, the globe's scarce resources are used up, and the carrying capacity of the planet is approached.

This is why it is so essential to pass out of the present economic age and into a future cultural age. What a cultural age provides is a way of addressing these problems — and others that have loomed up on the global horizon — in a holistic, humane, and egalitarian manner rather than a specialized, impersonal, and partisan manner. This makes it possible to situate economics and economies properly in context, recognize the crucial importance of the natural environment and history in global development and human affairs, and reduce the demands human beings are making on the world's scarce resources by achieving a better balance between activities that are high in material input and output and activities that are low in material input and output.

In a cultural age, strategic roles would be reserved for governments and international organizations, educational institutions, the cultural community, and people and civil society. Governments and international organizations could perform their role most effectively by utilizing a cultural model of development in government and the decision-making process, as well as by accelerating their efforts to reduce the gap between rich and poor countries and rich and poor people.

Educational institutions could execute their role most effectively by making a full commitment to cultural education, as well as by broadening and deepening understanding of cultural differences and facilitating as many exchanges as possible between the diverse peoples, cultures, and civilizations of the world.

The cultural community would also have a key role to play in a cultural age. It is required to spearhead the renaissance that is so badly needed in the future. In order to perform this role, the community will have to be much more consolidated and cohesive than it is today. It will also have to be much more vocal. As Melina Mercouri put it when she was Culture Minister for Greece (p. 6): "It is time for our voice to be heard as loud as that of the technocrats. Culture, art, and creativity are not less important than technology, commerce, and the economy."

But the most important role would be reserved for people and civil society. The world system will not change until people and civil society become much more fully and actively involved in the quest to change it, largely by taking a cultural approach to life. For culture is much more than a career, a profession, or a vocation. It is a way of life — a way of life that spans the gamut of possibilities, from how people visualize the world and organize themselves to how they conduct their affairs, elevate and embellish life, and position themselves in the world.

With developments like these and others in place, it is possible to see the pale outlines of a cultural age. Based on developing all the various cultures of the world and instituting the necessary safeguards and precautions, it is an age predicated on ensuring that culture's highest, wisest, and most enduring values and ideals receive the attention and priority they deserve in the world system of the future. In such an age, artistic creation, scientific discovery, respect for the natural environment and each other, life-long learning, spirituality, friendship, family life, and human love would be the most essential things in life, the things that bring peace and fulfilment as well as harmony and happiness. As the Indonesian philosopher Takdir Alisjahbana put it (1983, pp. 12–13):

> In the great movement of time which we call human history, we must ask ourselves the question, "Where are we, and where is our road leading to?" in the hope that through an understanding of the growths and declines, of the successes and the failures of cultures, we will acquire some clues that will lead us to the right decisions in our time.

Let us hope that we discover the clues that are necessary to make "the right decisions in our time." What is at stake here is the quality of life, environmental sustainability, and human well-being. This is why making the transition from an economic age to a cultural age is so essential: The future of humanity and the world depend on it.

Bibliography

For each of the items where two years are shown, the first year is that of the edition consulted during the writing of this book and the second is that of the first edition of the original text.

Abdel-Malek, Anisuzzaman, and Anouar Abdel-Malek. (1983). *Culture and Thought in the Transformation of the World*. London: Macmillan.

Agnew, John A., John Mercer, and David E. Sopher, ed. (1984). *The City in Cultural Context*. London and Boston: Allen & Unwin.

Alisjahbana, S. Takdir. (1983). *Sociocultural Creativity in the Converging and Restructuring Process of the New Emerging World*. Jakarta: Penerbit Dian Rakyat.

Alisjahbana, S. Takdir. (1986). *Values as Integrating Forces in Personality, Society and Culture*. Kuala Lumpur: University of Malaya Press.

Allport, Gordon. (1963). *Pattern and Growth in Personality*. New York: Holt, Rinehardt & Winston.

Amin, Samir. (1990). *Maldevelopment: Anatomy of a Global Failure*. New York: United Nations University Press and Zed Books.

Amin, Samir, Giovanni Arrighi, André Gunder Frank, and Immanuel Wallerstein. (1990). *Transforming the Revolution: Social Movements and the World-System*. New York: *Monthly Review* Press.

Anderson, Victor. (1991). *Alternative Economic Indicators*. London: Routledge.

Arensberg, Conrad M., and Solon T. Kimball. (1965). *Culture and Community*. New York: Harcourt, Brace & World.

Arndt, H. W. (1987). *Economic Development: The History of an Idea*. Chicago: University of Chicago Press.

Arnold, Matthew. (1981). *Culture and Anarchy* [1869], ed. John Dover Wilson. Cambridge and New York: Cambridge University Press.

Asad, Talal, ed. (1995). *Anthropology and the Colonial Encounter*. New York: Prometheus Books.

Ashton, Thomas S., and Pat Hudson. (1998). *The Industrial Revolution*. Oxford and New York: Oxford University Press.

Barber, William J. (1991). *A History of Economic Thought*. London: Penguin.

Barer-Stein, Thelma. (1979). *You Eat What You Are: A Study of Ethnic Food Traditions*. Toronto: McClelland & Stewart.

Bateson, Gregory. (2002). *Steps to an Ecoloy of Mind: Collected Essays in Anthropology, Evolution, and Epistemology*. Chicago: University of Chicago Press.

Batstone, David. (2003). *Saving the Corporate Soul*. New York: Jossey–Bass.

Bauman, Zygmunt. (1973). *Culture as Praxis*. London: Routledge & Kegan Paul.

Bauman, Zygmunt. (1998). *Globalization: The Human Consequences*. New York: Columbia University Press.

Baumol, William J. and William G. Bowen. (1966). *The Performing Arts: The Economic Dilemma*. New York: Twentieth Century Fund.

Behar, Ruth, and Deborah A. Gordon, ed. (1995). *Women Writing Culture: Twentieth Century Women American Anthropologists*. Berkeley and Los Angeles: University of California Press.

Bell, Daniel, and Irving Kristol, ed. (1981). *The Crisis in Economic Theory*. New York: Basic Books.

Benedict, Ruth. (1963). *Patterns of Culture*. [1934] London: Routledge and Kegan Paul.

Benedict, Ruth. (1946). *The Chrysanthemum and the Sword: Patterns of Japanese Culture*. Boston: Houghton Mifflin.

Bennett, Tony. (2001). *Cultural Policy and Cultural Diversity: Mapping the Policy Domain*. Strasbourg: Council of Europe.

Berger, Peter L., and Samuel Huntington, ed. (2002). *Many Globalizations: Cultural Diversity in the Contemporary World*. New York: Oxford University Press.

Bernardi, Bernardo, ed. (1977). *The Concept and Dynamics of Culture*. The Hague: Mouton Publishers.

Berry, Thomas. (1988). *Dream of the Earth*. San Francisco: Sierra Club Books.

Bickley, Verner, and John Philip Puthenparampil, ed. (1981). *Cultural Relations in the Global Community: Problems and Prospects*. New Delhi: Abhinav.

Bird, Jon, et al., ed. (1993). *Mapping the Futures: Local Cultures, Global Change*. London: Routledge.

Birket-Smith, Kaj. (1965). *The Paths of Culture: A General Ethnology*. trans. Karin Fennow. Madison and Milwaukee: University of Wisconsin Press.

Blaug, Marc. (1985). *Great Economists Since Keynes*. Totowa, NJ: Barnes & Noble.

Bloom, William, ed. (2000). *Holistic Revolution: The Essential New Age Reader*. London and New York: Allen Lane.

Bookchin, Murray, and Dave Foreman. (1991). *Defending the Earth*. Montreal and New York: Black Rose.

Boserup, Ester. (1970). *Women's Role in Development*. New York: St. Martin's Press.

Boulding, Elise (1994). *Building a Global Culture: Education for an Interdependent World*. Syracuse, NY: Syracuse University Press.

Boulding, Elise (1998). *Abolishing War: Cultures and Institutions*. Cambridge, MA: Boston Research Centre for the Twenty-first Century.

Boulding, Elise. (2000). *Cultures of Peace: The Hidden Side of History*. Syracuse, NY: Syracuse University Press.

Boulding, Kenneth E. (1981). *Evolutionary Economics*. London: Sage.

Boxx, T. William, and Gary M. Quinlivan, ed. (1994). *The Cultural Context of Economics and Politics*. Landan, MD: University Press of America.

Bradford, Gigi, Michael Gary, and Glenn Wallach, ed. (2000). *The Politics of Culture: Policy Perspectives for Individuals, Institutions and Communities*. New York: New Press and Center for Arts and Culture.

Braisted, Paul J. (1944). *Cultural Cooperation: Keynote of the Coming Age*. New Haven, CT: Edward W. Hazen Foundation.

Braisted, Paul J., Soedjatmoko, and Kenneth W. Thompson, ed. (1972). *Reconstituting The Human Community*. New Haven, CT: Hazen Foundation.

Braudel, Fernand. (1995). *A History of Civilizations* [1962], trans. Richard Mayne. Harmondsworth and New York: Penguin.

Brook, Peter. (1976). "The Three Cultures of Modern Man." *Cultures* 3:4. Paris: UNESCO and La Baconnière.

Bunzel, Ruth. (1929). *The Pueblo Potter*. New York: Columbia University Press.

Burckhardt, Jacob. (1958). *The Civilization of the Renaissance in Italy* [1860]. 2 vols. New York: Harper Torchbooks.

Burckhardt, Jacob. (1998). *The Greeks and Greek Civilization* [1872–85]. trans. Sheila Stern, ed. Oswyn Murray. New York: St. Martin's Press, and London: HarperCollins.

Burke, Peter. (1997). *Varieties of Cultural History*. Cambridge: Polity Press.

Burke, Peter. (1999). *The Italian Renaissance: Culture and Society in Italy* [1972]. 4th ed. Princeton, NJ: Princeton University Press.

Call, William. (2000). *Cultural Revolution: From the Decay of a Dying World Comes the Birth of a New Age*. Salt Lake City: Freethinker Press.

Canada Council Research and Evaluation Section. (1982). *A "Short-Hand" Technique for Estimating the Economic Impact of the Performing Arts*. 2nd ed. Ottawa: Canada Council.

Capra, Fritjof. (1982). *The Turning Point: Science, Society and the Rising Culture*. New York: Simon & Schuster.

Carson, Rachel. (1962). *Silent Spring*. Boston: Houghton Mifflin.

Castells, Manuel (2004). *The Power of Identity*. 2nd ed. Oxford: Blackwell.

Chamberlin, Edward H. (1933). *The Theory of Monopolistic Competition*. Cambridge, MA: Harvard University Press.

Chamberlin, E. R. (1976). *Awaking Giant: Britain and the Industrial Revolution.* London: B. T. Botsford.

Chambers, Robert. (1983). *Rural Development: Putting the Last First.* Harlow: Longman Scientific and Technical.

Chay, Jongsuk, ed. (1990). *Culture and International Relations.* New York: Praeger.

Chisholm, Anne. (1972). *Philosophers of the Earth: Conversations with Ecologists.* New York: Dutton.

Clement, W. R. (1998). *Quantum Jump: A Survival Guide for the New Renaissance.* Toronto: Insomniac Press.

Clifford, James, and George Marcus, ed. (1986). *Writing Culture: The Poetics and Politics of Ethnography.* Berkeley: University of California Press.

Clifford, James. (1988). *The Predicament of Culture: Twentieth-Century Ethnography, Literature and Art.* Cambridge, MA: Harvard University Press.

Clough, Shepard B. (1960). *Basic Values of Western Civilization.* New York and London: Columbia University Press.

Coate, Roger A., and Jerel A. Rosati, ed. (1988). *The Power of Human Needs in World Society.* Boulder, CO, and London: Lynne Rienner.

Cole, G. D. H. (1953–60). *A History of Socialist Thought.* 5 vols. London: Macmillan, and New York: St. Martin's Press.

Commission on Global Governance. (1995). *Our Global Neighbourhood.* New York: Oxford University Press.

Commoner, Barry. (1971). *The Closing Circle: Nature, Man and Technology.* New York: Alfred A. Knopf.

Condorcet, Marie-Jean-Antoine-Nicolas de Caritat, marquis de. (1955). *Sketch for a Historical Picture of the Progress of the Human Mind* [1795], trans. June Barraclough, with an introduction by Stuart Hampshire. New York: Noonday Press.

Crane, David. (1999, September 29). "Poverty Called Global Crisis." *Toronto Star,* p. E3.

Crane, David. (2000, July 22). "Chrétien and G8 Leaders Ignore Real Issues." *Toronto Star,* p. E2.

Cronk, Lee. (1999). *That Complex Whole: Culture and the Evolution of Human Behaviour.* Boulder, CO: Westview Press.

Cvjeticanin, Biserka, ed. (1995). *Directory of Institutions and Data Bases in the Field of Cultural Development.* Zagreb: IRMO/Culturelink.

Daly, Herman E. (1991). *Steady State Economics.* 2nd ed. Washington, DC: Island Press.

Daly, Herman E., and Kenneth N. Townsend. (1992). *Valuing the Earth: Economics, Ecology, Ethics.* Cambridge, MA: MIT Press.

Darwin, Charles. (1964). *On the Origin of Species* [1859]. Cambridge, MA: Harvard University Press.

Davis, Wade. (2000). *Light at the Edge of the World: Journey through the Realm of Vanishing Cultures.* Toronto: Douglas & McIntyre.

Dean, Phyllis. (1965). *The First Industrial Revolution*. Cambridge: Cambridge University Press.

de Soto, Hernando. (2003). *The Mystery of Capital: Why Capitalism Triumphs in the West and Fails Everywhere Else* [2000]. New York: Basic Books.

de Waal, Frans. (1996). *Good Natured*. Cambridge, MA: Harvard University Press.

Dirks, Nicholas B., Geoff Eley, and Sherry B. Ortner, ed. (1994). *Culture/Power/History: A Reader in Contemporary Social Theory*. Princeton, NJ: Princeton University Press.

Domar, Evsey D. (1957). *Essays in the Theory of Economic Growth*. Oxford and New York: Oxford University Press.

Doyal, Len, and Ian Gough. (1991). *A Theory of Human Need*. London: Gilford.

Easton, Stewart C. (1964). *The Rise and Fall of Western Colonialism: A Historical Survey from the Early Nineteenth Century to the Present*. New York: Praeger.

Ehrlich, Paul R.. (1971). *The Population Bomb*. revised ed. London: Pan.

Ehrlich, Paul R., and Anne Ehrlich. (1991). *Healing the Planet: Strategies for Resolving the Environmental Crisis*. Reading, MA: Addison–Wesley.

Eibl-Eibesfelt, Irennaus. (1972). *Love and Hate*. New York: Holt, Rinehart & Winston.

Elgin, Duane, and Colleen LeDrew. (1997, Winter). "Global Paradigm Report: Tracking the Shift Under Way." *YES! A Journal of Positive Futures*.

Eliot, T. S. (1948). *Notes Towards the Definition of Culture*. London: Faber.

Elkins, Paul, ed. (1987). *The Living Economy: A New Economics in the Making*. London and New York: Routledge & Kegan Paul.

Equitable Growth. (2000, Sept.15) *Toronto Star*. Editorial. p. A28.

Ergang, Robert Reingold. (1966). *Herder and the Foundations of German Nationalism*. New York: Octagon Books.

Etzioni, Amitai. (1988). *The Moral Dimension: Toward a New Economics*. New York: Free Press.

Evans-Pritchard, E. E. (1951). *Social Anthropology and Other Essays*. London: Cohen & West, and Glencoe, IL: Free Press.

Fanfani, Amintore. (1955). *Catholicism, Protestantism and Capitalism*. New York: Sheed & Ward.

Featherstone, Mike, ed. (1990). *Global Culture: Nationalism, Globalization and Modernity*. London: Sage.

Featherstone, Mike, ed. (1992). *Cultural Theory and Cultural Change*. London: Sage.

Featherstone, Mike, and Scott Lash, ed. (1999). *Spaces of Culture: City – Nation – World*. London: Sage.

Feibleman, James. (1968). *The Theory of Human Culture*. New York: Humanities Press.

Firth, Raymond. (1961). *Elements of Social Organization*. 2nd ed. Boston: Beacon Press.

Florida, Richard L. (2002). *The Rise of the Creative Class, and How It's Transforming Work, Leisure, Community and Everyday Life*. New York: Basic Books.

Frank, André Gunder. (1967). *Capitalism and Underdevelopment in Latin America*. New York: *Monthly Review* Press.

Freeman, Christopher, and Marie Jahoda, ed. (1978). *World Futures: The Great Debate*. New York: Universe Books.

Freire, Paulo. (1970). *Pedagogy of the Oppressed* [1968]. New York: Seabury Press.

Friedman, Jonathan (1994). *Cultural Identity and Global Process*. London: Sage.

Friedman, Milton, and Rose Friedman. (2002). *Capitalism and Freedom*. Chicago: University of Chicago Press.

Friedman, Thomas L. (2000). *The Lexus and the Olive Tree: Understanding Globalization*. New York: Anchor.

Gacs, Ute, et al., ed. (1988). *Women Anthropologists: A Biographical Dictionary*. Westport, CT: Greenwood Press.

Galbraith, John Kenneth. (1961). *The Good Society: The Human Agenda*. Boston: Houghton Mifflin.

Galbraith, John Kenneth. (1967). *The New Industrial State*. Boston: Houghton Mifflin.

Galtung, Johan. (1988). "International Development in Human Perspective," in Roger A. Coate and Jerel A. Rosati, ed. *The Power of Human Needs in World Society*. Boulder, CO, and London: Lynne Rienner.

Gandhi, Mahatma. (1949). *Communal Unity*. Ahmedabad: Navajivan.

Gandhi, Mahatma. (1962). *The Essential Gandhi: An Anthology*. New York: Random House.

Gao, Xian. (1996, November). "Culture and Development: Macro-Cultural Reflections on Development." *Culturelink* 20. Zagreb: Institute for International Relations.

Gao, Xian. (1998, April). "Culture and Development: The Sustainability of Sustainable Development." *Culturelink* 24. Zagreb: Institute for International Relations.

Garcia Canclini, Néstor. (1995). *Hybrid Cultures: Strategies for Entering and Leaving Modernity*. Minneapolis: University of Minnesota Press.

Gardiner, Patrick, ed. (1959). *Theories of History*. Glencoe, IL: The Free Press.

Geertz, Clifford. (1973). *Interpretation of Cultures*. New York: Basic Books.

Girard, Augustin. (1972). *Cultural Development: Experience and Policies*. Paris: UNESCO.

Goar, Carol. (2001, June 6). "A Measure of Progress." *Toronto Star*, p. K6.

Godwin, William (1946). *An Enquiry Concerning Political Justice and Its Influence on General Virtue and Happiness* [1793], ed. F. E. L. Priestley, 3 vols. Buffalo, NY: University of Toronto Press.

Goulet, Denis. (1985). *The Cruel Choice: A New Concept in the Theory of Development*. Lanham, MD: University Press of America.

Grossberg, Lawrence, Cary Nelson, and Paula Treichler, ed. (1992). *Cultural Studies*. London: Routledge.

Gunn, Giles. (1987). *The Culture of Criticism and the Criticism of Culture*. New York: Oxford University Press.

Hall, Edward. (1959). *The Silent Language*. Garden City, NY: Doubleday.

Hall, Edward. (1966). *The Hidden Dimension*. Garden City, NY: Doubleday.

Hall, Edward. (1976). *Beyond Culture*. Garden City, NY: Anchor Press/Doubleday.

Hallowell, Irving A. (1995). *Culture and Experience*. Philadelphia: University of Pennsylvania Press.

Hansen, Alvin H. (1927). *Business Cycle Theory*. Boston: Ginn & Company.

Haq, Mahbub ul. (1995). *Reflections on Human Development*. New York and Oxford: Oxford University Press.

Harman, Willis. (1998). *Global Mind Change*. 2nd ed. San Francisco: Berrett–Koehler.

Harris, Marvin. (1968). *The Rise of Anthropological Theory: A History of Theories of Culture*. New York: Thomas Y. Crowell.

Harris, Marvin. (1999). *Theories of Culture in Postmodern Times*. Walnut Creek, CA, London, and New Delhi: Altamira Press.

Harrison, Lawrence E., and Samuel P. Huntington, ed. (2001). *Culture Matters: How Values Shape Human Progress*. New York: Basic Books.

Harrod, Roy. (1948). *Towards a Dynamic Economics*. London: Macmillan.

Hartwell, R. M., ed. (1970). *The Industrial Revolution*. Oxford: Blackwell.

Hayek, Friedrich A. von. (1949). *Individualism and Economic Order*. London: Routledge & Kegan Paul.

Heckscher, Eli F. (1955). *Mercantilism*. Revised ed. by E. F. Söderlund, 2 vols. New York: Macmillan.

Heilbroner, Robert. L. (1986). *The Worldly Philosophers: The Lives, Times and Ideas of the Great Economic Thinkers*. New York: Simon & Schuster.

Henderson, Hazel. (1981). *The Politics of the Solar Age: Alternatives to Economics*. New York: Anchor Press/Doubleday.

Herder, Johann Gottfried von. (1803). *Outlines of a Philosophy of the History of Man* [1791], trans. T. O. Churchill. London: Hansard.

Herskovits, Melville. (1963). *Cultural Anthropology*. New York: Alfred A. Knopf.

Hicks, John R. (1939). *Value and Capital*. Oxford: Clarendon Press.

Hicks, John R. (1971). *The Social Framework: An Introduction to Economics*. 3rd ed. Oxford: Clarendon Press.

Hillman-Chartrand, Harry. (1983). *An Economic Impact Assessment of the Fine Arts*. Ottawa: Canada Council.

Hirsch, Fred. (1976). *Social Limits to Growth*. Cambridge, MA: Harvard University Press.

Hirschberg, Stuart, and Terry Hirschberg. (2001). *One World, Many Cultures*. 4th ed. Boston: Allyn & Bacon.

Hirschman, Albert O. (1958). *The Strategy of Economic Development*. New Haven, CT: Yale University Press.

Hobson, J. A. (1902). *Imperialism: A Study*. New York: James Pott.

Hofstede, Geert. (2001). *Culture's Consequences: Comparing Values, Behaviours, Institutions and Organizations Across Nations*. London: Sage.

Hollander, Samuel. (1973). *The Economics of Adam Smith*. Buffalo, NY: University of Toronto Press.

Hollander, Samuel. (1988). *Classical Economics*. Oxford and New York: Blackwell.

Honigmann, John J. (1954). *Culture and Personality*. New York: Harper & Row.

Honigmann, John J. (1963). *Understanding Culture*. New York: Harper & Row.

Honigmann, John J. (1967). *Personality in Culture*. New York: Harper & Row.

Honigmann, John J. (1976). *The Development of Anthropological Ideas*. Homewood, IL: Dorsey Press.

Hoselitz, Bert F. (1960). *Theories of Economic Growth*. New York: Free Press.

Huizinga, Johan. (1954). *The Waning of the Middle Ages* [1919], trans. Fritz Hopman. Harmondsworth: Penguin.

Hunt, Susan. (1989, Winter). "The Alternative Economics Movement." *INTERculture* 22:1.

Huntington, Samuel P. (1993, Summer). "The Clash of Civilizations?" *Foreign Affairs*.

Huntington, Samuel P. (1996). *The Clash of Civilizations and the Remaking of World Order*. New York: Touchstone Books.

Iriye, Akira. (1997). *Cultural Internationalism and World Order*. Baltimore, MD: Johns Hopkins University Press.

Jacobs, Jane. (2000). *The Nature of Economies*. Toronto: Random House Canada.

Jameson, Fredric, and Masao Miyoshi. (1998). *Cultures of Globalization*. Durham, NC: Duke University Press.

Jencks, Chris. (1993). *Culture: Key Ideas*. London: Routledge.

Jevons, William Stanley. (1970). *The Theory of Political Economy* [1871], ed. R. D. Collison Black. Harmondsworth: Penguin.

Johnson, Leslie. (1979). *The Cultural Critics: From Matthew Arnold to Raymond Williams*. London: Routledge & Kegan Paul.

Kahn, Joel S. (1995). *Culture, Multiculture, Postculture*. London: Sage.

Kaldor, Nicholas. (1989). *Collected Economic Essays*. 9 vols. London: Holmes & Meier.

Kalecki, Michal. (1969). *Theory of Economic Dynamics: An Essay on Cyclical and Long-Run Changes in Capitalist Economy*. 2nd ed. London: Augustus M. Kelley.

Kapur Surya Foundation. (1995). *Culture and Development: Abbreviation of a Three-Day Dialogue on Culture and Development*. New Delhi: Kapur Surya Foundation.

Kardiner, Abram, ed. (1939). *The Individual and His Society*. New York: Columbia University Press.

Kaufmann, Walter. (1976). *Religion in Four Dimensions: Existential, Aesthetic, Historical, Comparative*. New York: *Reader's Digest* Press.

Keeley, Lawrence. (1996). *War Before Civilization*. New York: Oxford University Press.

Keung, Nicholas. (2000, March 10). "Nations Urged to Invest in Solving Water Crisis." *Toronto Star*, p. A21.

Keynes, John Maynard. (1930). *Treatise on Money*. 2 vols. London: Macmillan, and New York: Harcourt, Brace & World.

Keynes, John Maynard. (1936). *The General Theory of Employment, Interest and Money*. London: Macmillan, and New York: Harcourt, Brace & World.

King, A. D., ed. (1991). *Culture, Globalization and the World System*. London: Macmillan.

Ki-Zerbo, Joseph, ed. (1981). *General History of Africa*, Vol. 1, *Methodology and African Prehistory*. Paris: UNESCO, Los Angeles: University of California Press, and London: Heinemann.

Klein, Naomi. (2000). *No Logo: Taking Aim at the Brand Bullies*. New York: Picador USA.

Klein, Richard G., and Blake Edgar. (2002). *The Dawn of Human Culture*. New York: John Wiley.

Korten, David C. (1995). *When Corporations Rule the World*. West Hartford, CT: Kumarian Press, and San Francisco: Berrett–Koehler.

Korten, David C. (1999). *The Post-Corporate World: Life After Capitalism*. San Francisco and West Hartford, CT: Berrett–Koehler, and San Francisco: Kumarian Press.

Kroeber, Alfred L. (1952). *The Nature of Culture*. Chicago: University of Chicago Press.

Kroeber, Alfred L., and Clyde Kluckhohn. (1963). *Culture: A Critical Review of Concepts and Definitions*. [1952], New York: Vintage.

Kroeber, Alfred L. (1969). *Configurations of Culture Growth*. Berkeley: University of California Press.

Kuper, Adam. (1999). *Culture: The Anthropologist's Account*. Cambridge, MA: Harvard University Press.

Kurtz, Seymour. (1975). *The World Guide to Antiquities*. New York: Crown Publishers.

Landes, David S. (1998). *The Wealth and Poverty of Nations: Why Some Are So Rich and Some So Poor*. New York: W. W. Norton.

Landry, Charles. (2002). "Culturally Creative Cities," in Colin Mercer, ed. *Convergence, Creative Industries and Civil Society: The New Cultural Policy*, Special Issue of *Culturelink*. Zagreb: Institute for International Relations, 2002.

Langness, L. L.. (1974). *The Study of Culture*. San Francisco: Chandler & Sharp.

Latouche, Serge. (1986). *Faut-il refuser de développement?* Paris: Presses Universitaires Françaises.

Latouche, Serge. (1996). *The Westernization of the World*. Cambridge: Polity Press.

Leibenstein, Harvey. (1957). *Economic Backwardness and Economic Growth*. London: Chapman & Hall, and New York: John Wiley.

Lemkow, Anna F. (1990). *The Wholeness Principle: Dynamics of Unity Within Science, Religion and Society*. Wheaton, IL: Quest Books.

Lévi-Strauss, Claude. (1958). *Anthropologie Structurale*. Paris: Plon.

Lévy-Bruhl, Lucien. (1910). *Les functions mentales dans les sociétiés inférieures*. Paris: F. Alcon.

Lewis, Arthur. (1955). *The Theory of Economic Growth*. London: Allen & Unwin.

Lewis, Jeff. (2002). *Cultural Studies: The Basics*. London: Sage.

Linton, Ralph. (1945). *The Cultural Background of Personality*. New York: Appleton Century Crofts.

Linton, Ralph. (1955). *The Tree of Culture*. New York: Alfred A. Knopf.

Locke, John. (2003). *The Classical Utilitarians: Bentham and Mill*. London: Hackett Publishing.

Lovelock, James. (1979). *Gaia*. Oxford: Oxford University Press.

Lovelock, James. (1995). *Gaia: A New Look at Life on Earth*. Oxford: Oxford University Press.

Mair, Douglas, and Anne G. Miller, ed. (1991). *A Modern Guide to Economic Thought*. Aldershot, Hants: Edward Elgar.

Malinowski, Bronislaw. (1922). *Argonauts of the Western Pacific*. London: George Routledge, and New York: E. P. Dutton.

Malinowski, Bronislaw. (1965). *A Scientific Theory of Culture* [1944]. Chapel Hill: University of North Carolina Press.

Malitza, Mircea. (1976). "Culture and the New Order: A Pattern of Integration." *Cultures* 3:4. Paris: UNESCO and La Baconnière.

Malthus, Thomas Robert. (1983). *An Essay on the Principle of Population as It Affects the Future Improvement of Society, with Remarks on the Speculations of Mister Godwin, Monsieur Condorcet and Other Writers* [1798], ed. Anthony Flew, 2 vols. New York: Penguin.

Malthus, Thomas Robert. (1987). *Works*, ed. E. A. Wrigley and David Sounden. 8 vols. London: Pickering & Chatto.

Mantoux, Paul. (1934). *The Industrial Revolution in the Eighteenth Century*. New York: Harcourt, Brace.

Margalis, Lynn, and Dorion Sagan. (1995). *What Is Life?* New York: Simon & Schuster.

Marshall, Alfred. (1920). *Principles of Economics* [1890]. 8th ed. London and New York: Macmillan.

Marx, Karl. (1970). *A Contribution to the Critique of Political Economy* [1859]. Moscow: Progress Publishers.

Marx, Karl. (1976). *Capital*. 3 vols [1867–94]. Harmondsworth: Penguin.

Masini, Eleonora Barbieri, coordinator. (1991). *The Futures of Culture*. 2 vols. Paris: UNESCO.

Masini, Eleonora Barbieri, and Yogesh Atal, ed. (1993). *The Futures of Asian Cultures*. Bangkok: UNESCO Principal Regional Office for Asia and the Pacific.

Masini, Eleonora Barbieri, ed. (1994). *The Futures of Cultures*. Paris: UNESCO.

Mazrui, Ali A. (1976). *A World Federation of Cultures: An African Perspective*. New York: Free Press.

McHale, John. (1969). *The Future of the Future*. New York: George Braziller.

McKibbon, Bill. (1989). *The End of Nature*. New York: Random House.

McQuaig, Linda. (2001). *All You Can Eat: Greed, Lust and The New Capitalism*. Toronto: Penguin Viking.

Mead, Margaret. (1928). *Coming of Age in Samoa*. New York: Morrow.

Mead, Margaret. (1970). *Culture and Commitment: A Study of the Generation Gap*. Garden City, NY: National History Press/Doubleday.

Meadows, D. H., D. L. Meadows, J. Randers, and W. W. Behrens III. (1972). *The Limits to Growth*. New York: New American Library.

Meek, Ronald, ed. (1937). *Precursors of Adam Smith, 1750–1775*. Totowa, NJ: Rowman & Littlefield.

Meek, Ronald. (1963). *The Economics of Physiocracy*. Cambridge, MA: Harvard University Press.

Meier, Gerald M., and Dudley Seers, ed. (1984). *Pioneers in Development*. Oxford and New York: Oxford University Press.

Menger, Carl. (1950). *Principles of Economics* [1871], ed. J. Dingwall and B. F. Hoselitz with an introduction by Frank H. Knight. New York: Free Press.

Mercer, Colin. (2002). *Towards Cultural Citizenship: Tools for Cultural Policy and Development*. Hedemora: Bank of Sweden Tercentenary Foundation, and Sida and Gidlunds Förlag.

Mercouri, Melina. (2000). Speech to the First Informal Meeting of Culture Ministers of the European Union, Athens, November 1983, as reported in *Blizzart* 4:4. Ottawa: Canadian Conference of the Arts.

Mill, John Stuart. (1961). *The Principles of Political Economy, with Some of their Applications to Social Philosophy* [1848]. New York: Augustus M. Kelley.

Miller, John. (1988). *The Holistic Curriculum*. Toronto: Ontario Institute for Studies in Education Press.

Mishan, E. J. (1967). *The Costs of Economic Growth*. London: Staples Press.

Mitchell, J. M. (1986). *International Cultural Relations*. London: Allen & Unwin in association with the British Council.

Mitchell, Wesley Clare. (1967 and 1969). *Types of Economic Theory: From Mercantilism to Institutionalism*, ed. with an introduction by Joseph Dorfman. 2 vols. New York: Augustus M. Kelley.

Moggridge, D. E. (1976). *Keynes*. London: Macmillan.

Mohammadian, Mansour. (2000). *Bioeconomics: Biological Economics: Interdisciplinary Study of Biology, Economics and Education*. Madrid: Edición personal.

Morgan, L. H. (1877). *Ancient Society*. New York: World Publishing.

Mumford, Lewis. (1938). *The Culture of Cities*. New York: Harcourt, Brace & World.

Murdock, George P. (1959). *Africa—Its People and Their Culture*. New York: McGraw–Hill.

Myerscough, John (1988). *The Economic Importance of the Arts in Britain*. London: Policy Studies Institute.

Myrdal, Gunnar. (1957). *Economic Theory and the Underdeveloped Regions*. London: Duckworth.

Myrdal, Gunnar. (1968). *Asian Drama: An Inquiry into the Poverty of Nations*. London: Allen Lane, and New York: Pantheon.

Myrdal, Gunnar. (1970). *The Challenge of World Poverty*. Harmondsworth and New York: Penguin.

Naess, Arne. (1989). *Ecology, Community and Lifestyle*. Cambridge: Cambridge University Press.

Nef, John U. (1957). *Industry and Government in France and England, 1540–1640*. Ithaca, NY: Great Seal Books.

Nisbet, Robert. (1979). *History of the Idea of Progress*. New York: Basic Books.

Northrop, F. S. C. (1946). *The Meeting of East and West: An Enquiry Concerning World Understanding*. New York: Macmillan.

Nurkse, Ragnar. (1953). *Problems of Capital Formation in Underdeveloped Countries*. Oxford: Oxford University Press.

Okun, Bernard, and Richard W. Richardson. (1961). *Studies in Economic Development*. New York: Holt, Rinehart & Winston.

Ormerod, Paul. (1997). *The Death of Economics*. London and New York: John Wiley.

Ostry, Bernard. (1978). *The Cultural Connection*. Toronto: McClelland & Stewart.

Pareto, Vilfredo. (1971). *Manual of Political Economy* [1906], trans. Anne S. Schwier, ed. Anne S. Schwier and Alfred N. Page. Clifton, NJ: Augustus M. Kelley.

Peacock, James L. (2001). *The Anthropological Lens: Harsh Light, Soft Focus*. 2nd ed. Cambridge: Cambridge University Press.

Pérez de Cuéllar, Javier. (1994, February 22). Address to the Inaugural Session of the Third Meeting of the World Commission on Culture and Development, San José, Costa Rica.

Petrie, W. M. F. (1911). *The Revolutions of Civilisation*. London: Harper, and New York: Haskell House.

Pigou, Arthur C. (1920). *The Economics of Welfare*. London: Macmillan.

Pilon, Robert. (2001, April 6). "Culture in an Age of Free Trade." *Toronto Star*.

Pitman, Walter. (1998). *Learning the Arts in an Age of Uncertainty*. Toronto: Arts Education Council of Ontario.

Pitt-Rivers, A. L-F. (1906). *The Evolution of Culture and Other Essays*, ed. J. L. Myers. Oxford: Clarendon Press.

Polanyi, Karl. (1944). *The Great Transformation: The Political and Economic Origins of Our Times.* Boston: Beacon Press.

Powys, John Cowper. (1929). *The Meaning of Culture.* London: Jonathan Cape, and New York: W. W. Norton.

Prebisch, Raúl. (1962, February). "The Economic Development of Latin America and Its Principal Problems." *Economic Bulletin for Latin America* 7.

Radcliffe-Brown, A. R. (1958). *Method in Social Anthropology: The Major Writings on Method by the Founder of the Scientific Study of Social Anthropology.* Chicago: University of Chicago Press.

Ray, Lawrence James, and Andrew Sayer, ed. (1999). *Culture and Economy After the Cultural Turn.* London: Sage.

Redfield, Robert. (1962). *The Little Community: Viewpoints for the Study of a Human Whole.* Chicago: University of Chicago Press.

Reid, David. (1995). *Sustainable Development: An Introductory Guide.* London: Earthscan.

Ricardo, David. (1951–55). *The Works and Correspondence,* ed. Piero Sraffa with the collaboration of M. H. Dobb. 10 vols. Cambridge: Cambridge University Press.

Ricardo, David. (1971). *Principles of Political Economy and Taxation* [1817]. Harmondsworth: Penguin.

Rist, Gilbert. (1997). *The History of Development: From Western Origins to Global Faith,* trans. Patrick Camiller. London and New York: Zed Books.

Rivers, R. W. H. R. (1922). *History and Ethnology.* New York: Macmillan.

Robbins, Richard. (1999). *Global Problems and the Culture of Capitalism.* Boston: Allyn & Bacon.

Robertson, H. M. (1933). *Aspects of the Rise of Economic Individualism.* Cambridge: Cambridge University Press.

Robinson, Joan. (1933). *The Economics of Imperfect Competition.* London: Macmillan.

Róheim, Géza. (1966). *Psychoanalysis and Anthropology.* New York: International University Press.

Roll, Eric. (1973). *A History of Economic Thought.* 4th ed. London: Faber.

Rosaldo, Renato. (1990). *Culture and Truth: The Remaking of Social Analysis.* Boston: Beacon Press.

Rosenstein-Rodan, Paul N. (1943, June–September). "Problems of Industrialization of Eastern and South-Eastern Europe." *Economic Journal* 53.

Rostow, W. W. (1991). *The Stages of Economic Growth: A Non-Communist Manifesto.* [1960] 3rd ed. Cambridge: Cambridge University Press.

Rostow, W. W. (1990). *Theorists of Economic Growth from David Hume to the Present, with a Perspective on the Next Century.* Oxford and New York: Oxford University Press.

Sachs, Wolfgang. (1990, Fall). "The Archaeology of the Development Idea." *INTERculture* 23:4.

Sachs, Wolfgang. (1992). *The Development Dictionary: A Guide to Knowledge as Power*. London: Zed Books.

Sachs, Wolfgang, ed. (1993). *Global Ecology: A New Arena of Political Conflict*. London: Zed Books.

Sahtouris, Elisabet. (1995). *Earthdance: Living Systems in Evolution*. Santa Barbara, CA: Metolog Books.

Said, Edward W. (1994). *Cultural Imperialism*. New York: Vintage.

Samuelsson, Kurt. (1957). *Religion and Economic Action*, trans. E. Geoffrey French, ed. with an introduction by D. C. Coleman. Stockholm: Scandinavian University Books.

Schafer, D. Paul. (1998a). *Culture—Beacon of the Future*. London: Adamantine Press.

Schafer, D. Paul. (1998b). *Culture and Politics in Canada: Towards a Culture for All Canadians*. Markham, ON: World Culture Project.

Schumacher, E. F. (1973). *Small is Beautiful: Economics as if People Mattered*. London: Blond & Briggs, and New York: Harper & Row.

Schumpeter, Joseph A. (1961). *The Theory of Economic Development: An Inquiry into Profits, Capital, Credit, Interest, and the Business Cycle* [1911], tr. Redvers Opie. Oxford and New York: Oxford University Press.

Schumpeter, Joseph A. (1939). *Business Cycles*. New York: McGraw–Hill.

Schumpeter, Joseph A. (1942). *Capitalism, Socialism and Democracy*. New York: Harper & Row.

Scitovsky, Tibor. (1977). *The Joyless Economy*. Oxford: Oxford University Press.

Seligman, Edwin R. A. (1907). *The Economic Interpretation of History*. 2nd ed. New York and London: Columbia University Press.

Sen, Amartya. (1989). *On Ethics and Economics*. London: Blackwell.

Sen, Amartya, and James E. Foster. (1997). *On Economic Inequality*. Oxford: Clarendon Press.

Sennett, Richard, ed. (1969). *Classic Essays on the Culture of Cities*. Englewood Cliffs, NJ: Prentice Hall.

Sessions, George, ed. (1994). *Deep Ecology for the Twenty-first Century: Readings on the Philosophy and Practice of the New Environmentalism*. Boston and London: Shambhala.

Shaw, William H., and Vincent Barry, ed. (1997). *Moral Issues in Business*. 7th ed. Belmont, CA.: Wadsworth.

Smith, Adam. (1986). *The Wealth of Nations, Books I-III*, with an introduction by Andrew Skinner. London: Penguin. For the complete publication, see:

Smith, Adam. (1937). *An Inquiry into the Nature and Causes of the Wealth of Nations* [1776], ed. Edwin Cannan, with an introduction by Max Lerner. New York: Random House.

Sorokin, Pitirim. (1957). *Social and Cultural Dynamics: A Study of Change in Major Systems of Art, Truth, Ethics, Law and Social Relationships*. Boston: Porter Sargent.

Sorokin, Pitirim. (1963). *Modern Historical and Social Philosophies*. New York: Dover.

Soyinka, Wole. (1992, April 2–3). "Culture, Memory and Development." Address to the International Conference on Culture and Development in Africa. Washington, DC: World Bank.

Spengler, Oswald. (1962). *The Decline of the West* [1918]. New York: Alfred A. Knopf.

Spiegel, Henry William. (1991). *The Growth of Economic Thought*. 3rd ed. Durham, NC, and London: Duke University Press.

Sraffa, Piero. (1960). *Production of Commodities by Means of Commodities*. Cambridge: Cambridge University Press.

Steward, Julian. (1955). *Theory of Culture Change: The Methodology of Multilineal Evolution*. Urbana: University of Illinois Press.

Stiglitz, Joseph E. (2003). *Globalization and its Discontents*. New York: W. W. Norton.

Streeten, Paul, with S. J. Burki, Mahbub ul Haq, Norman Hicks, and Frances Stewart. (1981). *First Things First: Meeting Basic Human Needs in Developing Countries*. London: Oxford University Press.

Suzuki, David, and Holly Dressel. (2002). *Good News For A Change: Hope For A Troubled Planet*. Toronto: Stoddart.

Svob-Dokic, Nada. (1991). "Culture as a System: Identity, Development, and Communications." *Razvoj/Development International* 6:2–3. Zagreb: Institute of Development and International Relations.

Svob-Dokic, Nada, ed. (2001). *Redefining Cultural Identities: The Multicultural Contexts of the Central European and Mediterranean Regions*. Zagreb: Institute for International Relations, Royaumont Process.

Sweezy, Paul M. (1956). *The Theory of Capitalist Development: Principles of Marxian Political Economy*. New York: *Monthly Review* Press.

Swimme, Brian, and Thomas Berry. (1994). *The Universe Story*. New York: HarperCollins.

Tagore, Rabindranath. (1992). *Creative Unity* [1922]. London: Macmillan.

Tawney, R. H. (1926). *Religion and the Rise of Capitalism: A Historical Study*. London: John Murray, and New York: Harcourt, Brace & World.

Thurow, Lester. (1983). *Dangerous Currents: The State of Economics*. New York: Random House.

Thurow, Lester. (1997). *The Future of Capitalism*. New York: Penguin.

Tinbergen, Jan, and H. C. Bos. (1958). *The Design of Development*. Baltimore, MD: Johns Hopkins Press.

Toffler, Alvin. (1967). "The Art of Measuring the Arts." *Annals of the American Academy of Political and Social Sciences*.

Toffler, Alvin, and Heidi Toffler. (1994). *Creating a New Civilization*. Atlanta, GA: Turner Publishing.

Tomlinson, John. (1991). *Cultural Imperialism*. London: Pinter.

Tomlinson, John. (1999). *Globalization and Culture*. Cambridge: Polity Press.

Toynbee, Arnold Joseph. (1934). *A Study of History*. London: Oxford University Press.

Toynbee, Arnold. (1956). *The Industrial Revolution* [1884]. Boston: Beacon Press.

Turgot, Anne-Robert-Jacques. (1898). *Reflections on the Formation and the Distribution of Riches* [1776]. New York: Macmillan.

Tylor, Edward Burnett. (1958). *Primtive Culture* [1871], reissued in 2 vols as Vol. I, *The Origins of Culture*, and Vol. 2, *Religion in Primitive Culture*. New York: Harper & Row.

UNESCO. (1976, November 26). "Recommendation on Participation by the People at Large in Cultural Life and Their Contribution to It, Adopted by the General Conference of UNESCO at its Nineteenth Session, Nairobi." Paris: UNESCO.

UNESCO. (1981). *Cultural Development: Some Regional Experiences*. Paris: UNESCO.

UNESCO. (1982). *Mexico City Declaration on Cultural Policies: Final Report*. Paris: UNESCO.

UNESCO. (1987) *A Practical Guide to the World Decade for Cultural Development 1988–1997*. Paris: UNESCO.

UNESCO. (1994). *Rethinking Development: World Decade for Cultural Development 1988–1997*. Paris: UNESCO.

United Nations. (2007). Intergovernmental Panel on Climate Change. Fourth Assessment Report. *Climate Change 2007: The Physical Science Basis*. New York: United Nations.

United Nations. (2007). *Millennium Development Goals Report 2007*. New York: United Nations.

Veblen, Thorstein. (1937). *The Theory of the Leisure Class* [1899]. New York: Random House/Modern Library.

Veblen, Thorstein. (1934). *The Portable Veblen*, with an introduction by Max Lerner. New York: Viking Press.

Wager, Warren W. (1991). *The Next Three Futures: Paradigms of Things to Come*. New York: Praeger.

Wallace, Anthony F. C. (1970). *Culture and Personality*. New York: Random House.

Wallerstein, Immanuel. (1974). *The Modern World System*. New York: Academic Press.

Wallerstein, Immanuel. (1987). *The Capitalist World-Economy*. Cambridge and New York: Cambridge University Press.

Walras, Léon. (1954). *Elements of Pure Economics, or The Theory of Social Wealth* [1874], trans. W. Jaffé. Homewood, IL: Richard D. Irwin.

Ward, Barbara. (1979). *Progress for a Small Planet*. New York and London: W. W. Norton.

Watson, Lyall. (1965). *Dark Nature*. New York: Harper & Row.

Webber, Jude. (2000, April 6). "World Must Act Now to Aid Famine: UN." *Toronto Star*, p. B1–2.

Weber, Max. (1958). *The Protestant Ethic and the Spirit of Capitalism* [1905], trans. Talcott Parsons. New York: Charles Scribner's Sons.

Weil, Andrew (1995). *Spontaneous Healing: How to Discover and Enhance Your Body's Natural Ability to Maintain and Heal Itself.* New York: Fawcett Columbine.

Weingartner, Rudolph H. (1962). *Experience and Culture: The Philosophy of Georg Simmel.* Middletown, CT: Wesleyan University Press.

Weintraub, E. Roy. (1985). *General Equilibrium Analysis.* Cambridge and New York: Cambridge University Press.

Weintraub, Karl J. (1966). *Visions of Culture: Voltaire, Guizot, Burckhardt, Lamprecht, Huizinga and Ortega y Gasset.* Chicago: University of Chicago Press.

White, Leslie A. (1975). *The Concept of Cultural Systems: A Key to Understanding Tribes and Nations.* New York: Columbia University Press.

Williams, Raymond. (1958). *Culture and Society, 1780–1950.* London: Chatto & Windus.

Williams, Raymond. (1961). *The Long Revolution.* London: Chatto & Windus, and New York: Columbia University Press.

Williams, Raymond. (1980). *Problems in Materialism and Culture.* London: Verso.

Williams, Raymond. (1981). *Culture.* Glasgow: Collins, and, as *The Sociology of Culture* (1982), New York: Schocken.

Wilson, Charles. (1958). *Mercantilism.* London: Routledge & Kegan Paul for the Historical Association.

Witt, Ulrich. (1988). *Evolutionary Economics.* Cambridge: Cambridge University Press.

Wittgenstein, Ludwig. (1980). *Culture and Value: A Selection from the Posthumous Remains.* ed. Georg Henrik von Wright in collaboration with Heikki Nyman, trans. Peter Winch. Oxford: Blackwell, and Chicago: University of Chicago Press.

Wojciechowski, Jerzy A. (1977). "Cultural Pluralism and National Identity." *Cultures* 4:4. Paris: UNESCO and La Baconnière.

Woodward, Kathryn, ed. (1997). *Identity and Difference.* London: Sage.

World Bank. (2007). *Global Economic Prospects Report 2007.* Washington, DC: World Bank.

World Commission on Culture and Development. (1995). *Our Creative Diversity.* Paris: UNESCO.

World Commission on Environment and Development. (1987). *Our Common Future.* Oxford and New York: Oxford University Press.

Worsley, Peter. (1984). *The Three Worlds: Culture and World Development.* Chicago: University of Chicago Press.

INDEX

population growth and production, 43

quasi-rent and potential profits, 68

rebellion by, 44

standard of living improvement, 18

surplus value on capital, 52

taxation issues, 46

Capra, Fritjof, 145, 265

Carlyle, Thomas, 34, 42, 186

carrying capacity of Earth

material inputs and outputs, 126

natural environment, damage to, 131

polices for future, 88

population growth, global, 1, 88–89, 132, 197, 206, 215

renewable and non-renewable resources consumption, 145, 260

Carson, Rachel, 144, 265

Catholicism, 28, 30

centrality of economics, 31, 35, 56, 79, 82, 95, 125

Chamberlin, E. H., 23, 70, 265–66

Chicago school of economics, 86, 88

child

deaths from water-borne disease, 126

equality, 152

exploitation, 152

labour, 38–39, 52–53, 127, 225

Child, Julia, 245

Child, Sir Josiah, 11, 21

children's rights, 153

China, 185

classless society, 55

Clement, W. R., 242–43, 266

Club of Rome, 88–89

cokeblasting process, 24

Cole, G. D. H., 57

Collection of Traditional Music of the World, 245

colonialism, 11, 36, 54, 83, 151, 154, 183

colonies, 23, 30, 35–36, 45, 73

commercial elites, 87

commercial revolution, 24, 184

communications age, 3, 5

communism, 54, 57, 63

The Communist Manifesto (Marx and Engels), 10, 54, 81

competition

capitalists or manufacturers, 53

consumption *vs.* conservation, 135, 157

cooperation *vs.*, 206, 225

corporate, 225–26

corporate capitalist monopoly, 223

dehumanized and impersonal, 131–32

dominant force in society, 102

economic and political liberalism, 45

environmental conditions, 51

excessive, 211

free-trade world, 31

for high incomes, 113

in humanized economies, 194

imperfect, 70, 72, 77

markets, 58

monopolistic, 70, 86

motivation of people, 206

perfect, 65, 70, 87, 106

producers and consumers, 31

profit motive, 106

profits and profit margins, 18

vigorous, 68–69

in vigorous economy, 206

virtues of, 106

Concheiro, Antonio Alonso, 232

Condorcet, Marie-Jean-Antoine-Nicolas de, 38, 40, 181, 266

conservation, 135, 157, 206, 211, 222, 246, 255

conspicuous consumption, 108

consumer and producer satisfaction, 66

consumer goods, 34

E

Ebadi, Shirin, 152
economic age
  balance sheet on, 130–35
  capitalism, 3
  classical economics, 39–51
  consumption, 93, 131
  contemporary economics, 85–91
  development economics, 78–84
  distribution, 120–22
  dominant forces of society, 102–13
  economic growth, 3, 120, 123–24,
    200, 202
  economic model of development,
    10f1, 98–102
  economic worldview, 93–98
  environmental crisis, 1, 120, 131,
    133
  globalization, 111
  industrial revolution in Britain,
    23–27
  investment, 105
  Keynesian economics, 37, 54, 72–
    79, 85–88, 95, 123, 146
  Marxian economics, 37, 51–58,
    65–66, 70, 72, 76, 146
  modern world systems, 113–18
  natural environment, 124, 133
  neoclassical economics, 58–72
  post-Keynesian economics, 54,
    87–88, 95
  religion and the rise of capitalism,
    27–30
  shortcomings, 124–31, 134, 152
  strengths of, 120–24
  The Wealth of Nations, 10–22
  world system, 31–36, 134, 201
economic and political liberalism, 13,
    16, 31, 34, 45, 65
economic base, 54, 98–100, 100f1,
    101
economic growth
  Americanization path, 255

classic economics, 39, 49
consumer needs, 131, 224
contemporary economics, 85
of countries in the world, 114
by developing countries, 127
developmental economics, 79
economic age, 3, 120, 123–24
economic age, dominant forces,
    200, 202
economic model of development,
    101–3, 105–6
economic worldview, 94
environment pressures, 199
environmental crisis, 123
environmentalists, concern of, 125
excessive rates of, 202
gap between rich and poor
    countries, 133
global new economy, 97–98
government, role of, 226–28
Harrod and Domar's ideas, 79
Hirschman's ideas, 80
industrial revolution in Britain,
    26, 38
international infrastructure, 115
Keynes's ideas, 72–73, 75–78, 87,
    95, 107–8
Malthus's ideas, 41
Marx's ideas, 60, 66
Mill's ideas, 48
modern world system, 31, 116
multidimensional process, 141
natural environment, 131
neoclassical economics, 70, 72
Nurkse's ideas, 80
organic collectivities, 130
post World War II, 79
preoccupation with increasing, 122,
    124
Protestant ethic, 35
Ricardo's ideas, 43–44
Rostow's ideas, 81–82
shortcomings in, 90–91

gender equality, 153
The General Theory of Employment, Interest and Money (Keynes), 73, 271
The German Ideology (Marx), 55
Gibbon, Edward, 181
Girard, Augustin, 204, 231, 268
Global Economic Prospects Report, 127, 279
global economy, 5, 34, 85, 90, 97, 114, 126, 207
global ecosystem, 1, 124–25, 132, 216
global equilibrium, 89
global ethics, 231
global village, 111, 248, 250, 253
global warming, 5, 120, 124, 127, 131, 144–45, 199
globalization
    as an intrusive force, 111
    as colonialism, 154
    contemporary economics, 85–86, 90, 94
    countervailing forces against, 249
    cultures are more open today, 175
    cultures as victims of, 195, 198–99
    debates about, 111
    development of, 112
    dominant force in society, 103
    economic age, 111
    economic systems and cultures, changes in, 163
    factors accounting for, 112
    human condition, transformation of, 3
    identity assertion, 154
    identity erosion, 154
    intercultural interaction, 156, 175, 199
    international trade and free trade, 48, 83–84
    planetary networks, 205
    power concentrated into few hands, 131

    promotion of financial and commercial interests, 131
    protests against, 155, 211, 226
    regional trade zones, 248–49
    specialization, demand for, 201
    trading blocs, 205
    United States influence, 115–16
    urbanization growth, 117
    violent reaction to, 202
    world as dynamic whole, 141
    world conflict, 2
    world system, current, 3
Godwin, William, 37–38, 40, 268
Goethe, Johann Wolfgang von, 181, 186
Gore, Al, 144
Gossen, Hermann Heinrich, 60
Goulet, Denis, 250, 257, 268
government involvement in the economy and markets, 12, 34, 49, 69, 71, 77–78
Graebner, Fritz, 187
Great Depression, 42, 73–75, 108, 123
The Great Transformation: The Political and Economic Origins of Our Time (Polanyi), 109–10, 275
Greek culture, ancient, 181, 185
greenhouse gases, 124, 215, 246
Greenpeace, 144, 215
Greenwood Publishing, 233
Greer, Germaine, 152
gross
    domestic expenditure, 32
    domestic income, 32
    domestic product, 32, 113–14, 126, 218, 239
    national product (GNP), 148
guild system of production, 30
Guizot, François, 181
Gunn, Giles, 167, 269
Gutenberg, Johannes, 243

H

Hall, Edward, 9, 161, 171–72, 189
Hallowell, Irving, 186
hand pump, 27
Haq, Mahbub ul, 145–46, 150, 269
Harding, John, 186
Hargreaves, James, 24–25
Harris, Marvin, 143, 269
Harrod, Sir Roy, 79, 269
Hartwell, R. M., 23, 269
Hayek, Friedrich A. von, 63
Heckscher, Eli F., 11, 30, 269
Heilbroner, Robert L., 42, 73, 269
Herder, Johann Gottfried von, 145,
    173–75, 269
Hicks, John, 71, 122, 269
high tariff walls, 84
Hildebrand, Bruno, 50
Hirschman, Albert, 80, 270
historians
    Ashley, William, 30
    Bagehot, Walter, 50
    Braudel, Fernand, 189, 265
    Brentano, Lujo, 30
    Burckhardt, Jacob, 180–81, 189,
        246, 265
    Burke, Joseph, 189, 242, 265
    Fanfani, Amintore, 30, 267
    Gibbon, Edward, 181
    Hildebrand, Bruno, 50
    Huizinga, Johan, 181, 189, 194,
        211, 270
    Ingram, John, 50
    Jones, Richard, 50
    Ki-Zerbo, Joseph, 189, 271
    Knies, Karl, 50
    Leslie, Cliffe, 50
    List, Friedrich, 50
    Michelet, Jules, 244
    Nef, John, 12, 23, 274
    Petrie, W. M. F., 189, 274
    Polanyi, Karl, 109–10, 129, 275
    Robertson, H. M., 30, 275

Roscher, Wilhelm, 50
Sombart, Werner, 30, 50
Spengler, Oswald, 179, 181, 189,
    277
Spiethoff, Arthur, 50
Tawney, R. H., 30, 277
Toynbee, Arnold, 23, 181, 189,
    278
Weintraub, Karl, 180, 189, 194,
    211, 246, 279
holism, 143, 193, 201, 206
holistic medicine, 140
homelessness, 112, 157, 218, 237, 256
Honigmann, John, 186
Howe, Elias, 24
Hugo, Victor, 21
Huizinga, Johan, 181, 189, 194, 211,
    270
human capital, 105
Human Development Index (HDI),
    148
Human Genome Project, 141
human rights, 93, 203–4, 230–31
    abuses, 153, 225, 256
    legislation, 152
Hume, David, 21, 146
hunger, 120, 126, 157, 194, 218, 224,
    256
Hunt, Susan, 93, 270
Huntington, Samuel P., 237–38, 270
Hutcheson, Francis, 21

I

identity, 153–55
imperialism, 54, 83, 183, 195
import substitution, 83
income per capita, 32
income stream, 18, 74, 76
An Inconvenient Truth (Gore), 144
industrial revolution, 23–28, 31,
    34–37, 44, 50–51, 53, 57, 80,
    90–91, 107, 170, 201
industrial society, 23
information age, 3

University of Ottawa Press Governance series

17. Gilles Paquet 2008
    Deep Collective Diversity – A Governance Challenge
16. D. Paul Schafer 2008
    Revolution or Renaissance: Making the Transition from an Economic Age to a Cultural Age.
15. Gilles Paquet 2008
    Tableau d'avancement – Petite ethnographie interprétative d'un certain Canada français
14. Tom Brzustowski 2008
    The Way Ahead – Meeting Canada's Productivity Challenge
13. Jeffrey Roy 2007
    Business and Government in Canada
12. N. Brown, L. Cardinal (Eds) 2007
    Managing Diversity – Practices of Citizenship
11. R. Hubbard, G. Paquet 2007
    Gomery's Blinders and Canadian Federalism
10. Emmanuel Brunet-Jailly (Ed.) 2007
    Borderlands – Comparing Border Security in North America and Europe
 9. C. Rouillard, E. Montpetit, I. Fortier, A.G. Gagnon 2006
    Reengineering the State – Toward an Impoverishment of Quebec Governance
 8. Jeffrey Roy 2006
    E-Government in Canada
 7. Gilles Paquet 2005
    The New Geo-Governance – A Baroque Approach
 6. C. Andrew, M. Gattinger, M.S. Jeannotte, W. Straw (Eds) 2005
    Accounting for Culture – Thinking Through Cultural Citizenship
 5. P .Boyer, L. Cardinal, D. Headon (Eds) 2004
    From Subjects et Citizens – A Hundred Years of Citizenship in Australia and Canada
 4. L. Cardinal, D. Headon (Eds) 2002
    Shaping Nations – Constitutionalism and Society in Australia and Canada
 3. L. Cardinal, C. Andrew (sld) 2001
    La démocratie à l'épreuve de la gouvernance
 2. Gilles Paquet 1999
    Governance Through Social Learning
 1. David McInnes 1999, 2005
    Taking it to the Hill – The Complete Guide to Appearing Before Parliamentary Commitees

Colophon

Printed and bound in May 2008
by l'Imprimerie Gauvin, Gatineau, Quebec,
for THE UNIVERSITY OF OTTAWA PRESS

Typeset in 9.5 pt. Adobe Garamond Pro
on 13 pt. leading by Kevin Matthews
Edited by Patrick Heenan
Proofread by Alex Anderson
Cover designed by Kevin Matthews

Printed on Rolland Opaque Natural 60 lb paper